MODERN AMERICAN DRAMA

The Beginnings of American Literature

The Growing Years of American Literature

Modern American Prose

Modern American Poetry

Modern American Drama

❧ ❧

MODERN AMERICAN DRAMA

Revised Edition

SISTER M. AGNES DAVID, S.S.J.
John W. Hallahan Catholic Girls' High School
Philadelphia, Pennsylvania

The Macmillan Company   New York

ACKNOWLEDGMENTS

For permission to use material in this book, grateful acknowledgment is made to the following:

The Dramatic Publishing Company: For *Twelve Angry Men* by Reginald Rose. Copyright, 1955, by Reginald Rose. Based upon the Television Show, *Twelve Angry Men*. Printed in the United States of America. All rights reserved.

Permission to give amateur performances of *Twelve Angry Men* must be obtained in advance of the performance from The Dramatic Publishing Company, 179 North Michigan Avenue, Chicago 1, Illinois. All performances of this work require the payment of a royalty fee, whether the work is presented for charity or gain, and whether admission is charged or not.

Harcourt, Brace & World, Inc.: For *I Remember Mama*, copyright, 1944, 1945, by John Van Druten. Copyright, 1952, by John Van Druten (revised). Reprinted by permission of Harcourt, Brace & World, Inc.

CAUTION: Professionals and amateurs are hereby warned that *I Remember Mama*, being fully protected by copyright, is subject to royalty. All rights, including professional, amateur, motion picture, talking motion picture, radio broadcasting, television, recitation, public reading, and the rights of translation into foreign languages, are strictly reserved. All inquiries should be addressed to the author's agent, Monica McCall, Inc., 667 Madison Avenue, New York, N. Y. 10021, except that in the case of amateur rights, inquiries should be addressed to the Dramatists Play Service, Inc., 14 East 38th Street, New York, N. Y. 10016.

Hill and Wang, Inc., Publishers: For *Billy Budd* by Louis O. Coxe and Robert Chapman. Copyright 1947 by Louis O. Coxe and Robert Chapman, as an unpublished play under the title *Uniform of Flesh*. Copyright 1949 by Louis O. Coxe and Robert Chapman, a revised version under the title *Billy Budd* as an unpublished play. Copyright © 1951 by Louis O. Coxe and Robert Chapman. Reprinted by permission of Hill and Wang, Inc.

Little, Brown and Company: For *Visit to a Small Planet* by Gore Vidal. Copyright, © 1956, by Gore Vidal.

❧ CONTENTS

INTRODUCTION

The theater . . . is a vivid and vibrant expression of truths and ideas. . . . It helps to make life whole.*

The Drama as Literature

Moss Hart, in his autobiography, *Act One*, wrote, "The vital scenes of a play are played as much by the audience, I suppose, as by the actors on the stage." It is this participation by the audience that makes the play on the stage so different from the same play in print. A play is written to be acted, to be seen, to be felt by an audience that carries it along with them. There is no substitute for this experience of the play as a member of the audience. Yet, the reading of plays can be exciting and rewarding. The careful reader who sets the stage in his mind's eye and hears the words spoken in his inner ear can become his own one-man audience. He can experience the play as a human conflict, a conflict between two or more people, or a conflict between a man and the circumstances around him.

The importance of close reading cannot be overemphasized. There are no descriptive passages and no long paragraphs of exposition to help you. There are only the dialogue and the brief stage directions. From these you must create the appearance and personality of the characters, their relation to each other, and the action that arises from these relationships. Every line in a play has its purpose—to characterize, to explain the situation, or to move the action forward. The playwright is limited by the two or three hours of the stage performance. He must make each word count. For this reason, the reader must be quick and alert to pick up clues to character and the clues to action that lie ahead.

You, the reader, will shape the play in your own mind as you read.

* Brooks Atkinson, "Why Have Theatre?" *Production Calendar*, October, 1948.

What the play means to you—what you get out of it—depends upon the curiosity, the alertness, and the sympathy with which you read it.

The Roots of American Drama

When the Puritans landed in 1620, they brought with them a positive abhorrence for the theater, an abhorrence based on their strongly Calvinistic philosophy. This distaste, together with the rigors of pioneer life, the sparse population, and the immediacy of physical danger, made the drama and the theater an almost totally forgotten art in seventeenth-century America.

But even in the time of the colonies there were faint stirrings of life. The first drama written in America and performed on the professional stage appeared in 1759 when twenty-four-year-old Thomas Godfrey of Philadelphia wrote *The Prince of Parthia,* a tragic play in blank verse. Charlestown and Williamsburg had theaters before the Revolutionary War, and both New York and Philadelphia had established theaters by 1776. In spite of these early signs of activity, there was no American drama being written; all plays were imported from England. In 1787, however, a comedy, *The Contrast,* by Royall Tyler, was produced in New York. Here, for the first time, audiences saw a play that was American in scene, in character, and in theme. *The Contrast* was also the first play to characterize the typical Yankee—shrewd, dry, naive, and forthright.

The early nineteenth century was a time of growth and optimism for young America, just beginning to feel its size and strength. All over the rapidly expanding country, scores of theaters were built. "Name" stars became famous; dramatic successes from Europe were imported and presented to capacity audiences. On the frontiers, traveling groups of players acted before stagecoach audiences. Along the Mississippi, the showboats moored at main landings; people poured aboard; companies af actors gave performances on the ship; and drama came alive.

Despite all of this theatrical activity, no really great American plays were written in this period. There was little attempt at realism; romanticism was the order of the day. Yet a few good plays did attain success. Audiences could not easily forget the dramatic impact of Otis Skinner's interpretation of *Uncle Tom's Cabin,* and Joseph Jefferson's name became synonymous with his sympathetic portrayal of the leading role in *Rip Van Winkle*. In addition to serious plays, farces and melodramas made audiences laugh and weep.

After the Civil War, the drama underwent major changes. With the realities of war, the rapid development of industry, and the tremendous Westward Movement, playwrights began to formulate a new outlook on life, a *realistic* outlook. In addition, the technique of staging improved rapidly. Men like Augustin Daly, playwright and stage manager, worked continually and constructively to make improvements in setting, lighting, and stage properties.

The growing interest in realism and in social drama was apparent when, in 1888, Bronson Howard's *Shenandoah* probed the problems of peacetime adjustment that had arisen after the Civil War. As the nineteenth century met the twentieth, writers like James Herne, author of *Shore Acres*, and Clyde Fitch, famous for *The Girl with the Green Eyes*, faced directly the problems of realism. But it was not until the twentieth century that the theater turned fully in this direction.

In Our Time

Modern American drama, although slow to come of age, profited by the experiences of Ibsen, Chekhov, Strindberg, and Shaw. These experimenters in the drama of the Western world revealed the possibilities of realism and naturalism in the theater. Other playwrights, such as Maurice Maeterlinck, turned to symbolism and expressionism. In America, these varied elements fused, but no single principle or style dominated. Instead, the experiments and strivings of several decades of theatrical pioneering are telescoped in the drama of the last forty years.

Only slowly did modern ideas in the theater acquire literary value, but soon the American drama began to contribute to the European stage rather than merely to borrow from it. By the 1930's, American drama was easily as vital as the English stage; in the years from 1930 to 1950, American drama was well ahead of the German, Italian, and Russian theater. Indeed, one may conclude, in spite of the diverse character of the American theater, that it was on a par with any other national drama after 1920.

To view the works of American dramatists during the twentieth century is to trace the "isms" prevalent in modern society. Some dramatists emphasized socialism; others, communism; still others, naturalism. These concepts give only a partial picture of man; and, in the extreme, some dramatists considered only the abnormal or exceptional man as typical. The influence of the psychology of Sigmund Freud and the political theories of Karl Marx on twentieth-century drama cannot be overestimated.

Technically, tremendous advances were made in the drama. Lighting, staging, and design achieved creative prominence under the influence of designers like Robert Edmond Jones, Lee Simonson, and Jo Mielziner. Critics like Alexander Woollcott and Heywood Broun established the high standards set for present-day reviewers. *Theatre Arts*, a magazine of the drama, publicized advanced ideas and made modern theater trends more widely known.

The great depression of the 1930's inspired strong plays of social protest. Organizations like the Group Theater, the Mercury Theater, and the Federal Theater presented these dramas, and names like Elmer Rice, Sidney Howard, and Clifford Odets became identified with the "new" drama. Looking back, however, the finest plays that emerge from this period are those dealing with the great universals of living and dying, like Thornton Wilder's *The Skin of Our Teeth* and Marc Connelly's *Green Pastures*.

Although the paralyzing impact of a new kind of warfare made possible by Hiroshima precluded any great American war literature of the Second World War, serious plays like *Watch on the Rhine* by Lillian Hellman and *There Shall Be No Night* by Robert Sherwood reflected the mood of the day. In the 1940's, William Saroyan expressed a lyrical trust in the common man in plays like *My Heart's in the Highlands*, although his undisciplined talent has not given proof of its early promise. Musical comedy and the music drama flourished with unparalleled vigor and originality. Perhaps the best known is *Oklahoma!*, first presented in 1943, a folk play which began a trend that is still growing today.

Modern American Playwrights

In our time, certain playwrights stand out as particularly noteworthy. The following are just a few of the outstanding figures that have dominated the theatrical scene in the first half of the twentieth century.

Eugene O'Neill (1888–1953), considered America's major dramatist, devoted much of his life to writing plays of tragic power and intensity. His works reveal the unsatisfied searching of a soul for truth. O'Neill's early one-act plays, like *Bound East for Cardiff*, show a deep love of the sea. His full-length play, *Beyond the Horizon*, which won a Pulitzer Prize in 1920, is a somber study of thwarted idealism. In all of his plays, including *Mourning Becomes Electra* and *Strange Interlude*, O'Neill shows a preoccupation with the unusual in human experience, and an attempt to solve the mystery of existence through various inadequate means. In *The Emperor Jones, The Great God Brown*, and *Desire Under the Elms*, there is the search for meaning in life with the sense of frustration. *Long Day's Journey into Night*, produced after his death, is a last powerful showing of this man's tragic view of life.

Eugene O'Neill dominated the scene in the American theater by his refusal to accept any easy answers. He did not let the American theater become trivial. Again and again he explored man's alienation in a world bereft of spiritual ideals and his capacity to feel and suffer greatly. O'Neill casts a long shadow; for, although he never reached great heights of expression, he voiced man's longings and anxieties.

Thornton Wilder (1897–   ), an experimentalist in the theater, won the Pulitzer Prize in 1938 with the still popular and moving play, *Our Town*. On a bare stage, characters who are almost symbolic act out a testimony of belief in human dignity and the nobility of life. The Stage Manager, who acts as the narrator in the play, says:

> I don't care what they say with their mouths—everybody knows that *something* is eternal. And it ain't houses, and it ain't names, and it ain't earth, and it ain't even the stars . . . everybody knows in their bones that something is eternal, and that something has to do with human beings. All the greatest people ever lived have been telling us that for five thousand years, and yet you'd be surprised how people are always losing hold of it. There's something way down deep that's eternal about every human being.

Wilder has reacted in a positive manner against materialism, and constantly asserts his belief in the power of man's personality.

Maxwell Anderson (1888–1959) displayed great versatility and deep interest in the problems of society. Most critics agree, however, that his finest plays are his historical dramas, such as *Elizabeth the Queen* and *Mary of Scotland*. Anderson is unique in his use of the poetic drama in such contemporary themes as *Winterset*, a bold and original tragedy.

Lillian Hellman (1905–   ) has also shown power and craftsmanship in examining the problems of modern society. One of her most outstanding plays, *The Little Foxes*, is a chilling study of the effects of greed on a Southern family.

These are but a few of America's fine and influential dramatists. The contemporary drama is impossible to evaluate with any finality. Literature demands the test of time. It is significant to note, however, a renewed interest in the "play with music." Collaborators like Rodgers and Hammerstein and Lerner and Loewe have contributed musicals of definite literary value. Notable are *The King and I* with its exotic charm and *My Fair Lady* with its brilliant sophistication.

New Voices

Among the most important serious dramatists who have emerged since World War II are Tennessee Williams, Arthur Miller, William Inge, and Edward Albee. Williams's first Broadway production, *The Glass Menagerie*, probes the psychological problem of a widow and her shy, crippled daughter who live in a dream world. In *All My Sons*, Miller shows his interest in social problems as he examines the life of a dishonest manufacturer during the Second World War. William Inge is a more traditional playwright, but he uses symbolism as a dramatic technique in plays like *The Dark at the Top of the Stairs*. Edward Albee is among the first of the new playwrights in America to show the influence of the theater of the absurd.

The theater of the absurd has been described in various ways as "the school of the grotesque," "the voice of cultivated disenchantment," "the expression of revulsion against materialism." Perhaps this new approach to drama has been described best by Thomas Barbour who writes that here "sense is spoken as nonsense, and nonsense as sense; the ordinary is shocking and the shocking is ordinary." European playwrights, such as Samuel Beckett, Eugene Ionesco, Harold Pinter, and Jean Genet form the avant-garde of this new trend in playwriting. A number of their plays, such as *Waiting for Godot, Rhinoceros, The Caretaker,* and *The Maids,* are powerful expressions of disillusionment. It is a theater to watch in the years to come.

Two major voices in the theater of today, Tennessee Williams and Arthur Miller, state most clearly what the drama today wants to explore.

The bird that I catch in the net of this play is . . . the true quality of experience in a group of people, that cloudy, flickering, evanescent, fiercely charged interplay of live human beings in the thundercloud of common crisis.

—Tennessee Williams

This is a world in which the human being can live as a naturally political, naturally private, naturally engaged person, a world in which once again a true tragic victory may be scored.

—Arthur Miller

Reginald Rose

Twelve Angry Men

A young boy is accused of murder, and his life hangs in the balance as a jury debates the evidence. The reactions of the twelve individuals to the facts in the case is the stuff of which this drama is made. The accused boy, unseen during the entire play, is the silent pivot around which the action revolves; and the playwright has asked, "What manner of men are these sitting in judgment on a person's life?"

In the last analysis, Reginald Rose has preached a strong lesson in the dignity of the individual. This nameless boy whose life depends on the verdict of twelve men is an individual. So is each juror whose personality is dramatically revealed in the tension of the locked jury room. Unconsciously, each reader of this drama must ask, "Which juror am I? Which one?"

◄§ §►

TWELVE ANGRY MEN

CHARACTERS

FOREMAN OF THE JURY: He is a small, petty man who is impressed with the authority he has and handles himself quite formally. He is not overly bright, but dogged.

JUROR NO. TWO: He is a meek, hesitant man who finds it difficult to maintain any opinions of his own. He is easily swayed and usually adopts the opinion of the last person to whom he has spoken.

JUROR NO. THREE: He is a very strong, very forceful, extremely opinionated man within whom can be detected a streak of sadism. Also, he is a humorless man who is intolerant of opinions other than his own, and accustomed to forcing his wishes and views upon others.

JUROR NO. FOUR: He seems to be a man of wealth and position, and a practiced speaker who presents himself well at all times. He seems to feel a little bit above the rest of the jurors. His only concern is with the facts in this case and he is appalled with the behavior of the others.

JUROR NO. FIVE: He is a naive, very frightened young man who takes his obligations in this case very seriously but who finds it difficult to speak up when his elders have the floor.

JUROR NO. SIX: He is an honest but dull-witted man who comes upon his decisions slowly and carefully. He is a man who finds it difficult to create positive opinions, but who must listen to and digest and accept those opinions offered by others which appeal to him most.

JUROR NO. SEVEN: He is a loud, flashy, glad-handed salesman type who has more important things to do than to sit on a jury. He is quick to show temper and equally quick to form opinions on things about which he knows nothing. He is a bully, and, of course, a coward.

JUROR NO. EIGHT: He is a quiet, thoughtful, gentle man—a man who sees all sides of every question and constantly seeks the truth. He is a man of strength tempered with compassion. Above all, he is a man who wants justice to be done, and will fight to see that it is.

JUROR NO. NINE: He is a mild, gentle old man, long since defeated by life, and now merely waiting to die. He recognizes himself for what he is, and mourns the days when it would have been possible to be courageous without shielding himself behind his many years.

JUROR NO. TEN: He is an angry, bitter man—a man who antagonizes almost at sight. He is also a bigot who places no values on any human life save his own. Here is a man who has been nowhere and is going nowhere and knows it deep within him.

JUROR NO. ELEVEN: He is a refugee from Europe. He speaks with an accent and is ashamed, humble, almost subservient to the people around him. He will honestly seek justice because he has suffered through so much injustice.

JUROR NO. TWELVE: He is a slick, bright advertising man who thinks of human beings in terms of percentages, graphs and polls, and has no real understanding of people. He is a superficial snob, but trying to be a good fellow.

PLACE: A *jury room.*
TIME: *The present. Summer.*

ACT I: *Late afternoon.*
ACT II: *A second or two later.*
ACT III: *Immediately following Act II.*

ACT I

AT RISE OF CURTAIN: *The curtain comes up on a dark stage; then as the lights start to come up on the scene we hear the voice of the* JUDGE, *offstage.*

JUDGE (*offstage*). Murder in the first degree . . . premeditated homicide . . . is the most serious charge tried in our criminal courts. You have heard a long and complex case, gentlemen, and it is now your duty to sit down to try and separate the facts from the fancy. One man is dead. The life of another is at stake. If there is a reasonable doubt in your minds as to the guilt of the accused—then you must declare him not guilty. If—however—there is no reasonable doubt, then he must be found guilty. Whichever way you decide, the verdict must be unanimous. I urge you to deliberate honestly and thoughtfully. You are faced with a grave responsibility. Thank you, gentlemen.

(*There is a long pause. The lights are now up full in the jury room. There is a door left and a window in the right wall of the room. Over the door left is an electric clock. A water cooler is down right, with a wastebasket beside it. A container with paper cups is attached to the wall nearby. A long conference table is slightly upstage of center stage. About it are twelve uncomfortable-looking straight chairs. There is a chair at either end of the table, seven at the upstage side and three at the downstage side of the table. There are two more straight chairs against the wall down left and one on the up right corner of the room. It is a bare, unpleasant room. After the pause the door left opens and the* GUARD *walks in. As he opens the door the lettering "Jury Room" can be seen on the outside of the door. The* GUARD *walks across the room and opens the window right as a* CLERK *drones out, offstage left.*)

5

CLERK (*offstage left*). The jury will retire.
GUARD (*surveying room, shaking his head*). He doesn't stand a chance. (*Moves left again.*)

(*The JURORS file in left. The GUARD stands upstage of the door and counts them. Four or five of the jurors light cigarettes as they enter the room. JUROR FIVE lights a pipe which he smokes constantly. JURORS TWO, NINE, and TWELVE go to the water cooler for a drink. JUROR SEVEN goes to the window and opens it wider. The rest of the JURORS begin to take seats around the table, though some of them stand and lean forward, with both hands on the back of the chair. JUROR SEVEN produces a pack of gum and offers a piece to the men by the water cooler.*)

SEVEN. Chewing gum? Gum? Gum?
NINE. Thank you, but no. (*Jurors TWO and TWELVE shake their heads.*)
SEVEN. Y'know something?
TWELVE. I know lots of things. I'm in advertising.
SEVEN (*tugging at collar*). Y'know, it's hot.
TWELVE. (*to TWO, mildly sarcastic*). I never would have known that if he hadn't told me. Would you?
TWO (*missing sarcasm*). I suppose not. I'd kind of forgotten.
TWELVE. All I've done all day is sweat.
THREE (*calling out*). I bet you aren't sweating like that kid who was tried.
SEVEN. You'd think they'd at least air-condition the place. I almost dropped dead in court.
TWELVE. My taxes are high enough.
SEVEN. This should go fast, anyway. (*Moves to table, as EIGHT goes to window.*)
NINE (*nodding to himself, then, as he throws his paper water cup into wastebasket*). Yes, it's hot.
GUARD. Okay, gentlemen. Everybody's here. If there's anything you want, I'm right outside. Just knock. (*Goes out left, closing door. They all look at door, silently. The lock is turned.*)
THREE. Did he lock that door?
FOUR. Yes, he did.
THREE. What do they think we are, crooks?

FOREMAN *(seated at table)*. They lock us up for a little while. . . .

THREE *(breaking in)*. And then they lock that kid up forever and that's okay by me.

FIVE *(motioning toward door)*. I never knew they did that.

TEN *(blowing his nose)*. Sure, they lock the door. What did you think?

FIVE *(a bit irritated)*. I just didn't know. It never occurred to me.

FOUR. Shall we all admit right now that it is hot and humid and our tempers are short?

EIGHT *(turning from window)*. It's been a pretty hard week. *(Turns back and continues looking out.)*

THREE. I feel just fine.

TWELVE. I wonder what's been going on down at the office. You know how it is in advertising. In six days my job could be gone, and the whole company, too. They aren't going to like this. *(JURORS start to take off their suit coats and hang them over backs of chairs.)*

FOREMAN. Well, figure this is our duty.

TWELVE. I didn't object to doing my duty. I just mentioned that I might not have a job by the time I get back. *(He and NINE move to table and take their places. NINE sits near right end of table.)*

THREE *(motioning to FOUR)*. Ask him to hire you. He's rich. Look at the suit!

FOREMAN *(to FOUR, as he tears off slips of paper for a ballot)*. Is it custom-tailored?

FOUR. Yes, it is.

FOREMAN. I have an uncle who's a tailor. *(FOUR takes his jacket off, places it carefully over back of chair and sits.)*

FOUR. How does he do?

FOREMAN *(shaking his head)*. Not too well. Y'know, a friend of his, that's a friend of my uncle, the tailor—well—this friend wanted to be on this jury in my place.

SEVEN. Why didn't you let him? I would have done anything to miss this.

FOREMAN. And get caught, or something? Y'know what kind of a fine you could pay for anything like that? Anyway, this friend of my uncle's was on a jury once, about ten years ago—a case just about like this one.

TWELVE. So what happened?

FOREMAN. They let him off. Reasonable doubt. And do y'know, about eight years later they found out that he'd actually done it, anyway. A guilty man—a murderer—was turned loose in the streets.

THREE. Did they get him?

FOUR. They couldn't.

THREE. Why not?

FOUR. A man can't be held in double jeopardy. Unless it's a hung jury, they can't try a man twice for the same crime.

SEVEN. That isn't going to happen here.

THREE. Six days. They should have finished it in two. (*Slapping back of one hand into palm of other.*) Talk! Talk! Talk! (*Gets up and starts for water cooler.*) Did you ever hear so much talk about nothing?

TWO (*laughing nervously*). Well—I guess—they're entitled . . .

THREE. Everybody gets a fair trial. . . . (*Shakes his head.*) That's the system. (*Downs his drink.*) Well, I suppose you can't say anything against it. (*Tosses his water cup toward wastebasket and misses.* TWO *picks cup up and puts it in wastebasket as* THREE *returns to his seat.*)

SEVEN (*to* TEN). How did you like that business about the knife? Did you ever hear a phonier story?

TEN (*wisely*). Well, look, you've gotta expect that. You know what you're dealing with. . . .

SEVEN. He bought a switch knife that night. . . .

TEN (*with a sneer*). And then he lost it.

SEVEN. A hole in his pocket.

TEN. A hole in his father.

TWO. An awful way to kill your father—a knife in his chest. (*Crosses to table.*)

TEN. Look at the kind of people they are—you know them. (*Gets handkerchief out again.*)

SEVEN. What's the matter? You got a cold?

TEN (BLOWING). A lulu! These hot weather colds can kill you.

SEVEN. I had one last year, while I was on vacation, too.

FOREMAN (*briskly*). All right, gentlemen. Let's take seats.

SEVEN. Right. This better be fast. I've got tickets to—(*Insert name of any current Broadway hit.*)—for tonight. I must be the only guy in the world who hasn't seen it yet. (*Laughs and sits down, as do others still not seated.*) Okay, your honor, start the show.

FOREMAN (*to* EIGHT, *who is still looking out window*). How about sitting down? (EIGHT *doesn't hear him.*) The gentleman at the window. (EIGHT *turns, startled.*) How about sitting down?

EIGHT. Oh, I'm sorry. (*Sits at right end of table, opposite* FOREMAN.)

TEN. It's tough to figure, isn't it? A kid kills his father. Bing! Just like that. Well, it's the element. They let the kids run wild. Maybe it serves 'em right.

FOUR. There are better proofs than some emotion you may have—perhaps a dislike for some group.

SEVEN. We all agreed that it was hot.

NINE. And that our tempers will get short.

THREE. That's if we disagree—but this is open and shut. Let's get it done.

FOREMAN. All right. Now—you gentlemen can handle this any way you want to. I mean, I'm not going to make any rules. If we want to discuss it first and then vote, that's one way. Or we can vote right now and see how we stand.

SEVEN. Let's vote now. Who knows, maybe we can all go home.

TEN. Yeah. Let's see who's where.

THREE. Right. Let's vote now.

EIGHT. All right. Let us vote.

FOREMAN. Anybody doesn't want to vote? (*Looks around table. There is a pause as* ALL *look at each other.*)

SEVEN. That was easy.

FOREMAN. Okay. All those voting guilty raise your hands. (JURORS THREE, SEVEN, TEN *and* TWELVE *put their hands up instantly. The* FOREMAN *and* TWO, FOUR, FIVE *and* SIX *follow a second later. Then* ELEVEN *raises his hand and a moment later* NINE *puts his hand up.*) Eight—nine—ten—eleven—that's eleven for guilty. Okay. Not guilty? (EIGHT's *hand goes up.* ALL *turn to look at him.*)

THREE. Hey, you're in left field!

FOREMAN. Okay. Eleven to one. Eleven guilty, one not guilty. Now we know where we stand.

THREE (*rising, to* EIGHT). Do you really believe he's not guilty?

EIGHT (*quietly*). I don't know.

SEVEN (*to* FOREMAN). After six days, he doesn't know.

TWELVE. In six days I could learn calculus. This is A, B, C.

EIGHT. I don't believe that it is as simple as A, B, C.

THREE. I never saw a guiltier man in my life. (*Sits again.*)

EIGHT. What does a guilty man look like? He is not guilty until we say he is guilty. Are we to vote on his face?

THREE. You sat right in court and heard the same things I did. The man's a dangerous killer. You could see it.

EIGHT. Where do you look to see if a man is a killer?

THREE (*irritated by him*). Oh, well! . . .

EIGHT (*with quiet insistence*). I would like to know. Tell me what the facial characteristics of a killer are. Maybe you know something I don't know.

FOUR. Look! What is there about the case that makes you think the boy is innocent?

EIGHT. He's nineteen years old.

THREE. That's old enough. He knifed his own father. Four inches into the chest. An innocent little nineteen-year-old kid.

FOUR (*to* THREE). I agree with you that the boy is guilty but I think we should try to avoid emotionally colored arguments.

THREE. All right. They proved it a dozen different ways. Do you want me to list them?

EIGHT. No.

TEN (*rising, putting his feet on seat of chair and sitting on back of it, then, to* EIGHT). Well, do you believe that stupid story he told?

FOUR (*to* TEN). Now, now.

TEN. Do you believe the kid's story?

EIGHT. I don't know whether I believe it or not. Maybe I don't.

SEVEN. So what'd you vote not guilty for?

EIGHT. There were eleven votes for guilty—it's not so easy for me to raise my hand and send a boy off to die without talking about it first.

SEVEN. Who says it's easy for me?

FOUR. Or me?

EIGHT. No one.

FOREMAN. He's still just as guilty, whether it's an easy vote or a hard vote.

SEVEN (*belligerently*). Is there something wrong because I voted fast?

EIGHT. Not necessarily.

SEVEN. I think the guy's guilty. You couldn't change my mind if you talked for a hundred years.

EIGHT. I don't want to change your mind.

THREE. Just what are you thinking of?

EIGHT. I want to talk for a while. Look—this boy's been kicked around all his life. You know—living in a slum—his mother dead since he was nine. That's not a very good head start. He's a tough, angry kid. You know why slum kids get that way? Because we knock 'em over the head once a day, every day. I think maybe we owe him a few words. That's all. (*Looks around table. He is met by cold looks.* NINE *nods slowly while* FOUR *begins to comb his hair.*)

FOUR. All right, it's hard, sure—it was hard for me. Everything I've got I fought for. I worked my way through college. That was a long time ago, and perhaps you do forget. I fought, yes, but I never killed.

THREE. I know what it's like. I never killed nobody.

TWELVE. I've been kicked around, too. Wait until you've worked in an ad agency and the big boy that buys the advertising walks in. We all know.

ELEVEN (*who speaks with an accent*). In my country, in Europe, kicking was a science, but let's try to find something better than that.

TEN (*to* EIGHT). I don't mind telling you this, mister. We don't owe the kid a thing. He got a fair trial, didn't he? You know what that trial cost? He's lucky he got it. Look, we're all grown-ups here. You're not going to tell us that we're supposed to believe him, knowing what he is. I've lived among 'em all my life. You can't believe a word they say. You know that.

NINE (*to* TEN, *very slowly*). I don't know that. What a terrible thing for a man to believe! Since when is dishonesty a group character-istic? You have no monopoly on the truth!

THREE (*interrupting*). All right. It's not Sunday. We don't need a sermon.

NINE (*not heeding*). What this man says is very dangerous. (EIGHT *puts his hand on* NINE's *arm and stops him.* NINE *draws a deep breath and relaxes.*)

FOUR. I don't see any need for arguing like this. I think we ought to be able to behave like gentlemen.

SEVEN. Right!

TWELVE (*smiling up at* FOUR). Oh, all right, if you insist.

FOUR (*to* TWELVE). Thank you.

TWELVE. Sure.

FOUR. If we're going to discuss this case, why, let's discuss the facts.

FOREMAN. I think that's a good point. We have a job to do. Let's do it.

ELEVEN. If you gentlemen don't mind, I'm going to close the window. (*Gets up and does so, then, apologetically as he moves back to table.*) It was blowing on my neck. (TEN *blows his nose fiercely as he gets down from back of chair and sits again.*)

SEVEN. If you don't mind, I'd like to have the window open.

ELEVEN. But it was blowing on me.

SEVEN. Don't you want a little air? It's summer—it's hot.

ELEVEN. I was very uncomfortable.

SEVEN. There are twelve of us in this room; it's the only window. If you don't mind!

ELEVEN. I have some rights, too.

SEVEN. So do the rest of us.

FOUR (*to* ELEVEN). Couldn't you trade chairs with someone at the other end of the table?

ELEVEN. All right, I will open the window, if someone would trade. (*Goes to window and opens it.* TWO *gets up and goes to* ELEVEN's *chair, near right end of table.*)

TWO (*motioning*). Take my chair.

ELEVEN. Thank you. (*Goes to* TWO's *chair, near left end of table.*)

FOREMAN. Shall we get back to the case?

THREE. Yeah, let's.

TWELVE. I may have an idea here. I'm just thinking out loud now, but it seems to me that it's up to us to convince this gentleman— (*Motioning toward* EIGHT.)—that we're right and he's wrong. Maybe if we each talk for a minute or two. You know—try it on for size.

FOREMAN. That sounds fair enough.

FOUR. Very fair.

FOREMAN. Supposing we go once around the table.

SEVEN. Okay—let's start it off.

FOREMAN. Right. (*To* TWO.) We'll start with you.

TWO (*timidly*). Oh. Well . . . (*There is a long pause.*) I just think he's guilty. I thought it was obvious.

EIGHT. In what way was it obvious?

TWO. I mean that nobody proved otherwise.

EIGHT (*quietly*). Nobody has to prove otherwise; innocent until proven guilty. The burden of proof is on the prosecution. The defendant doesn't have to open his mouth. That's in the Constitution. The Fifth Amendment. You've heard of it.

FOUR. Everyone has.

TWO (*flustered*). Well, sure—I've heard of it. I know what it is . . . I . . . what I meant . . . well, anyway . . . I think he's guilty!

EIGHT (*looking at* TWO, *shaking his head slowly*). No reasons—just guilty. There is a life at stake here.

THREE. Okay, let's get to the facts. Number one: let's take the old man who lived on the second floor right underneath the room where the murder took place. At ten minutes after twelve on the night of the killing he heard loud noises in the upstairs apartment. He said it sounded like a fight. Then he heard the kid say to his father, "I'm gonna kill you." A second later he heard a body falling, and he ran to the door of his apartment, looked out and saw the kid running downstairs and out of the house. Then he called the police. They found the father with a knife in his chest.

FOREMAN. And the coroner fixed the time of death at around midnight.

THREE. Right. Now what else do you want?

EIGHT. It doesn't seem to fit.

FOUR. The boy's entire story is flimsy. He claimed he was at the movies. That's a little ridiculous, isn't it? He couldn't even remember what picture he saw.

THREE. That's right. Did you hear that? (*To* FOUR.) You're absolutely right.

FIVE. He didn't have any ticket stub.

EIGHT. Who keeps a ticket stub at the movies?

FOUR (*to* FIVE). That's true enough.

FIVE. I suppose, but the cashier didn't remember him.

THREE. And the ticket taker didn't, either.

TEN. Look—what about the woman across the street? If her testimony don't prove it, then nothing does.

TWELVE. That's right. She saw the killing, didn't she?

FOREMAN (*rapping on table*). Let's go in order.

TEN (*loudly*). Just a minute. Here's a woman who's lying in bed and can't sleep. It's hot, you know. (*Gets up and begins to walk around at left stage, blowing his nose and talking.*) Anyway, she wakes up and she looks out the window, and right across the street she sees the kid stick the knife into his father.

EIGHT. How can she really be sure it was the kid when she saw it through the windows of a passing elevated train?

TEN (*pausing down left*). She's known the kid all his life. His window is right opposite hers—across the el tracks—and she swore she saw him do it.

EIGHT. I heard her swear to it.

TEN. Okay. And they proved in court that you can look through the windows of a passing el train at night, and see what's happening on the other side. They proved it.

EIGHT. Weren't you telling us just a minute or two ago that you can't trust *them*? That you can't believe *them*.

TEN (*coldly*). So?

EIGHT. Then I'd like to ask you something. How come you believed her? She's one of *them*, too, isn't she? (TEN *crosses up to* EIGHT.)

TEN. You're a pretty smart fellow, aren't you?

FOREMAN (*rising*). Now take it easy. (THREE *gets up and goes to* TEN.)

THREE. Come on. Sit down. (*Leads* TEN *back to his seat.*) What're you letting him get you all upset for? Relax. (TEN *and* THREE *sit down.*)

FOUR. Gentlemen, they did take us out to the woman's room and we looked through the windows of a passing el train—(*To* EIGHT.) —didn't we?

EIGHT. Yes. (*Nods.*) We did.

FOUR. And weren't you able to see what happened on the other side?

EIGHT. I didn't see as well as they told me I would see, but I did see what happened on the other side.

TEN (*snapping at* EIGHT). You see—do you see?

FOREMAN (*sitting again*). Let's calm down now. (*To* FIVE.) It's your turn.

FIVE. I'll pass it.

FOREMAN. That's your privilege. (*To* SIX.) How about you?

SIX (*slowly*). I don't know. I started to be convinced, you know, with the testimony from those people across the hall. Didn't they say something about an argument between the father and the boy around seven o'clock that night? I mean, I can be wrong.

ELEVEN. I think it was eight o'clock. Not seven.

EIGHT. That's right. Eight o'clock.

FOUR. They heard the father hit the boy twice and then saw the boy walk angrily out of the house.

SIX. Right.

EIGHT. What does that prove?

SIX. Well, it doesn't exactly prove anything. It's just part of the picture. I didn't say it proved anything.

FOREMAN. Anything else?

SIX. No. (*Rises, goes to water cooler for a drink and then sits again.*)

SEVEN. I don't know—most of it's been said already. We can talk all day about this thing, but I think we're wasting our time.

EIGHT. I don't.

FOUR. Neither do I. Go on.

SEVEN. Look at the kid's record. He stole a car. He's been arrested for mugging. I think they said he stabbed somebody in the arm.

FOUR. They did.

SEVEN. He was picked up for knife fighting. At fifteen he was in reform school.

THREE. And they sent him to reform school for stabbing someone!

SEVEN (*with sarcasm*). This is a very fine boy.

EIGHT. Ever since he was five years old his father beat him up regularly. He used his fists.

SEVEN. So would I! On a kid like that.

THREE. You're right. It's the kids. The way they are—you know? They don't listen. (*Bitterly.*) I've got a kid. When he was eight years old he ran away from a fight. I saw him. I was *so* ashamed. I told him right out, "I'm gonna make a man out of you or I'm gonna bust you up into little pieces trying." When he was fifteen he hit me in the face. He's big, you know? I haven't seen him in three years. Rotten kid! I hate tough kids! You work your heart out. . . . (*Pauses.*) All right. Let's get on with it. . . . (*Gets up and goes to window, very embarrassed.*)

FOUR. We're missing the point here. This boy—let's say he's a product of a filthy neighborhood and a broken home. We can't help that. We're not here to go into the reasons why slums are breeding grounds for criminals; they are. I know it. So do you. The children who come out of slum backgrounds are potential menaces to society.

TEN. You said it there. I don't want any part of them, believe me. (*There is a dead silence for a moment, and then* FIVE *speaks haltingly.*)

FIVE. I've lived in a slum all my life. . . .

TEN. Now wait a second!

FIVE. I used to play in a backyard that was filled with garbage. Maybe it still smells on me.

FOREMAN. Now, let's be reasonable. There's nothing personal——

FIVE (*rising, slamming his hand down on table*). There is something personal! (*Then he catches himself, and, seeing* EVERYONE *looking at him, sits down, fists clenched.*)

THREE (*turning from window*). Come on, now. He didn't mean you, feller. Let's not be so sensitive. (*There is a long pause.*)

EIGHT (*breaking silence*). Who did he mean?

ELEVEN. I can understand this sensitivity.

FOREMAN. Now let's stop the bickering.

TWELVE. We're wasting time.

FOREMAN (*to* EIGHT). It's your turn.

EIGHT. All right. I had a peculiar feeling about this trial. Somehow I felt that the defense counsel never really conducted a thorough cross-examination. Too many questions were left unasked.

FOUR. While it doesn't change my opinion about the guilt of the kid, still, I agree with you that the defense counsel was bad.

THREE. S-o-o-o? (*Crosses back to table and sits.*)

EIGHT. This is a point.

THREE. What about facts?

EIGHT. So many questions were never answered.

THREE. (*annoyed*). What about the questions that were answered? For instance, let's talk about that cute little switch knife. You know, the one that fine upright kid admitted buying.

EIGHT. All right, let's talk about it. Let's get it in here and look at it. I'd like to see it again, Mr. Foreman. (FOREMAN *looks at him questioningly and then gets up and goes to door left.*)

(*During the following dialogue the* FOREMAN *knocks. The* GUARD *unlocks the door and comes in left and the* FOREMAN *whispers to him. The* GUARD *nods and leaves, locking the door. The* FOREMAN *returns to his seat.*)

THREE. We all know what it looks like. I don't see why we have to look at it again. (*To* FOUR.) What do·you think?

FOUR. The gentleman has a right to see exhibits in evidence.

THREE (*shrugging*). Okay with me.

FOUR (*to* EIGHT). This knife is a pretty strong piece of evidence, don't you agree?

EIGHT. I do.

FOUR. Now let's get the sequence of events right as they relate to the switch knife.

TWELVE. The boy admits going out of his house at eight o'clock, after being slapped by his father.

EIGHT. Or punched.

FOUR. Or punched. (*Gets up and begins to pace at right stage, moving down right to up right and back again.*) He went to a neighborhood store and bought a switch knife. The storekeeper was arrested the following day when he admitted selling it to the boy.

THREE. I think everyone agrees that it's an unusual knife. Pretty hard to forget something like that.

FOUR. The storekeeper identified the knife and said it was the only one of its kind he had in stock. Why did the boy get it?

SEVEN (*sarcastically*). As a present for a friend of his, he says.

FOUR (*pausing in his pacing*). Am I right so far?

EIGHT. Right.

THREE. You bet he's right. (*To* ALL.) Now listen to this man. He knows what he's talking about.

FOUR (*standing at right stage*). Next, the boy claims that on the way home the knife must have fallen through a hole in his coat pocket, that he never saw it again. Now there's a story, gentlemen. You know what actually happened. The boy took the knife home, and a few hours later stabbed his father with it and even remembered to wipe off the fingerprints.

(*The door left opens and the* GUARD *walks in with an oddly-designed knife with a tag on it.* FOUR *crosses left and takes the knife from him. The* GUARD *goes out left, closing and locking the door.*)

FOUR (*at left center, holding up knife*). Everyone connected with the case identified this knife. Now are you trying to tell me that someone picked it up off the street and went up to the boy's house and stabbed his father with it just to be amusing?

EIGHT. No. I'm saying that it's possible that the boy lost the knife, and that someone else stabbed his father with a similar knife. It's possible. (FOUR *flips knife open and jams it into wall just down-stage of door left.*)

FOUR (*standing back to allow others to see*). Take a look at that knife. It's a very strange knife. I've never seen one like it before in my life. Neither had the storekeeper who sold it to him. (EIGHT *reaches casually into his pocket and withdraws an object. No one notices him. He stands up.*) Aren't you trying to make us accept a pretty incredible coincidence?

EIGHT (*moving toward* FOUR). I'm not trying to make anyone accept it. I'm just saying it's possible.

THREE (*rising, shouting*). And I'm saying it's not possible! (EIGHT *swiftly flicks open blade of a switch knife, jams it into wall next to first knife and steps back. They are exactly alike. There are several gasps and* EVERYONE *stares at knife. There is a long silence.* THREE *continues, slowly, amazed.*) What are you trying to do?

TEN (*loudly*). Yeah, what is this? Who do you think you are? (*A flow of ad lib conversation bursts forth.*)

FIVE. Look at it! It's the same knife!

FOREMAN. Quiet! Let's be quiet. (JURORS *quiet down.* THREE *sits again.*)

FOUR. Where did you get it?

EIGHT. I got it in a little junk shop around the corner from the boy's house. It cost two dollars.

THREE. Now listen to me!

EIGHT (*turning to him*). I'm listening.

THREE. You pulled a real smart trick here, but you proved absolutely zero. Maybe there are ten knives like that, so what?

EIGHT. Maybe there are.

THREE. The boy lied and you know it.

EIGHT. (*crossing back to his seat, sitting*). And maybe he didn't lie. Maybe he did lose the knife and maybe he did go to the movies. Maybe the reason the cashier didn't see him was because he sneaked into the movies, and maybe he was ashamed to say so. (*Looks around.*) Is there anybody here who didn't sneak into the movies once or twice when they were young? (*There is a long silence.*)

ELEVEN. I didn't.

FOUR. Really, not even once?

ELEVEN. We didn't have movies.

FOUR. Oh. (*Crosses back to his place and sits.*)

EIGHT. Maybe he did go to the movies—maybe he didn't. And—he may have lied. (*To* TEN.) Do you think he lied?

TEN (*violently*). Now that's a stupid question. Sure, he lied!

EIGHT (*to* FOUR). Do you?

FOUR. You don't have to ask me that. You know my answer. He lied.

EIGHT (*to* FIVE). Do you think he lied? (FIVE *can't answer immediately. He looks around nervously.*)

FIVE. I—I don't know.

SEVEN. Now wait a second. What are you—the guy's lawyer? Listen—there are still eleven of us who think he's guilty. You're alone. What do you think you're going to accomplish? If you want to be stubborn and hang this jury he'll be tried again, and found guilty sure as he's born.

EIGHT. You're probably right.

SEVEN. So what are you going to do about it? We can be here all night.

NINE. It's only one night. A man may die.

SEVEN. Oh, now. Come on.

EIGHT (*to* NINE). Well, yes, that's true.

FOREMAN. I think we ought to get on with it now.

THREE. Right. Let's get going here.

TEN (*to* THREE). How do you like this guy? (THREE *shrugs and turns to* EIGHT.)

THREE. Well, what do you say? You're the one holding up the show.

FOUR (*to* EIGHT). Obviously you don't think the boy is guilty.

EIGHT. I have a doubt in my mind.

FOUR. But you haven't really presented anything to us that makes it possible for us to understand your doubt. There's the old man downstairs. He heard it. He heard the kid shriek it out. . . .

THREE. The woman across the el tracks—she saw it!

SEVEN. We know he bought a switch knife that night and we don't know where he really was. At the movies?

FOREMAN. Earlier that night the kid and his father did have a fight.

FOUR. He's been a violent kid all the way, and while that doesn't prove anything . . .

TEN. Still, you know . . .

EIGHT (*standing*). I've got a proposition to make. (FIVE *stands and puts his hands on back of his chair. Several jurors glare at him. He sinks his head down a bit, then sits down.*) I want to call for a vote. I want you eleven men to vote by secret ballot. I'll abstain.

If there are still eleven votes for guilty, I won't stand alone. We'll take in a guilty verdict right now.

SEVEN. Okay. Let's do it.

FOREMAN. That sounds fair. Is everyone agreed?

FOUR. I certainly am.

TWELVE. Let's roll it.

ELEVEN (*slowly*). Perhaps this is best. (EIGHT *walks over to window and stands there for a moment looking out, then turns as* FORE-MAN *passes ballot slips down table to all of them.* EIGHT *tenses as* JURORS *begin to write. Then folded ballots are passed back to* FOREMAN. *He flips through folded ballots, counts them to be sure he has eleven and then he begins to open them, reading verdict each time.*)

FOREMAN. Guilty. Guilty. Guilty. Guilty. Guilty. Guilty.

THREE. That's six.

FOREMAN. Please. (*Fumbles with one ballot.*) Six guilty. Guilty. Guilty. Guilty. (*Pauses for a moment at tenth ballot and then reads.*) Not guilty. (THREE *slams his hand down hard on table.* EIGHT *starts for table, as* FOREMAN *reads final ballot.*) Guilty.

TEN (*angrily*). How do you like that!

SEVEN (*standing, snarling*). Who was it? I think we have a right to know. (*Looks about. No one moves.*)

CURTAIN

ACT II

AT RISE OF CURTAIN: *It is only a second or two later. The* JURORS *are in the same positions as they were at the end of Act I.*

THREE (*after brief pause*). All right! Who did it? What idiot changed his vote?

EIGHT. Is that the way to talk about a man's life? (*Sits at his place again.*)

THREE. Whose life are you talking about? The life of the dead man or the life of a murderer?

SEVEN. I want to know. Who?

THREE. So do I.

ELEVEN. Excuse me. This was a secret ballot.

THREE. No one looked while we did it, but now I want to know.

ELEVEN. A secret ballot; we agreed on that point, no? If the gentleman wants it to remain a secret——

THREE (*standing up angrily*). What do you mean? There are no secrets in here! I know who it was. (*Turns to* FIVE.) What's the matter with you? You come in here and you vote guilty and then this—(*Nods toward* EIGHT.)—slick preacher starts to tear your heart out with stories about a poor little kid who just couldn't help becoming a murderer. So you change your vote. If that isn't the most sickening——(FIVE *edges away in his chair.*)

FOREMAN. Now hold it. (SEVEN *sits again slowly.*)

FOUR (*to* THREE). I agree with you that the man is guilty, but let's be fair.

THREE. Hold it? Be fair? That's just what I'm saying. We're trying to put a guilty man into the chair where he belongs—and all of a sudden we're paying attention to fairy tales.

FIVE. Now, just a minute——

THREE (*bending toward* FIVE, *wagging finger at him*). Now, you listen to me——

FOREMAN. (*rapping on table*). Let's try to keep this organized, gentlemen.

FOUR. It isn't organized, but let's try to be civilized.

ELEVEN. Please. I would like to say something here. I have always thought that a man was entitled to have unpopular opinions in this country. This is the reason I came here. I wanted to have the right to disagree.

THREE. Do you disagree with us?

ELEVEN. Usually, I would. In this one case I agree with you, but the point I wish to make is that in my own country, I am ashamed to say——

TEN. Oh, now-w-w, what do we have to listen to—the whole history of your country? (THREE *sits again in disgust.*)

FOUR. It's always wise to bear in mind what has happened in other countries, when people aren't allowed to disagree; but we are, so let's stick to the subject.

SEVEN. Yeah, let's stick to the subject. (*To* FIVE.) I want to ask you, what made you change your vote?

THREE. I want to know, too. You haven't told us yet.

FIVE. Why do you think I did change my vote?

SEVEN. Because I do. Now get on with it.

NINE (*quietly*). There's nothing for him to tell you. He didn't change his vote. I did. (ALL *look at* NINE.)

FIVE (*to* THREE). I was going to tell you, but you were so sure of yourself.

THREE. Sorry. (*To* NINE.) Okay, now. . . .

NINE. Maybe you'd like to know why.

THREE (*not giving him a chance*). Let me tell you why that kid's a——

FOREMAN. The man wants to talk. (THREE *subsides*.)

NINE (*to* FOREMAN). Thank you. (*Points at* EIGHT.) This gentleman chose not to stand alone against us. That's his right. It takes a great deal of courage to stand alone even if you believe in something very strongly. He left the verdict up to us. He gambled for support and I gave it to him. I want to hear more. The vote is ten to two. (JURORS TWO *and* FOUR *get up at about the same instant and walk to water cooler as* TEN *speaks*.)

TEN. That's fine. If the speech is over, let's go on. (FOREMAN *gets up, goes to door left, pulls tagged knife from wall and then knocks on door*.)

(*The door is opened by the* GUARD. *The* FOREMAN *hands the* GUARD *the tagged switch knife. The* GUARD *goes out and the* FOREMAN *takes the other switch knife, closes it and puts it in the middle of the table. He sits again. The other* JURORS *talk on, in pantomime, as* TWO *and* FOUR *stand by the water cooler*.)

FOUR (*filling cup*). If there was anything in the kid's favor I'd vote not guilty.

TWO. I don't see what it is.

FOUR (*handing cup to* TWO, *then drawing drink for himself*). Neither do I. They're clutching at straws.

TWO. As guilty as they get—that's the kid, I suppose.

FOUR. It's that one juror that's holding out, but he'll come around. He's got to and, fundamentally, he's a very reasonable man.

TWO. I guess so.

FOUR. They haven't come up with one real fact yet to back up a not guilty verdict.

TWO. It's hard, you know.

FOUR. Yes, it is. And what does "guilty beyond a reasonable doubt" really mean?

TWO. What's a reasonable doubt?

FOUR. Exactly. When a life is at stake, what is a reasonable doubt? You've got to have law and order; you've got to draw the line somewhere; if you don't, everyone would start knifing people.

TWO. Not much doubt here.

FOUR. Two men think so. I wonder why. I really wonder why.

TWO. You do hear stories about innocent men who have gone to jail—or death, sometimes—then years later things turn up.

FOUR. And then on the other hand some killers get turned loose and they go and do it again. They squeeze out on some technicality and kill again. (*Throws his cup into wastebasket, walks back and sits. We then hear* THREE *say to* FIVE.)

THREE. Look, buddy, now that we've kind of cooled off, why—ah—I was a little excited a minute ago. Well, you know how it is—I didn't mean to get nasty. Nothing personal. (TWO *trails back to his place and sits again.*)

FIVE (*after staring at* THREE *for a moment*). Okay.

SEVEN (*to* EIGHT). Look. Supposing you answer me this. If the kid didn't kill him, who did?

EIGHT. As far as I know, we're supposed to decide whether or not the boy on trial is guilty. We're not concerned with anyone else's motives here.

SEVEN. I suppose, but who else had a motive?

EIGHT. The kid's father was along in years; maybe an old grudge.

NINE. Remember, it is "guilty beyond a reasonable doubt." This is an important thing to remember.

THREE (*to* TEN). Everyone's a lawyer. (*To* NINE.) Supposing you explain to us what your reasonable doubts are.

NINE. This is not easy. So far, it's only a feeling I have. A feeling. Perhaps you don't understand.

THREE (*abruptly*). No. I don't.

TEN. A feeling! What are we gonna do, spend the night talking about your feelings? What about the facts?

THREE. You said a mouthful. (*To* NINE.) Look, the old man heard the kid yell, "I'm gonna kill you." A second later he heard the father's body falling, and he saw the boy running out of the house fifteen seconds after that.

SEVEN. Where's the reasonable doubt in that?

TWELVE. That's right. And let's not forget the woman across the street. She looked into the open window and saw the boy stab his father. She saw it!

THREE. Now, if that's not enough for you——

EIGHT. (*quietly firm*). It's not enough for me.

FOUR. What is enough for you? I'd like to know.

SEVEN. How do you like him? It's like talking into a dead 'phone.

FOUR. The woman saw the killing through the windows of a moving elevated train. The train had five cars and she saw it through the windows of the last two cars. She remembers the most insignificant details.

THREE. Well, what have you got to say about that?

EIGHT. I don't know. It doesn't sound right to me.

THREE. Well, supposing you think about it. (*To* TWELVE.) Lend me your pencil. (TWELVE *hands him a pencil.*) Let's play some tic-tac-toe. (*Draws an X on a piece of paper, then hands pencil and paper to* TWELVE.) We might as well pass the time.

EIGHT. This isn't a game. (*Rises and snatches paper away.* THREE *jumps up.*)

THREE. Now, wait a minute!

EIGHT. This is a man's life.

THREE (*angrily*). Who do you think you are?

SEVEN (*rising*). All right, let's take it easy. (EIGHT *sits again.*)

THREE. I've got a good mind to walk around this table and belt him one!

FOREMAN. Now, please. I don't want any fights in here.

THREE. Did you see him? The nerve! The absolute nerve!

TEN. All right. Forget it. It don't mean anything.

SIX. How about sitting down?

THREE. "This isn't a game." Who does he think he is? (SIX *and* TEN *urge* THREE *back into his seat.* SEVEN *sits again, and* ALL *are seated once more.*)

FOUR (*when quiet is restored*). Weren't we talking about elevated trains?

EIGHT. Yes, we were.

FOUR. So?

EIGHT. All right. How long does it take an elevated train going at top speed to pass a given point?

FOUR. What has that got to do with anything?

EIGHT. How long would it take? Guess.

FOUR. I wouldn't have the slightest idea.

SEVEN. Neither would I.

NINE. I don't think they mentioned it.

EIGHT (*to* FIVE). What do you think?

FIVE. About ten or twelve seconds—maybe.

EIGHT. I'd say that was a fair guess. (*Looks about.*) Anyone else?

ELEVEN. I would think about ten seconds, perhaps. . . .

TWO (*reflectively*). About ten seconds, yes.

FOUR. All right, we're agreed. Ten seconds. (*To* EIGHT.) What are you getting at?

EIGHT. This. An el train passes a given point in ten seconds. That given point is the window of the room in which the killing took place. You can almost reach out of the window of that room and touch the el. Right?

FOREMAN. That's right. I tried it.

FOUR. So?

EIGHT. All right. Now let me ask you this. Did anyone here ever live right next to the el tracks?

FIVE. I've lived close to them.

EIGHT. They make a lot of noise, don't they? (FIVE *nods.*) I've lived right by the el tracks. When your window is open, and the train goes by, the noise is almost unbearable. You can't hear yourself think.

TEN (*impatiently*). Okay. You can't hear yourself think. Get to the point.

EIGHT. The old man who lived downstairs heard the boy say——

THREE (*interrupting*). He didn't *say it*, he screamed it.

EIGHT. The old man heard the boy scream, "I'm going to kill you," and one second later he heard a body fall. (*Slight pause.*) One second. That's the testimony. Right?

TWO. Right.

EIGHT. The woman across the street looked through the windows of the last two cars of the el and saw the body fall. Right?

FOUR. Right.

TWELVE. So?

EIGHT (*slowly*). The last two cars. (*Slight pause, then repeats.*) The last two cars.

TEN. What are you giving us here?

EIGHT. An el train takes ten seconds to pass a given point, or two seconds per car. That el had been going by the old man's window for at least six seconds and maybe more *before the body fell*, according to the woman. The old man would have had to hear the boy say, "I'm going to kill you," while the front of the el was roaring past his nose. It's not possible that he could have heard it.

THREE. What do you mean! Sure, he could have heard it.

EIGHT. With an el train going by?

THREE. He said the boy yelled it out.

EIGHT. An el train makes a lot of noise.

THREE. It's enough for me.

FOUR. It's enough for me, too.

NINE. I don't think he could have heard it.

TWO. Maybe the old man didn't hear it. I mean with the el noise. . . .

THREE. What are you people talking about? Are you calling the old man a liar?

EIGHT (*shaking his head*). Something doesn't fit.

FIVE. Well, it stands to reason——

THREE. You're crazy! Why would he lie? What's he got to gain?

NINE. Attention . . . maybe.

THREE. You keep coming up with these bright sayings. Why don't you send one in to a newspaper? They pay two dollars.

EIGHT (*hard, to* THREE). What does that have to do with a man's life? (*Then, to* NINE.) Why might the old man have lied? You have a right to be heard.

NINE (*after moment's hesitation*). It's just that I looked at him for a very long time. The seam of his jacket was split under his arm. Did you notice that? He was a very old man with a torn jacket, and he carried two canes. (*Gets up, moves right and leans against wall.*) I think I know him better than anyone here. This is a quiet, frightened, insignificant man who has been nothing all his life—who has never had recognition—his name in the newspapers. Nobody knows him after seventy-five years. This is a very sad thing. A man like this needs to be recognized—to be questioned, and listened to, and quoted just once. This is very important. . . .

TWELVE. And you're trying to tell us he lied about a thing like this just so he could be important?

NINE. No, he wouldn't really lie. But perhaps he'd make himself believe that he heard those words and recognized the boy's face.

THREE. Well—(*Loud and brassy.*)—that's the most fantastic story I've ever heard. How can you make up a thing like that?

NINE (*doggedly*). I'm not making it up.

THREE. You must be making it up. People don't lie about things like that.

NINE. He made himself believe he told the truth.

THREE. What do you know about it?

NINE (*low but firm*). I speak from experience.

SEVEN. What!

NINE. I am the same man.

FOUR. I think we all understand now. Thank you. (NINE *moves slowly back to table and sits.*)

THREE (*as* NINE *sits*). If you want to admit you're a liar, it's all right by me.

EIGHT. Now, that is too much!

THREE. He's a liar. He just told us so.

EIGHT. He did not say he was a liar; he was explaining.

THREE (*to* NINE). Didn't you admit that you're a liar?

EIGHT (*to* THREE). Please—he was explaining the circumstances so that we could understand why the old man might have lied. There is a difference.

THREE. A liar is a liar, that's all there is to it.

EIGHT. Please—have some compassion.

FOREMAN. Gentlemen, please, we have our job and our duty here.

FOUR. I think they've covered it.

EIGHT. I hope we have.

FOREMAN (*to* EIGHT). All right. Is there anything else? (TWO *holds up a box of cough drops and speaks to* FOREMAN.)

TWO. Cough drop?

FOREMAN (*waving it aside*). No, thank you.

TWO (*hesitantly*). Anybody—want a cough—drop? (*Offers box around.*)

FOREMAN (*sharply*). Come on. Let's get on with it.

EIGHT. I'll take one. (TWO *hands him box.*) Thank you. (*Takes one and returns box.*) Now—there's something else I'd like to point out here. I think we proved that the old man couldn't have heard the boy say, "I'm going to kill you."

THREE. Well, I disagree.

FOUR (*to* THREE). Let's hear him through, anyway.

EIGHT. But supposing the old man really did hear the boy say "I'm going to kill you." This phrase—how many times has each of you used it? Probably hundreds. "If you do that once more, Junior, I'm going to murder you." "Come on, Rocky, kill him!" We say it every day. This doesn't mean that we're really going to kill someone.

FOUR. Don't the circumstances alter that somewhat?

TWELVE. The old man was murdered.

THREE. One thing more. The phrase was "I'm going to kill you." And the kid screamed it out at the top of his lungs.

FOUR. That's the way I understand it.

THREE. Now don't try and tell me he didn't mean it. Anybody says a thing like that the way he said it—they mean it.

TEN. And how they mean it!

EIGHT. Well, let me ask you this. Do you really think the boy would shout out a thing like that so the whole neighborhood would hear it? I don't think so. He's much too bright for that.

TEN (*exploding*). Bright! He's a common ignorant slob. He don't even speak good English!

ELEVEN (*slowly*). He *doesn't* even speak good English.

FOUR. The boy is clever enough. (FOUR'S *line is spoken as* TEN *rises and glowers at* ELEVEN. *There is a momentary pause.* TEN *sits again as* FIVE *gets up and looks around. He is nervous.*)

FIVE. I'd like to change my vote to not guilty. (THREE *slams his fist into his hand, then walks to window and does it again.*)

FOREMAN. Are you sure?

FIVE. Yes. I'm sure.

FOREMAN. The vote is nine to three in favor of guilty.

FOUR (*to* FIVE). I'd like to know why you've changed your vote.

FIVE. I think there's a doubt.

THREE (*turning abruptly from window, snarling*). Where? What is the doubt?

FIVE. There's the knife. . . .

SEVEN (*slamming his hand down on table*). Oh, fine!

TEN. He—(*Motioning at* EIGHT.)—he talked you into believing a fairy tale.

FOUR (*to* FIVE). Go on. Give us the reasons.

FIVE. The old man, too. Maybe he didn't lie, but then just *maybe* he did. Maybe the old man doesn't like the kid.

SEVEN. Well, if that isn't the end.

FIVE. I believe that there is reasonable doubt. (*Sits again.*)

SEVEN. What are you basing it on? Stories that this guy—(*Indicates* EIGHT.)—made up! He ought to write for Amazing Detective Monthly. He'd make a fortune. Listen, the kid had a lawyer, didn't he? Why didn't his lawyer bring up all these points?

FIVE. Lawyers can't think of everything.

SEVEN. Oh, brother! (*To* EIGHT.) You sit in here and pull stories out of thin air. Now we're supposed to believe that the old man didn't get out of bed, run to the door and see the kid beat it downstairs fifteen seconds after the killing.

FOUR. That's the testimony, I believe.

SEVEN. And the old man swore to this—yes—he swore to this only so he could be important. (*Looks over at* NINE.)

FIVE. Did the old man say he *ran* to the door?

SEVEN. Ran. Walked. What's the difference? He got there.

FIVE. I don't remember what he said. But I don't see how he could run.

FOUR. He said he *went*. I remember it now. He *went* from his bedroom to the front door. That's enough, isn't it?

EIGHT. Where was his bedroom, again?

TEN (*disinterested*). Down the hall somewhere.

EIGHT (*mad*). Down the hall! Are we to send a man off to die because it's down the hall *somewhere*?

TEN. I thought you remembered everything. Don't you remember that?

EIGHT. No, I don't.

NINE. I don't remember, either.

EIGHT. Mr. Foreman, I'd like to take a look at the diagram of the apartment.

SEVEN. Why don't we have them run the trial over just so you can get everything straight?

EIGHT. The bedroom is down the hall somewhere. Do you *know*—do you know exactly where it is? Please. A man's life is at stake. Do you *know?*

SEVEN. Well, ah . . .

EIGHT. Mr. Foreman.

FOREMAN (*rising*). I heard you. (*Goes to door left and knocks on door.*)

(*During the ensuing dialogue the* GUARD *opens the door left. The* FOREMAN *whispers to him. The* GUARD *nods and then closes the door.*)

THREE (*stepping away from window, moving a few steps toward* EIGHT). All right. What's this one for? How come you're the only one in the room who wants to see exhibits all the time?

FIVE. I want to see this one, too.

NINE. So do I.

THREE. And I want to stop wasting time.

FOUR. Are we going to start wading through all that nonsense about where the body was found?

EIGHT. We're not. We're going to find out how a man who's had two strokes in the past three years and who walks with a pair of canes could get to his front door in fifteen seconds.

THREE. He said twenty seconds.

TWO. He said fifteen.

THREE. How does he know how long fifteen seconds is? You can't judge that kind of thing.

NINE. He said fifteen. He was very positive about it.

THREE (*angrily*). He's an old man. You saw that. Half the time he was confused. How could he be positive about—anything? (*Looks around sheepishly, unable to cover his blunder.*) Well, ah—you know.

EIGHT. No, I don't know. Maybe you know.

(*The door left opens and the* GUARD *walks in carrying a large pen-and-ink diagram of the apartment done on heavy drawing board stock. It is a railroad flat. A bedroom faces the el tracks. Behind it is a series of rooms off a long hall. In the front bedroom there is a mark where the body was found. At the back of the apartment we see the entrance into the apartment hall from the building hall. We see a flight of stairs in the building hall. The diagram is clearly labeled, and included in the information on it are the various dimensions of the various rooms. The* GUARD *gives the diagram to the* FOREMAN, *who has remained by the door left.*)

GUARD. Is this what you wanted?

FOREMAN. That's right. Thank you.

GUARD. Sure, that's my job. (*Nods and goes out left, closing and locking door as he goes.* EIGHT *rises and starts toward* FOREMAN.)

FOREMAN. You want this?

EIGHT. Yes, please. (FOREMAN *nods.* EIGHT *takes diagram and crosses up right. He takes chair from up right corner and brings it right center, half facing table. He sets diagram up on chair so that all can see it.* EIGHT *looks it over. Several* JURORS *get up to see it better.* FOREMAN *comes over to look.* THREE, TEN *and* SEVEN, *however, barely bother to look at it.* THREE *sits abruptly again at table.*)

SEVEN (*to* TEN). Do me a favor. (*Slumps in chair.*) Wake me up when this is over.

TEN. I looked at that diagram for two hours; enough is enough.

FOUR. Some of us are interested. Go ahead.

EIGHT. All right. This is the apartment in which the killing took place. The old man's apartment is directly beneath it, and exactly the same. (*Pointing.*) Here are the el tracks. The bedroom. Another bedroom. Living room. Bathroom. Kitchen. And this is the hall. Here's the front door to the apartment, and here are the steps. (*Points to front bedroom and then to front door.*) Now, the old man was in bed in this room. He says he got up, went out into the hall, down the hall to the front door and opened it and looked out just in time to see the boy racing down the stairs. Am I right?

FOUR. That's the story.

SEVEN. That's what happened!

EIGHT. Fifteen seconds after he heard the body fall.

ELEVEN. Correct. (FOREMAN *and other* JURORS *who have come over to look at diagram now drift back to table and sit again.*)

EIGHT (*still by diagram at right center*). His bed was at the window. (*Looking closer.*) It's twelve feet from his bed to the bedroom door. The length of the hall is forty-three feet six inches. He had to get up out of bed, get his canes, walk twelve feet, open the bedroom door, walk forty-three feet and open the front door—all in fifteen seconds. Do you think this possible?

TEN. You know it's possible.

FOUR. I don't see why not.

THREE. He would have been in a hurry. He did hear the scream.

ELEVEN. He can only walk very slowly. They had to help him into the witness chair.

THREE. You make it sound like a long walk. It's not. (EIGHT *goes down left and takes two chairs. He crosses down right, near water cooler, and puts them together to indicate a bed.*)

NINE. For an old man who uses canes it's a long walk.

THREE (*to* EIGHT). What are you doing?

EIGHT. I want to try this thing. Let's see how long it took him. I'm going to pace off twelve feet—the length of the bedroom. (*Begins to do so, pacing from down right, across stage, toward down center.*)

THREE. You're crazy! You can't re-create a thing like that.

ELEVEN. Perhaps if we could see it—this is an important point.

THREE (*angrily*). It's a ridiculous waste of time!

SIX. Let him do it.

FOUR. I can't see any harm in it. Foolish, but go ahead.

EIGHT. Hand me a chair, please. (NINE *pushes chair from right end of table to* EIGHT *and then sits again.*) All right. (*Places chair at point he has paced off.*) This is the bedroom door. How far would you say it is from here to the door of this room?

SIX (*as* ALL *look*). I'd say it was twenty feet. (*Several* JURORS, *excluding* THREE, SEVEN *and* TEN, *rise and stand near their places, watching.*)

TWO. Just about.

EIGHT. Twenty feet is close enough. All right, from here to the door and back is about forty feet. It's shorter than the length of the hall the old man had to move through. Wouldn't you say that?

NINE. A few feet, maybe.

TEN. Look, this is absolutely insane. What makes you think you can do this?

FOREMAN. We can't stop him.

EIGHT. Do you mind if I try it? According to you, it'll only take fifteen seconds. We can spare that. (*Walks over to two chairs and lies down on them.*) Who's got a watch with a second hand?

TWO. I have. (*Indicates wrist watch.*)

EIGHT. When you want me to start, stamp your foot. That'll be the body falling.

TWO. We'll time you from there.

EIGHT (*lying down on two chairs*). Let's say he keeps his canes right at his bedside. Right?

FOUR. Right!

EIGHT. Okay. I'm ready.

TWO (*explaining*). I'm waiting for the hand to get to sixty. (ALL *watch carefully; then* TWO *stamps his foot, loudly.* EIGHT *begins to get up. Slowly, he swings his legs over edges of chairs, reaches for imaginary canes and struggles to his feet.* TWO *stares at his watch.* EIGHT *walks as a crippled old man would walk now. He goes toward chair which is serving as bedroom door. He gets to it and pretends to open it.*)

TEN (*shouting*). Speed it up. He walked twice as fast as that. (EIGHT, *not having stopped for this outburst, begins to walk simulated forty-foot hallway, to door left and back to chair.*)

ELEVEN. This is, I think, even more quickly than the old man walked in the courtroom.

THREE. No, it isn't.

EIGHT. If you think I should go faster, I will.

FOUR. Speed it up a little. (EIGHT *speeds up his pace slightly. He reaches door left and turns now, heading back, hobbling as an old man would hobble, bent over his imaginary canes.* ALL *watch him tensely. He hobbles back to chair, which also serves as front door. He stops there and pretends to unlock door. Then he pretends to push it open.*)

EIGHT (*loudly*). Stop.

TWO (*his eyes glued to watch*). Right.

EIGHT. What's the time?

TWO. Fifteen—twenty—thirty—thirty-five—thirty-nine seconds, exactly. (*Moves toward* EIGHT. *Other* JURORS *now move in toward* EIGHT, *also.*)

THREE. That can't be!

ELEVEN. Thirty-nine seconds!

FOUR. Now, that's interesting.

SEVEN (*looking at* JURORS). Hey, now—you know. . . .

NINE. What do you think of that!

ELEVEN (*nodding*). Thirty-nine seconds. Thirty-nine.

FOUR. And the old cripple swore, on his oath, that it was fifteen.

ELEVEN (*pointing to* EIGHT). He may have been a little bit off on the speed that the old cripple moved at—but twenty-four seconds off . . . well, now, you know . . .

FOREMAN. Far be it from me to call anyone a liar, and even allowing for quite a difference in speed between the old man and you . . . (*Motions at* EIGHT.) Why, still, there's quite a——

FOUR. Quite a discrepancy.

EIGHT. It's my guess that the old man was trying to get to the door, heard someone racing down the stairs and *assumed* that it was the boy.

SIX. I think that's possible.

THREE (*infuriated*). Assumed? Now, listen to me, you people. I've seen all kinds of dishonesty in my day—but this little display takes the cake.

EIGHT. What dishonesty?

THREE (*to* FOUR). Tell him! (FOUR *turns away down right and sits silently in one of the two chairs there.* THREE *looks at him and then he strides to* EIGHT.) You come in here with your heart bleeding all over the floor about slum kids and injustice and you make up these wild stories, and you've got some soft-hearted old ladies listening to you. Well, I'm not. I'm getting real sick of you. (*To* ALL.) What's the matter with you people? This kid is guilty! He's got to burn! We're letting him slip through our fingers.

EIGHT (*calmly*). Our fingers. Are you his executioner?

THREE (*raging*). I'm one of 'em!

EIGHT. Perhaps you'd like to pull the switch.

THREE (*shouting*). For this kid? You bet I'd like to pull the switch!

EIGHT (*shaking his head sadly*). I'm sorry for you.

THREE (*shouting*). Don't start with me!

EIGHT. What it must feel like to want to pull the switch!

THREE. Shut up!

EIGHT. You're a sadist. . . .

THREE (*louder*). Shut up!

EIGHT (*his voice strong*). You want to see this boy die because you personally want it—not because of the facts. (*Spits out words.*) You are a beast. You disgust me.

THREE (*shouting*). Shut up! (*Lunges at* EIGHT, *but is caught by two of the* JURORS *and is held. He struggles as* EIGHT *watches calmly. Then he screams.*) Let me go! I'll kill him! I'll kill him!

EIGHT (*softly*). You don't really mean you'll kill me, do you? (THREE *stops struggling now and stares at* EIGHT, *and all the* JURORS *watch in silence.*)

CURTAIN

ACT III

AT RISE OF CURTAIN: *We see the same scene as at the end of Act II. There has been no time lapse.* THREE *glares angrily at* EIGHT. *He is still held by two* JURORS. *After a long pause* THREE *shakes himself loose and turns away. He walks to the window. The other* JURORS *move away and stand around the room now; they are shocked by this display of anger. There is silence. Then the door left opens and the* GUARD *enters. He looks around the room.*

GUARD. Is there anything wrong, gentlemen? I heard some noise.

FOREMAN. No. There's nothing wrong. (*Points to large diagram of apartment.*) You can take that back. We're finished with it. (GUARD *nods and takes diagram. He looks curiously at some of* JURORS *and then goes out.* JURORS *still are silent; some of them begin to sit down slowly at table.* FOUR *is still seated down right.* THREE *still stands at window. He turns around now.* JURORS *look at him.*)

THREE (*loudly*). Well, what are you looking at? (*They turn away. He goes back to his seat now.* EIGHT *puts his chair back at right end of table. Silently, rest of* JURORS, *including* FOUR *but excluding* ELEVEN, *take their seats.* TWELVE *begins to doodle on a piece of paper.* ELEVEN *moves down left and leans reflectively against wall.* TEN *blows his nose but no one speaks. Then, finally.*)

FOUR. I don't see why we have to behave like children here.

ELEVEN. Nor do I. We have a responsibility. This is a remarkable thing about democracy. That we are—what is the word? . . . ah, notified! That we are notified by mail to come down to this place—and decide on the guilt or innocence of a man; of a man we have not known before. We have nothing to gain or lose by our verdict. This is one of the reasons why we are strong. We should not make it a personal thing. . . .

NINE (*slowly*). Thank you, very much.

ELEVEN (*slight surprise*). Why do you thank me?

NINE. We forget. It's good to be reminded. (ELEVEN *nods and leans against wall again.*)

FOUR. I'm glad that we're going to be civilized about this.

TWELVE. Well, we're still nowhere.

EIGHT. No, we're somewhere, or getting there—maybe.

FOUR. Maybe.

TWELVE. Who's got an idea?

SIX. I think maybe we should try another vote. (*Turns to* FOREMAN.) Mr. Foreman?

FOREMAN. It's all right with me. Anybody doesn't want to vote? (*Looks around table. Most of them shake their heads.* ELEVEN *has moved to table and takes his seat.*)

FOUR. Let's vote.

TWELVE. Yes, vote.

SEVEN. So all right, let's do it.

THREE. I want an open ballot. Let's call out our votes. I want to know who stands where.

FOREMAN. That sounds fair. Anyone object? (*Looks around. There is a general shaking of heads.*) All right. I'll call off your jury numbers. (*Takes a pencil and paper and makes marks in one of two columns after each vote.*) I vote guilty. Number two?

TWO. Not guilty.

FOREMAN. Three?

THREE. Guilty.

FOREMAN. Four?

FOUR. Guilty.

FOREMAN. Five?

FIVE. Not guilty.

FOREMAN. Six?

SIX. Not guilty.

FOREMAN. Seven?

SEVEN. Guilty.

FOREMAN. Eight?

EIGHT. Not guilty.

FOREMAN. Nine?

NINE. Not guilty.

FOREMAN. Ten?

TEN. Guilty.

FOREMAN. Eleven?

ELEVEN. Not guilty.

FOREMAN. Twelve?

TWELVE. Guilty.

FOUR. That's six to six.

TEN (*mad*). I'll tell you something. The crime is being committed right in this room.

FOREMAN. The vote is six to six.

THREE. I'm ready to walk into court right now and declare a hung jury. There's no point in this going on any more.

FOUR (*to* ELEVEN). I'd like to know why you changed your mind. (*To* TWO.) And why you changed your mind. (*To* SIX.) And why you did. There are six men here who think that we may be turning a murderer loose in the streets. Emotion won't do. Why? (TWO, ELEVEN *and* SIX *look at each other*.)

SIX. It would seem that the old man did not see the boy run down-stairs. I do not think it likely that the old man heard someone scream, "I'm going to kill you." Old men dream. And if the boy did scream that he was going to kill, then we have the authority of this man—(*Motions at* THREE.)—to prove that it might not really mean he's going to kill.

SEVEN. Why don't we take it in to the judge and let the kid take his chances with twelve other guys?

FOREMAN. Six to six. I don't think we'll ever agree—on anything.

THREE. It's got to be unanimous—(*Motioning at* EIGHT.)—and we're never going to convince him.

EIGHT. At first I was alone. Now five others agree; there is a doubt.

THREE. You can't ever convince me that there's a doubt, because I know there isn't no doubt.

TWELVE. I tell you what, maybe we are a hung jury. It happens some-times.

EIGHT. We are not going to be a hung jury.

SEVEN. But we are, right now, a perfect balance. Let's take it in to the judge.

FOUR (*to* EIGHT). If there is a reasonable doubt I don't see it.

NINE. The doubt is there, in my mind.

FOREMAN. Maybe we should vote.

TWELVE. What do you mean—vote?

THREE. Not again!

TEN. I still want to know. Vote on what?

FOREMAN. Are we or aren't we a hung jury?

EIGHT. You mean that we vote yes, we are a hung jury, or no, we are not a hung jury?

FOREMAN. That's just what I was thinking of.

ELEVEN (*bitterly*). We can't even agree about whether or not the window should be open.

FOREMAN. Let's make it a majority vote. The majority wins.

FOUR. If seven or more of us vote yes, that we are a hung jury, then we take it in to the judge and tell him that we are a hung jury.

FOREMAN. Right. And if seven or more vote no, that means that we aren't a hung jury, and we go on discussing it.

FOUR. It doesn't seem quite right to me.

THREE. It's the only solution.

SEVEN. I agree, it's the only way.

TWELVE. Anything to end this.

FOREMAN (*looking around table*). Are we agreed then? Seven or more vote yes and we take it in to the judge. (ALL *nod.*)

THREE. Let's call our votes out.

FOREMAN. I vote yes, we're a hung jury. (*Makes a mark on a sheet of paper.*) Two?

TWO. No.

FOREMAN. Three?

THREE. Yes.

FOREMAN. Four?

FOUR. Yes.

FOREMAN. Five?

FIVE. No.

FOREMAN. Six?

SIX. No.

FOREMAN. Seven?

SEVEN. Yes.

FOREMAN. Eight?

EIGHT. No.

FOREMAN. Nine?

NINE. No.

FOREMAN. Ten?

TEN. Yes.

FOREMAN. Eleven?

ELEVEN. No.

FOREMAN. Twelve?

TWELVE. Yes.

THREE (*with a groan*). Oh, no!

FOREMAN. It's six to six.

NINE. We can't even get a majority to decide whether or not we're a hung jury.

FOUR (*rising*). I went along with the majority vote on this question. And I didn't agree with voting that way, not really, and I still don't. So I'm changing my vote. I say no, we are not a hung jury. I believe that the boy is guilty beyond a reasonable doubt. There are some things I want to find out from those gentlemen that changed their minds. (*Sits again.*)

FOREMAN. Then we aren't a hung jury—so we go on.

EIGHT. Good! We go on.

FOUR (*to* TWO). Why did you change your mind?

TWO (*hesitating a moment*). He—(*Points to* EIGHT.)—he seems so sure. And he has made a number of good points. While he—(*Points to* THREE.)—only gets mad and insults everybody.

FOUR. Does the anger and the insult change the guilt of the boy? He did do it. Are you going to turn a murderer loose because one of the jurors gets angry when he thinks a murderer is being turned loose?

TWO. That's true.

FIVE. There is a doubt.

FOUR. I don't think so. The track is straight in front of the window. Let's take that point. So the el train would have made a low rumbling noise. El trains screech when they go around curves. So the old man could have heard a scream, which is high-pitched. And it is a tenement and they have thin walls.

THREE. Good. Good. That's it. That's it.

FOUR. And what if the old man was wrong about the time it took him to get to the door but right about whom he saw? Please remember that there weren't any fingerprints on the knife, and it is summer, so gloves seem unlikely.

THREE (*to* EIGHT). Now I want you to listen to this man. (*Motions at* FOUR.) He's got the goods.

FOUR. And it might have taken a few seconds to get a handkerchief out and wipe the fingerprints away.

EIGHT. This is a point.

THREE. Why don't we just time this one, to see?

FIVE. Just what are we timing?

EIGHT. Yes, let's be exact, please.

FOUR. I am saying that the old man downstairs might have been wrong about how long it took him to get to the door but that he was right about whom he saw running down the stairs. Now it may have taken the murderer about thirty-nine seconds to wipe away all the fingerprints and get down the stairs to the place where the old man saw him—the boy, that is.

THREE. This is right.

FOREMAN. We reconstructed the old man getting out of bed and going to the door, and we timed that; now let's reconstruct the actual crime.

NINE. As well as we can reconstruct it.

SEVEN. I think a murderer could use up thirty or forty seconds pretty easily at that point.

FOUR. Let's reconstruct the killing.

SEVEN. Yes, let's.

THREE (*taking knife from table, giving it to* EIGHT). Here, you do the stabbing.

FOUR (*taking knife*). No, I'll do it.

THREE (*to* SEVEN). Why don't you be the one that gets stabbed? You're younger than I am. And don't forget, you take one second to fall.

FOUR (*rising, moving toward right, turning*). And he was found on his side—his right side—so fall and roll onto your right side. (*To* EIGHT.) If someone hates another person enough to kill them, don't you think that it's reasonable to suppose that the murderer would look at his victim for a second or two?

TWELVE (*to* EIGHT). Divorce yourself from this particular case—just human nature.

EIGHT. Yes, it seems reasonable.

THREE. Hey, wait a minute! (ALL *look at* THREE.) He falls and he ends up on his right side, the father did, but stabbing someone isn't like shooting them, even when it's right in the heart. The father would have worked around for a few seconds—lying there on the floor—writhing, maybe.

FOUR. That's quite possible. There would have been enough oxygen in his system to carry him for two or three seconds, I should think.

ELEVEN. Wouldn't the father have cried out?

THREE. Maybe the kid held his mouth.

EIGHT. That also seems possible.

FOUR. Also, there's another point we might bring out. Anyone who is clear enough mentally to wipe the fingerprints away after murdering someone, well, that person is also clear enough mentally to look around the apartment, or the room in this case, to see if there are any other clues. It would just be for a second or two, I should think, but still he would look around.

THREE. This gets better and better.

FOUR. We're trying to make it clear. One doesn't talk about quality when murder is involved. Well, let's do it.

FOREMAN. About this on the fingerprints—the kid wiped the fingerprints off the knife. Well, what about the doorknob? If I saw a man coming into my home, a man that hated me, and if he was wiping the doorknob with a handkerchief as he came in, it would give me an uneasy feeling. (ALL *smile*.) So the doorknobs must have been wiped after the killing, and this, too, would take some time.

FOUR (*to* TWO). You timed the last one. Why don't you time this one, too?

TWO. All right.

FOUR (*as* SEVEN *takes his position in front of* FOUR *at right stage;* FOUR *has knife in his hand*). Stamp your foot when you want me to start.

TWO (*waiting a few seconds*). I want the hand to be at sixty. (*Waits another second, then stamps foot.*)

FOUR (*not screaming, but still loud*). I'm going to kill you. (*Brings knife down, overhand. Blade is collapsed.* SEVEN *catches knife in his hands and falls to floor a second after shout. He writhes a bit, then rolls onto his right side.* FOUR *stares at him for a few moments, then digs into his pocket and produces a handkerchief.*

It takes him a moment or two to unfold handkerchief; then he bends down and wipes handle of knife. He looks about, as though checking to be sure that he has done everything. Then he rushes to door left that leads out of jury room and wipes doorknob. Then he turns around a full circle and wipes knob again.) He would have wiped both knobs. (*Then he rushes right and goes back to door of jury room and repeats double process on doorknob. Then he stamps his foot and cries out.*) Stop!

TWO (*checking watch*). Twenty—yeah, twenty, twenty-five—twenty-nine—about twenty-nine and a half seconds, I'd say.

FOUR (*moving to behind* FOREMAN's *chair at left end of table*). And whoever did murder the old man, and I think it was the kid, he still had to run down the hall and down the stairs—at least one flight of stairs.

THREE. You see! You see! (SEVEN *rises from floor and dusts himself off.*)

FOUR. The old man downstairs may have been wrong on the time, but in view of this I think it's quite reasonable to assume that he did see the kid run downstairs.

TWELVE (*to* EIGHT). So now both time sequences check—the one you did and the one we did; what with running downstairs and everything, it does pretty much check out on times.

SEVEN. Sure—he's an old man who wants attention. . . . (*Motions at* NINE.) He's probably right, but the old man feels the way everyone does—a life is at stake. (*Sits again at table, placing knife back on table.*)

FOUR. So the story of the old man may well be true.

EIGHT. Except for the fact that he absolutely swore, under oath, that it was only fifteen seconds.

NINE. We seem to all agree that it was twenty-five to forty seconds later.

EIGHT. You are now admitting that the old man lied in one case and told the truth in the other. I admit that this does tend to confirm the story of the old man, but in part he is now a proven liar—and this is by your own admission.

TWO (*to* EIGHT). That may be true, that the old man lies in part, but I think it will change my vote once more. (*To* FOREMAN.) Guilty.

THREE (*to* SIX). What about you? What do you think now?

SIX (*getting up, crossing to water cooler*). I'm not just sure what I think. I want to talk some more. At first I thought guilty, then I changed. Now—I'm sort of swinging back to guilty. (*Takes a drink.*)

THREE (*to* ELEVEN). And what about you?

ELEVEN. No. (*Shakes his head.*) I am now in real doubt—real doubt. . . .

FIVE. I say guilty. I was right the first time.

THREE. Now we're beginning to make sense in here.

FOREMAN. It seems to be about nine guilty to three not guilty. (FOUR *sits again.*)

EIGHT. One more question about the old man downstairs. How many of you live in apartment buildings? (*Eight hands go up, including his own.*)

ELEVEN (*to* EIGHT). I don't know what you're thinking but I know what I'm thinking.

FOUR (*to* ELEVEN). What's that?

ELEVEN. I do not live in a tenement, but it is close and there is just enough light in the hall so you can see the steps, no more—the light bulbs are so small—and this murder took place in a tenement. Remember how we stumbled on the steps?

EIGHT. The police officers were using big bulbs and one even had a flashlight. Remember?

ELEVEN. An old man who misjudged the time by twenty seconds, on this we all agree, this old man looked down the dark hallway of a tenement and recognized a running figure?

EIGHT. He was one hundred per cent wrong about the time; it took twice as long as he thought.

ELEVEN. Then could not the old man be one hundred per cent wrong about who he saw?

THREE. That's the most idiotic thing I've ever heard of. You're making that up out of thin air.

TWELVE. We're a hung jury. Let's be honest about it.

ELEVEN (*to* SEVEN). Do you truly feel that there is no room for reasonable doubt?

SEVEN. Yes, I do.

ELEVEN. I beg your pardon, but maybe you don't understand the term, "reasonable doubt."

SEVEN (*angrily*). What do you mean, I don't understand it? Who do you think you are to talk to me like that? (*To* ALL.) How do you like this guy? He comes over here running for his life, and before he can even take a big breath he's telling us how to run the show. The arrogance of him!

FOUR. No one here is asking where anyone came from.

SEVEN. I was born right here.

FOUR. Or where your father came from. (*Looks at* SEVEN, *who looks away.*)

EIGHT. Maybe it wouldn't hurt us to take a few tips from people who come running here! Maybe they learned something we don't know. We're not so perfect.

ELEVEN. Please. . . . I am used to this. . . . It's all right. Thank you.

EIGHT. It's not all right.

SEVEN. Okay—okay—I apologize. Is that what you want?

EIGHT (*grimly*). That's what I want.

FOREMAN. All right. Let's stop the arguing. Who's got something constructive to say?

TWO (*hesitantly*). Well, something's been bothering me a little. This whole business about the stab wound, and how it was made—the downward angle of it, you know?

THREE. Don't tell me we're going to start that. They went over it and over it in court.

TWO. I know they did—but I don't go along with it. The boy is five feet eight inches tall. His father was six feet two inches tall. That's a difference of six inches. It's a very awkward thing to stab *down* into the chest of someone who's half a foot taller than you are. (THREE *grabs knife from table and jumps up.*)

THREE (*moving left center*). Look, you're not going to be satisfied till you see it again. I'm going to give you a demonstration. Somebody get up. (*Looks toward table.* EIGHT *stands up and walks toward him.* THREE *closes knife and puts it in his pocket. They stand face to face and look at each other for a moment.*) Okay. (*To* TWO.) Now watch this. I don't want to have to do it again. (*Crouches down until he is quite a bit shorter than* EIGHT.) Is that six inches?

TWELVE. That's more than six inches.

THREE. Okay, let it be more. (*Reaches into his pocket and takes out knife. He flicks it open, changes its position in his hand and holds knife aloft, ready to stab. He and* EIGHT *look steadily into each other's eyes. Then he stabs downward, hard.*)

TWO (*shouting*). Look out! (*Reaches short just as blade reaches* EIGHT's *chest.* THREE *laughs.*)

SIX. That's not funny. (*Crosses back to table and sits.*)

FIVE. What's the matter with you?

THREE. Now just calm down. Nobody's hurt, are they?

EIGHT (*low*). No. Nobody's hurt. (*Turns, crosses back to his place but does not sit.*)

THREE. All right. There's your angle. Take a look at it. (*Illustrates.*) Down and in. That's how I'd stab a taller man in the chest, and that's how it was done. (*Crosses back to his place at table.*) Take a look at it, and tell me I'm wrong. (TWO *doesn't answer.* THREE *looks at him for a moment, then jams knife into table and sits down.* ALL *look at knife.*)

SIX. Down and in. I guess there's no argument. (EIGHT *picks knife out of table and closes it. He flicks it open and, changing its position in his hand, stabs downward with it.*)

EIGHT (*to* SIX). Did you ever stab a man?

SIX. Of course not.

EIGHT (*to* THREE). Did you?

THREE. All right, let's not be silly.

EIGHT (*insistently*). Did you?

THREE (*loudly*). No. I didn't!

EIGHT. Where do you get all your information about how it's done?

THREE. What do you mean? It's just common sense.

EIGHT. Have you ever seen a man stabbed?

THREE (*pausing, looking around rather nervously, finally*). No.

EIGHT. All right. I want to ask you something. The boy was an experienced knife-fighter. He was even sent to reform school for knifing someone. Isn't that so?

TWELVE. That's right.

EIGHT. Look at this. (*Closes knife, flicks it open and changes position of knife so that he can stab overhand.*) Doesn't it seem like an awkward way to handle a knife?

THREE. What are you asking me for? (EIGHT *closes blade and flicks it open, holding knife ready to slash underhanded.*)

FIVE. Wait a minute! What's the matter with me? Give me that knife. (*Reaches out for knife.*)

EIGHT. Have you ever seen a knife fight?

FIVE. Yes, I have.

EIGHT. In the movies? (*Passes knife to* FIVE.)

FIVE. In my backyard. On my stoop. In the vacant lot across the street. Too many of them. Switch knives came with the neighborhood where I lived. Funny that I didn't think of it before. I guess you try to forget those things. (*Flicks knife open.*) Anyone who's ever used a switch knife would never have stabbed downward. You don't handle a switch knife that way. You use it underhanded. (*Illustrates.*)

EIGHT. Then he couldn't have made the kind of wound that killed his father.

FIVE. I suppose it's conceivable that he could have made the wound, but it's not likely, not if he'd ever had any experience with switch knives, and we know that the kid had a lot of experience with switch knives.

THREE. I don't believe it.

TEN. Neither do I. You're giving us a lot of mumbo-jumbo.

EIGHT (*to* TWELVE). What do you think?

TWELVE (*hesitantly*). Well—I don't know.

EIGHT (*to* SEVEN). What about you?

SEVEN. Listen, I'll tell you all something. I'm a little sick of this whole thing already. We're getting nowhere fast. Let's break it up and go home.

EIGHT. Before we decide anything more, I would like to try to pull this together.

THREE. This should be good.

FOUR. He has a right. Let him go ahead.

TWO. Do you want me to time this, too? (EIGHT *looks at* TWO.)

FOREMAN. Let's hear him.

TWELVE (*getting comfortable*). I'm in advertising. I'm used to the big shots pulling things together. Let's chip up a few shots to see if any of them land on the green.

EIGHT. I want you all to look at this logically and consistently.

THREE. We have. Guilty.

EIGHT. I want to know—is the kid smart or is the kid dumb?

FOUR. What do you mean?

EIGHT (*moving up center, so that he is standing back of men at upstage side of table*). This is a kid who has gone to the reform school for knife fighting. The night of the murder he bought a knife, a switch knife. It would then take a very stupid kid to go and murder a man, his father, with an instrument that everyone would associate with the kid.

THREE. I quite agree, he's dumb.

EIGHT. However, if he were dumb, then why did he make the kind of wound that an inexperienced man would make with a knife?

FOREMAN. I'm not sure I understand.

EIGHT. To murder someone must take a great emotion, great hatred. (*Moves over to left of* FOREMAN.) And at that moment he would handle the knife as best he could, and a trained knife-fighter would handle it as he had been trained, underhand. . . . (*Makes underhanded motion.*) A man who had not been trained would go overhand. . . . (*Makes overhanded motion.*) But the kid is being very smart. Everyone knows that he is an experienced knife-fighter—so he is smart enough at that moment to make the wound that an amateur would make. That man is a smart man. Smart enough to wipe the fingerprints away, perhaps even smart enough to wait until an el train was going by in order to cover the noise. Now, is the kid smart, or is he dumb? (*Looks around.*)

THREE. Hey, now, wait a minute!

NINE. Well, the woman across the el tracks saw the murder through the el train, so someone in that el train could have seen the murder, too.

EIGHT. A possibility, but no one did that we know of.

NINE. It would take an awfully dumb man to take that chance, doing the murder as the train went by.

EIGHT. Exactly. A dumb man, a very stupid man, a man swept by emotion. Probably he heard nothing; he probably didn't even hear the train coming. And whoever did murder the father did it as well as he could.

FOUR. So?

EIGHT (*moving back to his place, at right end of table, not sitting*). The kid is dumb enough to do everything to associate himself with the switch knife—a switch knife murder—and then a moment after the murder he becomes smart. The kid is smart enough to make a kind of wound that would lead us to suspect someone else, and yet at the same instant he is dumb enough to do the killing as an el train is going by, and then a moment later he is smart enough to wipe fingerprints away. To make this boy guilty you have to say he is dumb from eight o'clock until about midnight and then about midnight he is smart one second, then dumb for a few seconds and then smart again and then once again he becomes stupid, so stupid that he does not think of a good alibi. Now is this kid smart or is he dumb? To say that he is guilty you have to toss his intelligence like a pancake. There is doubt, doubt, doubt. (*Beats table with fist as he emphasizes word* "*doubt.*")

FOUR. I hadn't thought of that.

EIGHT. And the old man downstairs. On the stand he swore that it was fifteen seconds; he insisted on fifteen seconds, but we all agree that it must have been almost forty seconds.

NINE. Does the old man lie half the time and then does he tell the truth the other half of the time?

EIGHT. For the kid to be guilty he must be stupid, then smart, then stupid and then smart and so on, and, also, for the kid to be guilty the old man downstairs must be a liar half of the time and the other half of the time he must tell the truth. You can reasonably doubt. (*Sits again. There is a moment of silence.*)

SEVEN (*breaking silence*). I'm sold on "reasonable doubt."

TWO. I think I am, too.

SIX. I wanted more talk, and now I've had it.

EIGHT (*fast*). I want another vote.

FOREMAN. Okay, there's another vote called for. I guess the quickest way is a show of hands. Anybody object? (*No one does.*) All right. All those voting not guilty raise your hands. (*Jurors* TWO, FIVE, SIX, SEVEN, EIGHT, NINE, ELEVEN *and* TWELVE *raise their hands immediately.* FOREMAN *looks around table carefully and then he, too, raises his hand. He looks around table, counting silently.*) Nine. (*Hands go down.*) All those voting guilty. (*Jurors* THREE, FOUR *and* TEN *raise their hands.*) Three. (*They lower their hands.*) The vote is nine to three in favor of acquittal.

TEN. I don't understand you people. How can you believe this kid is innocent? Look, you know how those people lie. I don't have to tell you. They don't know what the truth is. And let me tell you, they—(FIVE *gets up from table, turns his back to it and goes to window.*)—don't need any real big reason to kill someone, either. You know, they get drunk, and bang, someone's lying in the gutter. Nobody's blaming them. That's how they are. You know what I mean? Violent! (NINE *gets up and goes to window and looks out. He is followed by* ELEVEN.) Human life don't mean as much to them as it does to us. Hey, where are you all going? Look, these people're drinking and fighting all the time, and if somebody gets killed, so somebody gets killed. They don't care. Oh, sure, there are some good things about them, too. Look, I'm the first to say that. (EIGHT *gets up and then* TWO *and* SIX *follow him to window.*) I've known a few who were pretty decent, but that's the exception. Most of them, it's like they have no feelings. They can do anything. What's going on here? (FOREMAN *gets up and goes to window, followed by* SEVEN *and* TWELVE.) I'm speaking my piece, and you—listen to me! They're no good. There's not a one of 'em who's any good. We better watch out. Take it from me. This kid on trial . . . (THREE *sits at table toying with knife as* FOUR *gets up and starts toward* TEN. *All the other* JURORS *have their backs turned on* TEN.) Well, don't you know about them? Listen to me! What are you doing? I'm trying to tell you something. . . . (FOUR *stands over him as he trails off. There is a dead silence. Then* FOUR *speaks softly.*)

FOUR. I've had enough. If you open your mouth again I'm going to split your skull. (*Stands there and looks at him. No one moves or speaks.* TEN *looks at* FOUR *and then looks down at table.*)

TEN (*softly*). I'm only trying to tell you. . . . (*There is a long pause as* FOUR *stares down at* TEN.)

FOUR (*to* JURORS *at window*). All right. Sit down, everybody. (ALL *move back to their seats. When they are all seated* FOUR *takes a stand behind men on upstage side of table. He speaks quietly.*) I still believe the boy is guilty of murder. I'll tell you why. To me, the most damning evidence was given by the woman across the street who claimed she actually saw the murder committed.

THREE. That's right. As far as I'm concerned that's the most important testimony.

EIGHT. All right. Let's go over her testimony. What exactly did she say?

FOUR (*moving toward window*). I believe I can recount it accurately. She said that she went to bed at about eleven o'clock that night. Her bed was next to the open window and she could look out of the window while lying down and see directly into the window

across the street. She tossed and turned for over an hour, unable
to fall asleep. Finally she turned toward the window at about
twelve-ten and, as she looked out, she saw the boy stab his father.
As far as I can see, this is unshakable testimony.

THREE. That's what I mean. That's the whole case. (FOUR *takes off
his eyeglasses and begins to polish them as they all sit silently
watching him.*)

FOUR (*to all of them*). Frankly, in view of this, I don't see how you
can vote for acquittal. (*To* TWELVE *as he sits again.*) What do
you think about it?

TWELVE. Well—maybe. . . . There's so much evidence to sift. . . .

THREE. What do you mean, maybe? He's absolutely right. You can
throw out all the other evidence.

FOUR. That was my feeling. I don't deny the validity of the points
that he has made. (*Motions at* EIGHT.) Shall we say that on one
side of the tracks there is doubt? But what can you say about the
story of the woman? She saw it? (TWO, *while he is polishing his
glasses, too, squints at clock.*)

TWO. What time is it?

ELEVEN. Ten minutes of six.

SIX. You don't suppose they'd let us go home and finish it in the
morning. I've got a kid with mumps. . . .

FIVE. Not a chance.

EIGHT (*to* TWO). Can't you see the clock without your glasses?

TWO. Not clearly.

EIGHT. Oh.

FOUR. Glasses are a nuisance, aren't they?

EIGHT (*an edge of excitement in his tone*). Well, what do you
all do when you wake up at night and want to know what time
it is?

TWO. I put my glasses on and look at the clock.

FOUR. I just lie in bed and wait for the clock to chime. My father
gave it to me when we married, my wife and I. It was ten years
before we had a place to put it.

EIGHT (*to* TWO). Do you wear your glasses to bed?

TWO. Of course not. No one wears eyeglasses to bed.

EIGHT. The woman who testified that she saw the killing wears glasses.
What about her?

FOUR. Did she wear glasses?

ELEVEN (*excitedly*). Of course! The woman wore bifocals. I remember this very clearly. They looked quite strong.

NINE. That's right. Bifocals. She never took them off.

FOUR. Funny. I never thought of that.

EIGHT. I think it's logical to say that she was not wearing her glasses in bed, and I don't think she'd put them on to glance casually out the window. . . . She testified that the murder took place the instant she looked out, and that the lights went out a split second later. She couldn't have had time to put on her glasses then. Now perhaps this woman honestly thought she saw the boy kill his father. (*Rises.*) I say that she only saw a blur.

THREE. How do you know what she saw? Maybe she's farsighted. . . . (*Looks around. No one answers. Loudly.*) How does he know all these things? (*There is silence.*)

EIGHT. Does anyone think there still is not a reasonable doubt? (*Looks around room, then squarely at* TEN. TEN *looks down at table for a moment; then he looks up at* EIGHT.)

TEN. I will always wonder. But there is a reasonable doubt.

THREE (*loudly*). I think he's guilty!

EIGHT (*calmly*). Does anyone else?

FOUR (*quietly*). No. I'm convinced now. There is a reasonable doubt.

EIGHT (*to* THREE). You're alone.

FOREMAN. Eleven votes, not guilty; one, guilty.

THREE. I don't care whether I'm alone or not! I have a right. . . .

EIGHT. Yes, you have a right. (ALL *stare at* THREE.)

THREE. Well, I told you. I think the kid's guilty. What else do you want?

EIGHT. Your arguments. (ALL *look at* THREE *after glancing at* EIGHT.)

THREE. I gave you my arguments.

EIGHT. We're not convinced. We're waiting to hear them again. We have time. (*Sits down again.* THREE *runs to* FOUR *and grabs his arm.*)

THREE (*pleading*). Listen. What's the matter with you? You're the guy. You made all the arguments. You can't turn now. A guilty man's going to be walking the streets. A murderer! He's got to die! Stay with me! . . .

FOUR (*rising*). I'm sorry. I'm convinced. I don't think I'm wrong often, but I guess I was this once. (*Crosses right.*) There is a reasonable doubt in my mind.

EIGHT. We're waiting. . . . (THREE *turns violently on him.*)

THREE (*shouting*). You're not going to intimidate me! (*They are* ALL *staring at* THREE.) I'm entitled to my opinion! (*No one answers him.*) It's gonna be a hung jury! (*Turns abruptly and sits in his chair again.*) That's it!

EIGHT. There's nothing we can do about that except hope that some night, maybe in a few months, why, you might get some sleep.

FIVE. You're all alone.

NINE. It takes a great deal of courage to stand alone.

FOUR (*moving back to table, sitting*). If it is a hung jury there will be another trial and some of us will point these things out to the various lawyers. (THREE *looks around table at all of them. As* THREE's *glance goes from juror to juror each one of them shakes his head in his direction. Then, suddenly,* THREE's *face contorts and he begins to pound on table with his fist. He seems about to cry.*)

THREE (*thundering*). All right! (*Jumps up quickly and moves down right, his back to all of them as* FOREMAN *goes to door left and knocks. The other* JURORS *now rise.*)

(*The* GUARD *opens the door left and looks in and sees them all standing. The* GUARD *holds the door open for them as they all file past and out that is, all except* THREE *and* EIGHT. *The* GUARD *waits for them.* EIGHT *moves toward the door left, pausing at left center.*)

EIGHT (*to* THREE). They're waiting. (THREE *sees that he is alone. He moves to table and pulls switch knife out of table and walks over to* EIGHT *with it.* THREE *is holding knife in approved knife-fighter fashion.* THREE *looks long and hard at juror* EIGHT *and weaves a bit from side to side as he holds knife with point of it in direction of* EIGHT's *belly.* EIGHT *speaks quietly, firmly.*) Not guilty. (THREE *turns knife around and* EIGHT *takes it by handle.* EIGHT *closes knife and puts it away.*)

THREE. Not guilty! (THREE *walks out of room.* EIGHT *glances around quickly, sighs, then turns and moves out through door.* GUARD *goes out, closing door.*)

CURTAIN

For discussion

ACT I

1. The introductory notes on the characters (pages 3 and 4) are of major importance. Reread them. Throughout Act I, did you find these jurors consistent; that is, were their speech and actions in accord with their personalities as described by the playwright?
2. Point out how the circumstances of the murder are revealed through the conversations of the jurors.
3. At first, the mood in the jury room is casual; the tone is rather off-hand. How does the playwright create this effect?
4. Did the jury feel any doubt in the beginning concerning the boy's guilt? What small detail (on page 9) set a more serious tone among the men?
5. What was the general feeling of the jury when one man voted *not guilty*? Who was the man? Why did he vote this way?
6. Side comments are made concerning the influence of a slum environment. In your own words, present the feelings of any two jurors on this question of environment.
7. As Act I progresses, strong undercurrents of feeling are apparent among the jurors. Point out examples of these. What issues were arising that touched these men personally?
8. The other jurors felt strongly about the dissenting vote. By the end of Act I, did they still feel this way? Explain.
9. State briefly the circumstantial evidence given in court.
10. What dramatic gesture did Juror Eight use against the circumstantial evidence? What did this reveal about him?
11. How does the playwright create a feeling of suspense at the end of Act I?
12. From this act, what clues do you have about the theme of this play?

ACT II

1. Which juror had changed his mind that the boy was "guilty beyond a reasonable doubt"? Do you think this jurior was justified in changing his mind? Why or why not?
2. Juror Three called Juror Nine a liar. What was it Juror Three did not understand? What did it reveal about him? If you were one of the jurors, would you find Juror Nine's explanation about the old man valid? Why or why not?

3. What did the foreman of the jury ask the guard to bring into the jury room? Why?
4. What lack of consistency did Juror Eight find in the old man's story about hearing the boy threaten his father?
5. How did Juror Eight demonstrate the impossibility of accuracy in the old man's account of seeing the boy?
6. Describe the mood at the close of Act II. What clues prepared you for the behavior of Juror Three? How did his outburst support Juror Eight's argument earlier in the act? Explain the irony in this incident at the end of Act II.

ACT III

1. What was the result of the new vote that was taken? What did this show about the jury's state of mind at this point?
2. Explain Juror Eleven's bitter remark, "We can't even agree about whether or not the window should be open."
3. Describe briefly Juror Four's defense of the *guilty* verdict by reinterpreting the time discrepancy in the old man's testimony.
4. How did the light in a tenement stairway prove to be an important factor in the jury's deliberations?
5. What did Juror Seven reveal in his argument with Juror Eleven? Why was this important?
6. The manner in which the murder victim was stabbed became an important issue. Why did it matter whether he was killed by an underhanded or overhanded knife thrust?
7. Explain Juror Eight's question, "I want to know—is the kid smart or is the kid dumb?" What was the result of the jurors' exploration of this question?
8. Why did the other members of the jury react to Juror Ten's violent and impassioned speech as they did? Explain the importance of the speech in relation to the theme of the play.
9. What facts made the story of the woman across the street questionable? How did this affect the jury?
10. What was the final vote of the jury? Point out the irony in Juror Nine's final remark to Juror Three, "It takes a great deal of courage to stand alone." Where had Juror Nine said this earlier in the play? Contrast the circumstances under which it was said.

On the play as a whole

1. Four elements are necessary in a play: plot, character, setting, and theme. State which of these you feel is the most important in this play and why.

2. The judge says at the opening of the play, "If there is a reasonable doubt in your mind as to the guilt of the accused—then you must declare him not guilty." This might be called the key statement behind the action that follows. Why? Explain its significance.

3. At one point, Juror Eight says, "Too many questions were left unasked." Discuss some of these questions and their possible answers.

4. "Juror Eight is the protagonist in this play." Do you agree or disagree with this statement? State the reasons for your answer.

5. The main conflict in the play is between Juror Eight and Juror Three. Explain this conflict and give instances to illustrate the two jurors' positions as protagonist and antagonist. How does the incident of the knife, for example, have more dramatic value than simply as a piece of circumstantial evidence?

6. From your discussion of conflict in Question 5, what would you say is the theme of this play? Give reasons to support your answer. What important social problem does the playwright raise?

7. Some dramatists believe that modern man has lost his dignity as an individual, that he is just a toy in a mechanistic society. Does this play affirm or refute this idea? How?

8. Would you say that the chaotic and bickering atmosphere that permeated the jury room from time to time is an argument for or against our jury system? Why?

9. The setting of the play is a jury room in summer. Point out details which the author uses to indicate that the weather is hot. How is this minor point important in establishing the mood of the play?

10. In your opinion, which character in the play is strongest? Which is weakest? Most likeable? Most repugnant? Who is a leader? A leaner? A braggart? Discuss. Remember that your answers may vary on the basis of personal judgment.

11. In most serious drama, many of the characters grow and develop; that is, they are dynamic, not static. Trace through the play any one character (other than Juror Eight or Three) and show how he changes as the play progresses. Point out his strengths and weaknesses.

12. Here are some comments on the accused boy:
    EIGHT. He's much too bright for that.

TEN. Bright! He's a common ignorant slob.

FOUR. The boy is clever enough.

What do you think of the boy? Must you conclude, as many of the jurors did at first, that he is ignorant and stupid? Why or why not?

13. The accused boy is never seen; the audience does not know whether he is innocent or guilty. Describe the boy as you imagine him to be. Do you, personally, believe him to be innocent or guilty? Why?

14. Suspense is an important factor in good drama. Show how the playwright, Reginald Rose, uses suspense in character, plot, and setting in *Twelve Angry Men*.

15. The dialogue is swift and economical. Choose a brief section from Act II to read aloud as a sample of everyday speech that reveals character and advances the plot.

16. Irony is an important element in this play (see Glossary, page 245). Discuss the irony (a) in the incident about the second knife that looked exactly like the one used in the murder; (b) in the underlying feeling of barely contained violence that grew in the jury room. Point out other examples of irony in the play.

17. What did you learn about people from reading this play? Give specific examples to support your answer.

18. What did you learn about the jury system? For example, what is the responsibility of a jury? What is a hung jury? What is the function of a foreman? May the jury use evidence presented earlier in court? If you are interested in this subject, do some research on the jury system in American society and give a report on your findings.

For composition

1. In two well-organized paragraphs, compare and contrast the personalities of Juror Eight and Juror Three.

2. Juror Eleven knew foreign oppression from personal experience. Write an imaginative description of what his former life might have been like.

3. "It takes a great deal of courage to stand alone." Develop this idea in a paragraph of exposition. Your comments need not refer directly to this play.

4. Is a man's temperament revealed by his conversation? Write a short composition in which you express your ideas on this subject. Give at least two examples from *Twelve Angry Men* to illustrate your statements.

5. Is a man's character revealed by his actions under stress? Express your views on this question, using characters from the play to support your opinion.

John Van Druten

Comedy

I Remember Mama

Here is a warm and delightful picture of family life that combines humor and pathos. John Van Druten has shown, through a series of incidents skillfully woven together, how the ordinary occurrences of everyday life have within them more beauty and drama than we thought.

The playwright has succeeded in making these scenes of family life moving and gentle, without ever letting them become sentimental. There are dramatic moments, but the characters always remain convincing and true to life. Outstanding is the character of Mama, holding the family together with her quiet and luminous dignity, her understanding, and her humor. There is also the sensitive and charming daughter, Katrin, blustering Uncle Chris, timid Aunt Trina, and many others, all blended into a nostalgic American drama of life as it was lived early in the century.

Van Druten has chosen to tell his story through the "flashback" method. As the play opens, Katrin, a young woman, is writing about her family as she remembers them when she was growing up. The play consists of these memories. To achieve the effect of past and present flowing into each other, Van Druten has used certain technical devices in staging the play so that the change of scenes is accomplished without any break in the unity. These devices are explained in the stage directions.

In his book, *The Playwright at Work,* John Van Druten wrote the following words, which, while about playwriting in general, are particularly true for his own play *I Remember Mama:*

"Your play will be born in you because you have something to say. . . . Your play will say what to you seems beautiful and wise and important. . . . That is what is good about it."

I REMEMBER MAMA

CHARACTERS

KATRIN   MR. THORKELSON
MAMA   DR. JOHNSON
PAPA   ARNE
DAGMAR   A NURSE
CHRISTINE   ANOTHER NURSE
MR. HYDE   SODA CLERK
NELS   MADELINE
AUNT TRINA   DOROTHY SCHILLER
AUNT SIGRID   FLORENCE DANA MOORHEAD
AUNT JENNY   BELLBOY
UNCLE CHRIS   SCRUBWOMAN, NURSES, DOCTORS,
A WOMAN   AND HOTEL GUESTS

ACT I

The period of the play is around 1910.

SCENE. *On either side of the stage are two small turntables on which the shorter scenes are played against very simplified backgrounds. As each scene finishes, the lights dim and the table revolves out, leaving an unobstructed view of the main stage. The main stage is raised by two steps, above which traveler curtains open and close.*

When the curtain rises, KATRIN, *in a spotlight, is seated at a desk on the right turntable, facing the audience. She is writing and*

59

smoking a cigarette. KATRIN *is somewhere in her early twenties. She should be played by an actress who is small in stature, and capable of looking sufficiently a child not to break the illusion in subsequent scenes. She is a blonde. Her hair, when we see her first, is in a modern "up" style, capable of being easily loosened to fall to shoulder length for the childhood scenes. She wears a very short dress, the skirt of which is concealed for the prologue by the desk behind which she is seated.*

KATRIN *writes in silence for a few moments, then puts down her pen, takes up her manuscript, and begins to read aloud what she has written.*

KATRIN (*reading*). "For as long as I could remember, the house on Steiner Street had been home. Papa and Mama had both been born in Norway, but they came to San Francisco because Mama's sisters were here. All of us were born here. Nels, the oldest and the only boy—my sister Christine—and the littlest sister, Dagmar." (*She puts down her manuscript and looks out front.*) It's funny, but when I look back, I always see Nels and Christine and myself looking almost as we do today. I guess that's because the people you see all the time stay the same age in your head. Dagmar's different. She was always the baby—so I see her as a baby. Even Mama—it's funny, but I always see Mama as around forty. She couldn't always have been forty. (*She puts out her cigarette, picks up her manuscript and starts to read again.*) "Besides us, there was our boarder, Mr. Hyde. Mr. Hyde was an Englishman who had once been an actor, and Mama was very impressed by his flowery talk and courtly manners. He used to read aloud to us in the evenings. But first and foremost, I remember Mama." (*The light dims down, leaving* KATRIN *only faintly visible. Lights come up on the main stage, revealing the house on Steiner Street—a kitchen room. It has a black flat, with a dresser, holding china. On either side of the dresser is a door, one leading to the pantry, the other to the rest of the house. The wall on the left is a short one. It is the wall of the house, and contains a door leading into the street, being presumably the back door of the house, but the one most commonly used as the entry door. Beyond it the street is visible, with a single lamppost at left, just outside the house. Behind*

*the room rises the house itself with upper windows lighted, and
behind it a painted backdrop of the San Francisco hills, houses,
and telegraph posts. The furniture of the kitchen is simple. A
center table, with two chairs above it, armchairs at either end,
and a low bench below it. Against the right wall, a large stove,
below it another armchair. The window is below the door in
the left wall and has a low Norwegian chest under it.* KATRIN's
voice continuing in the half-dark, as the scene is revealed.) "I
remember that every Saturday night Mama would sit down by
the kitchen table and count out the money Papa had brought
home in the little envelope."

(*By now the tableau is revealed in full, and the light on* KATRIN
dwindles further. The picture is as she described. MAMA—*looking around forty—is in the armchair at right of the table, empty-
ing the envelope of its silver dollars and smaller coins.* PAPA—
looking a little older than MAMA—*stands above her. His English
throughout is better than hers, with less accent.*)

MAMA. You call the children, Lars. Is good they should know about
money.

(PAPA *goes to door at the back and calls.*)

PAPA. Children! Nels—Christine—Katrin!
CHILDREN'S VOICES (*off, answering*). Coming, Papa!
MAMA. You call loud for Katrin. She is in her study, maybe.
PAPA. She is where?
MAMA. Katrin make the old attic under the roof into a study.
PAPA (*amused*). So? (*shouting*) Katrin! Katrin!
KATRIN (*still at her desk*). Yes, Papa. I heard.
PAPA (*returning to the room*). A study now, huh? What does Katrin
study?
MAMA. I think Katrin wants to be author.
PAPA. Author?
MAMA. Stories she will write. For the magazines. And books, too,
maybe, one day.
PAPA (*taking out his pipe*). Is good pay to be author?
MAMA. I don't know. For magazines, I think maybe yes. For books,
I think no.

PAPA. Then she become writer for magazines.

MAMA. Maybe. But I like she writes books. Like the ones Mr. Hyde reads us. (DAGMAR *enters from the pantry. She is a plump child of about eight and carries an alley cat in her arms.*) Dagmar, you bring that cat in again?

DAGMAR. Sure, she's my Elizabeth—my beautiful Elizabeth! (*She crosses to the chest under the window, and sits, nursing the cat.*)

PAPA. Poor Elizabeth looks as if she had been in fight again.

DAGMAR. Not poor Elizabeth. *Brave* Elizabeth. Elizabeth's a Viking cat. She fights for her honor!

PAPA (*exchanging an amused glance with* MAMA). And just what is a cat's honor, little one?

DAGMAR. The honor of being the bravest cat in San Francisco. (CHRISTINE *comes in. She, like* KATRIN, *should be played by a small young actress, but not a child. Her hair is to her shoulders, her dress short, her age indeterminate. Actually, she is about thirteen at this time. She is the cool, aloof, matter-of-fact one of the family. She carries a box of crayons, scissors and a picture-book.*) Aren't you, Elizabeth?

CHRISTINE (*sitting above the table and starting to color the picture-book with the crayons*). That disgusting cat!

DAGMAR. She's not disgusting. She's beautiful. Beautiful as the dawn!

CHRISTINE. And when have *you* ever seen the dawn?

DAGMAR. I haven't seen it, but Mr. Hyde read to us about it. (MR. HYDE *comes in from back door. He is a slightly seedy, long-haired man in his fifties. Rather of the old-fashioned English "laddie" actor type. He wears a very shabby long overcoat, with a deplorable fur collar, and carries his hat. His accent is English.*) Didn't you, Mr. Hyde? Didn't you read to us about the dawn?

MR. HYDE. I did, my child of joy. The dawn, the rosy-finger-tipped Aurora . . .

DAGMAR. When can I get to *see* the dawn, Mama?

MAMA. Any morning you get up early.

DAGMAR. Is there a dawn every morning?

MAMA. Sure.

DAGMAR (*incredulous*). It's all that beautiful, and it happens every *morning*? Why didn't anyone *tell* me?

MR. HYDE. My child, that is what the poets are for. To tell you of *all* the beautiful things that are happening every day, and that no one sees until they tell them. (*He starts for the door.*)

MAMA. You go out, Mr. Hyde?

MR. HYDE. For a few moments only, dear Madam. To buy myself a modicum [1] of that tawny weed, tobacco, that I lust after, as Ben Jonson says. I shall be back in time for our nightly reading. (*He goes out and disappears down the street.*)

MAMA (*who has gone to the back door, calls with a good deal of sharpness and firmness*). Nels! Katrin! You do not hear Papa call you?

NELS (*from upstairs*). Coming, Mama!

KATRIN (*at her desk*). Yes, Mama. I'm coming. (*She rises. In her few moments in the dark, she has loosened her hair to her shoulders, and we see that her skirt is short as she walks from her desk, and up the steps into the set. As soon as she has left it, the turntable revolves out. Immediately after her,* NELS *comes in from the back. He is a tall, strapping young fellow—old enough to look eighteen or nineteen, or fifteen or sixteen, according to his dress, or demeanor.[2] Now, he is about fifteen.* KATRIN, *to* CHRISTINE.) Move over. (*She shares* CHRISTINE's *chair at the table with her.*)

PAPA. So now all are here.

MAMA. Come, then. (CHRISTINE, NELS *and* KATRIN *gather around the table.* DAGMAR *remains crooning to* ELIZABETH, *but rises and stands behind* PAPA. *Sorting coins.*) First, for the landlord. (*She makes a pile of silver dollars. It gets pushed down the table from one member of the family to the next, each speaking as he passes it.* PAPA *comes last.*)

NELS (*passing it on*). For the landlord.

KATRIN (*doing likewise*). For the landlord.

CHRISTINE (*passing it to* PAPA). The landlord.

PAPA. For the landlord. (*He dumps the pile at his end of the table, writing on a piece of paper, which he wraps around the pile.*)

MAMA (*who has been sorting*). For the grocer.

[1] **modicum:** small amount, portion
[2] **demeanor:** bearing, conduct

(*The business is repeated. During this repeat,* DAGMAR'S *crooning to the cat becomes audible, contrapuntally* [3] *to the repetitions of "For the Grocer."*)

DAGMAR (*in a crescendo* [4]). In all the United States no cat was as brave as Elizabeth. (*Fortissimo.* [5]) In all the *world* no cat was as brave as Elizabeth!

MAMA (*gently*). Hush, Dagmar. Quietly. You put Elizabeth back into the pantry.

DAGMAR (*in a loud stage whisper, as she crosses to pantry*). In Heaven or HELL no cat was as brave as Elizabeth! (*She goes out with the cat.*)

MAMA. For Katrin's shoes to be half-soled. (*She passes a half dollar.*)

NELS. Katrin's shoes.

KATRIN (*proudly*). *My* shoes!

CHRISTINE (*contemptuously*). Katrin's old shoes.

PAPA. Katrin's shoes.

CHRISTINE (*rising and coming to* MAMA). Mama, Teacher says this week I'll need a new notebook.

MAMA. How much it will be?

CHRISTINE. A dime.

MAMA (*giving her a dime*). For the notebook. You don't lose it.

CHRISTINE. I won't lose it. (*She wraps it in her handkerchief.*)

MAMA. You take care when you blow your nose.

CHRISTINE. I'll take care. (*She returns to her seat.*)

PAPA. Is all, Mama?

MAMA. Is all for this week. Is good. We do not have to go to the Bank. (*She starts to gather up the few remaining coins.* KATRIN *leaves the group, comes and sits on steps.*)

NELS (*rising*). Mama . . . (*She looks up, catching an urgency in his tone.* PAPA *suspends smoking for a moment.*) Mama, I'll be graduating from grammar school next month. Could I . . . could I go on to High, do you think?

MAMA (*pleased*). You want to go to high school?

NELS. I'd like to . . . if you think I could.

---

[3] **contrapuntally:** in the manner of music when one sound (or melody) accompanies another sound (or melody) independently

[4] **crescendo:** gradually louder tone

[5] **fortissimo:** very loud tone

MAMA. Is good.

(PAPA *nods approvingly.*)

NELS (*awkwardly*). It . . . it'll cost a little money. I've got it all written down. (*Producing a piece of paper from his pocket.*) Carfare, clothes, notebooks—things I'll really need. I figured it out with Cy Nichols. He went to High last year.

(PAPA *rises and comes behind* MAMA *to look at the paper* NELS *puts before them.*)

MAMA. Get the Little Bank, Christine.

(CHRISTINE *gets a small box from the dresser.*)

KATRIN (*from the steps—herself again, in the present—looking out front*). The Little Bank! That was the most important thing in the whole house. It was a box we used to keep for emergencies —like the time when Dagmar had croup and Papa had to go and get medicine to put in the steam kettle. I can *smell* that medicine now! The things that came out of the Little Bank! Mama was always going to buy herself a warm coat out of it, when there was enough, only there never was.

(*Meanwhile,* MAMA *has been counting the contents.*)

NELS (*anxiously*). Is there enough, Mama?

MAMA (*shaking her head*). Is not much in the Little Bank right now. We give to the dentist, you remember? And for your roller skates?

NELS (*his face falling*). I know. And there's your warm coat you've been saving for.

MAMA. The coat I can get another time. But even so . . . (*She shakes her head.*)

CHRISTINE. You mean Nels can't go to High?

MAMA. Is not enough here. We do not want to have to go to the Bank, do we?

NELS. No, Mama, no. I'll work in Dillon's grocery after school.

(MAMA *writes a figure on the paper and starts to count on her fingers.* PAPA *looks over, and does the sum in his head.*)

PAPA. Is not enough.

MAMA (*finishing on her fingers against her collarbone*). No, is not enough.

PAPA (*taking his pipe out of his mouth and looking at it a long time*). I give up tobacco.

(MAMA *looks at him, almost speaks, then just touches his sleeve, writes another figure and starts on her fingers again.*)

CHRISTINE. I'll mind the Maxwell children Friday nights. Katrin can help me.

(MAMA *writes another figure.* PAPA *looks over—calculates again, nods with satisfaction.*)

MAMA (*triumphantly*). Is good! Is enough!

NELS. Gee! (*He moves beside* PAPA *and starts to play with a wire puzzle.*)

MAMA. We do not have to go to the Bank.

(DAGMAR *returns, without the cat.*)

DAGMAR (*hearing the last line*). Where is the Bank?

CHRISTINE (*leaving the table, cutting out the picture which she colored*). Downtown.

DAGMAR. What's it look like?

CHRISTINE. Just a building.

DAGMAR (*sitting on the bench, below the table*). Like a prison?

CHRISTINE (*sharply*). No, nothing like a prison.

DAGMAR. Well, then, why does Mama always say "We don't want to go to the Bank"?

CHRISTINE. Because . . . well, because no one ever wants to go to the Bank.

DAGMAR. Why not?

CHRISTINE. Because if we went to the Bank all the time, there'd be no money left there. And then if we couldn't pay our rent, they'd turn us out like Mrs. Jensen down the street.

DAGMAR. You mean, it's like saving some of your candy for tomorrow?

MAMA (*busy with coffee and cups at the stove and the dresser*). Yes, my Dagmar. Is exactly like saving your candy.

DAGMAR. But if . . . if all the other people go to the Bank, then there won't be any money left for us, either.

NELS (*kindly*). It isn't like that, Dagmar. Everyone can only get so much.

DAGMAR. How much?

NELS. However much you've got there . . . put away. You see, it's *our* money that we put there, to keep safe.

DAGMAR. When did we put it there?

NELS. I . . . I don't know when. A long time back, I guess. Wasn't it, Mama?

MAMA. Is enough about the Bank.

DAGMAR. How much money have we got in the Bank?

NELS. I don't know. How much, Mama?

MAMA. Enough. (*During the last speeches* AUNT TRINA *appears from the wings. She is a timid, mouselike little woman of about forty, with some prettiness about her. She wears her hat and coat and a pathetic feather boa.*[6] *She comes up the street and knocks on the house door.* MAMA, *hearing the knock.*) Was the door?

CHRISTINE (*quickly moving*). If it's the aunts, I'm going to my boodwar.

KATRIN (*rising, entering the scene*). And I'm going to my study.

MAMA (*stopping them*). You cannot run away. We must be polite to the aunts. (*She opens the door.*) Why, is Trina!

PAPA. Trina, and all by herself!

MAMA. Say good evening to Aunt Trina, children.

CHILDREN (*together*). Good evening, Aunt Trina.

TRINA. Good evening, children. How well they all look. (*She comes to the table.*)

MAMA. You have a feather boa. Is new. (*Inspecting it.*) Beautiful.

TRINA (*simpering a little*). It was a present.

MAMA (*smiling*). A present! Look, Lars. Trina has a present.

PAPA (*feeling it*). Is fine. (*He puts* TRINA's *hat, coat and boa on the chest under the window.*)

MAMA. Jenny and Sigrid don't come with you, Trina?

TRINA (*embarrassed*). No, I . . . I didn't tell them I was coming. I want to talk to you, Marta.

MAMA (*smiling*). So? Sit then, and we talk. (*She puts her in* PAPA's *chair, at the left of the table.*)

TRINA (*nervously agitated*). Could we talk alone?

MAMA. Alone?

[6] **boa**: a long, round scarf of fur or feathers

TRINA. If you wouldn't mind.

MAMA. Children, you leave us alone a little. I call you. Dagmar, you go with Katrin.

KATRIN (*protesting*). Oh, but, Mama . . .

MAMA (*firmly*). Katrin, you take Dagmar!

KATRIN. Yes, Mama. (*Pushing* DAGMAR *resentfully*.) Come on.

(*The* CHILDREN *go out the back*.)

MAMA. Now—what is it, Trina?

TRINA (*looking down, embarrassed*). Marta . . .

MAMA (*helpfully*). Yes?

TRINA. Oh, no, I can't say it.

MAMA (*anxiously*). Trina, what is it?

TRINA. It's . . . something very personal.

MAMA. You want Lars should go outside?

TRINA. Would you mind, Lars? Just for a minute?

PAPA (*good-humoredly*). No, I go. I know what women's secrets are. (*Teasing.*) As your Uncle Chris say—"Vomen! Pff!"

MAMA. You have your pipe, Lars? Is fine night. (PAPA *takes out his pipe—then lays it down.*) What is it?

PAPA. I forget. I give up tobacco.

MAMA. Is still some tobacco in your pouch? (PAPA *nods.*) Then you do not give up tobacco till you have finish. You give up *more* tobacco—not the tobacco you already have.

PAPA. Is not right, Marta. (*He pats her, takes his pipe, and goes out, standing outside the house, under the lamppost, and looking up at the stars, smoking.*)

MAMA. So, Trina. Now. What is it?

TRINA. Marta . . . I want to get married.

MAMA. You mean . . . you want to get married, or there is someone you want to marry?

TRINA. There's someone I want to marry.

MAMA. Does *he* want to marry *you*?

TRINA (*sitting on bench*). He says he does.

MAMA (*delighted*). Trina! Is wonderful! (*She sits beside her.*)

TRINA (*crying a little*). I think it is.

MAMA. Who is?

TRINA. Mr. Thorkelson.

MAMA. From the funeral parlor? (TRINA *nods.* MAMA *nods, speculatively, but with less enthusiasm.*)

TRINA. I know he isn't very handsome or . . . or tall. I know it isn't what most people would think a very nice profession, but . . .

MAMA. You love him, Trina? (TRINA *nods ecstatically.*) Then is good. (*She pats* TRINA's *hand.*)

TRINA. Marta, will you . . . will you help me tell the others?

MAMA. Oh . . . Jenny and Sigrid . . . they do not know?

TRINA. No. I was afraid they'd laugh at me. But if *you* tell them . . .

MAMA. Jenny will not like you tell me first.

TRINA (*desperately*). I can't help that. You've got to tell them not to laugh at me. If they laugh at me, I'll . . . I'll kill myself.

MAMA (*with decision*). Jenny and Sigrid will not laugh. I promise you, Trina.

TRINA. Oh, thank you, Marta. And . . . Uncle Chris?

MAMA (*with some seriousness*). Ah!

TRINA. Will you talk to him?

MAMA. It is Mr. Thorkelson who must talk to Uncle Chris. Always it is the husband who must talk to the head of the family.

TRINA. Yes. I know, but . . . well, Uncle Chris is so very frightening. He's so big and black, and he shouts so. And Mr. Thorkelson is (*Gesturing a very small man.*) . . . well, kind of timid, really.

MAMA (*gently*). But, Trina, if he is to be your husband, he must learn not to be timid. You do not want husband should be timid. *You* are timid. Is not good when *both* are timid. (*Then firmly.*) No! Jenny and Sigrid I speak to, but Mr. Thorkelson must go to Uncle Chris.

PAPA (*re-enters the house*). Marta, Trina, I do not want to interrupt your talk, but Jenny and Sigrid are coming.

TRINA (*alarmed*). Oh, dear! (*She rises, quickly.*)

PAPA. I see them get off the cable car. They come up the hill.

TRINA (*in a flurry*). I'd better go to your room for a minute.

(*She starts for the door, turns back, gets her things from the chest, and runs out, carrying them. Meanwhile,* MAMA *has been whispering the news to* PAPA.)

MAMA. The coffee is ready—I get more cups.

(*During the above,* AUNTS JENNY *and* SIGRID *have entered from the front.* JENNY *is a domineering woman in her fifties,* SIGRID, *whining and complaining.*)

SIGRID (*in the street*). Wait, Jenny, I must get my breath. This hill kills me every time I climb it.

JENNY. You climbed bigger hills than that in the old country.

SIGRID. I was a *girl* in the old country.

(*They march to the door and knock—*SIGRID *following* JENNY.)

MAMA (*opening the door to them*). Jenny. Sigrid. Is surprise. (*To* SIGRID.) Where's Ole?

SIGRID. Working. He's always working. I never see anything of him at all.

MAMA (*crossing to the stove for coffeepot*). Is good to work.

SIGRID. It's good to see your husband once in a while, too. (*Sits near table.*)

JENNY (*no nonsense about her*). Has Trina been here? (*At the left of table.*)

MAMA (*at right of table*). Trina?

JENNY. She's gone somewhere. And she doesn't know anyone but *you.* . . .

MAMA. That is what *you* think.

JENNY. What do you mean by that?

MAMA. Give Lars your coat. I give you some coffee. Then we talk about Trina.

SIGRID (*as* PAPA *helps with coats*). She *has* been here?

MAMA. Yes, she has been here. (*Pouring coffee and passing cups.*)

JENNY. What did Trina want?

MAMA. She want to talk to me.

JENNY. What about?

MAMA. Marriage.

SIGRID. What?

MAMA (*pouring calmly*). Marriage. (*Passing* SIGRID'S *cup.*) Trina wants to get married.

JENNY (*seated at left of table*). That's no news. Of course she wants to get married. Every old maid wants to get married. (*She rolls up her veil.*)

MAMA. There is someone who wants to marry Trina.

JENNY. Who'd want to marry Trina?

MAMA. Mr. Thorkelson.

SIGRID. Peter Thorkelson? Little Peter? (*She gestures a midget.*)

MAMA. He is not so little.

SIGRID. He's hardly bigger than my Arne—and Arne is not ten yet.

MAMA. So he is hardly bigger than your Arne. Does every husband have to be big man?

JENNY. Trina's making it up. That happens with old maids when they get to Trina's age.

MAMA (*firmly*). No, Jenny—it is true. Mr. Thorkelson wants to marry Trina.

JENNY (*changing her tactics slightly*). Mr. Thorkelson. She'd be the laughing stock. (*She laughs, rising and moving to the left.*)

MAMA (*moving to her*). Jenny, Trina is here. She will come in in a minute. This is serious for her. You will not laugh at her.

JENNY. I shall do what I please.

MAMA. No, Jenny, you will not.

JENNY. And why won't I?

MAMA. Because I will not let you.

JENNY. And how will you stop me?

MAMA. If you laugh at Trina, I will tell her of the time before your wedding when your husband try to run away.

SIGRID (*rising, intrigued*). What is that?

JENNY. Who told you that?

MAMA. I know.

SIGRID (*intrigued—stealing around and below the table*). Erik . . . tried to run away?

JENNY. It's not true.

MAMA. Then you do not mind if I tell Trina.

JENNY. Uncle Chris told you.

SIGRID (*tenaciously [7]*). Tried to run away?

MAMA. It does not matter, Sigrid. Jenny will not laugh at Trina now. Nor will you! For if *you* laugh at her, I will tell her of your wedding night with Ole, when you cry all the time, and he send you back to Mother.

PAPA (*with sudden enjoyment*). This I do *not* know!

MAMA (*reprovingly*). Is no need you should know. I do not tell

---

[7] **tenaciously:** with persistence, stubbornly

these stories for spite—only so they do not laugh at Trina. Call
her, Lars. You like more coffee, Jenny? Sigrid?

(PAPA *goes to the back door, calls, "Trina."* MAMA *pours coffee
for* JENNY. MR. HYDE *reappears and lets himself into the house.
The* AUNTS *rise, standing in line with* MAMA.)

MR. HYDE (*seeing company*). Oh, I beg your pardon. I was not
aware . . .

MAMA. Mr. Hyde, these are my sisters.

MR. HYDE. Enchanted, ladies, Madame, Madame. The Three Graces.
(*He bows.* SIGRID *giggles coyly. He turns to leave the room.*)
You will excuse me?

MAMA. Sure, Mr. Hyde.

MR. HYDE. I shall be in my room. (*He goes out.*)

JENNY (*moving to table again*). So *that's* your famous boarder. Has
he paid you his rent yet? Three months he's been here, hasn't
he?

MAMA (*at the other side of the table*). Is hard to ask. Surely he
will pay soon.

JENNY (*with a snort*). Surely he won't! If I ran my boardinghouse
the way you run this place . . .

PAPA. Maybe your boarders wouldn't always leave you.

JENNY. If Marta thinks she's going to get the warm coat she's always talking about out of *that* one . . .

MAMA. Jenny, Mr. Hyde is a gentleman. He reads to us aloud. Wonderful books . . . Longfellow, and Charles Dickens, and Feni-
more Kipling. (TRINA *steals back.* MAMA, *seeing her hesitant in
the doorway.*) Come in, Trina. The coffee is getting cold. (*She
pours a cup. There is a silence.*) I tell them.

JENNY. Why did you come to Marta first?

PAPA (*beside her*). She thought Marta would understand.

JENNY. Aren't Sigrid and I married women, too?

PAPA. You have been married longer than Marta. She think maybe
you forget.

JENNY. What sort of a living does Mr. Thorkelson make?

TRINA (*on bench near table*). I . . . I haven't asked.

SIGRID (*at right of table*). Can he keep you?

TRINA. I don't think he would have asked me to marry him if he
couldn't.

JENNY. Maybe he thinks you are going to keep *him*.

MAMA (*warningly*). Jenny!

SIGRID. Maybe he thinks Trina will have a dowry [8] like the girls at home.

TRINA. Well, why shouldn't I? You all had dowries. . . .

JENNY. We were married in Norway. And our parents were alive. Where would your dowry come from, I'd like to know?

TRINA. Uncle Chris. He's head of the family.

JENNY. And who will ask him?

TRINA. He won't need asking. When Mr. Thorkelson goes to see him . . .

JENNY. Uncle Chris will eat him!

SIGRID (*giggling maliciously*). Little Peter and Uncle Chris!

MAMA (*with meaning*). Maybe Uncle Chris will tell him some family stories. He knows many, does Uncle Chris.

(*The* AUNTS *put down their cups, discomfited.*)

JENNY (*to change the subject*). Where are the children? Aren't we going to see them before we go?

PAPA. Of course. I'll call them. (*He goes to the door and does so, shouting.*) Children! Your aunts are *leaving!*

CHILDREN'S VOICES (*eagerly shouting back*). Coming, Papa!

JENNY. You come with us, Trina?

MAMA. I think maybe Trina like to stay here and listen to Mr. Hyde read to us. You like, Trina?

TRINA. Well, if I wouldn't be in the way. I asked Mr. Thorkelson to call for me here. He'll see me home. I'll help you with the coffee things. (*She takes the tray of coffee cups and goes into the pantry.*)

(KATRIN *returns from her study. She carries her diary.* DAGMAR *follows her, and behind them,* CHRISTINE.)

KATRIN *and* DAGMAR (*curtseying*). Good evening, Aunt Sigrid. Good evening, Aunt Jenny.

(CHRISTINE *sketches a perfunctory* [9] *curtsey without speaking.*)

JENNY. Where have *you* all been hiding yourselves?

---

[8] **dowry:** property that a woman brings to her husband at marriage
[9] **perfunctory:** indifferent, without interest

DAGMAR (*going into the pantry*). We've been in Christine's bood-war.

JENNY. Her *what?*

MAMA. Christine makes the little closet into a boudoir. I give her those bead portieres,[10] Jenny, that you lend us when we come from the old country.

SIGRID. And what does she do there?

CHRISTINE (*impertinently*). What people usually do in boudoirs.

MAMA. Christine, that is rude. It is her little place to herself.

(NELS *enters.*)

NELS. Hello, Aunt Sigrid. Hello, Aunt Jenny.

SIGRID (*shaking hands*). Good evening, Nels. My, how tall he is getting!

MAMA (*proudly*). Yes, is almost as tall as his Papa.

(NELS *sits on the chest under the windows.*)

SIGRID. He looks to me as if he was outgrowing his strength. Dagmar was looking pale, too. (DAGMAR *returns now, carrying the cat again.* SIGRID, *jumping.*) Goodness, what a horrid-looking cat.

DAGMAR. She's not. She's beautiful.

PAPA. Is her new friend. She goes with Dagmar everywhere.

CHRISTINE (*seated, above table*). She does. First thing you know, she'll have the cat sleeping with her.

DAGMAR (*eagerly*). Oh, Mama, can I? Can I, Mama? (*She comes to the bench and sits.*)

JENNY. Certainly not. Don't you know a cat draws breath from a sleeping child? You wouldn't want to wake up some morning *smothered*, would you?

DAGMAR. I wouldn't care. Elizabeth can have *all* my breath! (*She blows into the cat's face.*) There!

JENNY (*putting on gloves*). Elizabeth—what a very silly name for a cat.

NELS (*rising*). It's a very silly name for *that* cat. It's a Tom.

MAMA. Nels, how you know?

NELS. I looked!

DAGMAR. How can you tell?

NELS. You can.

[10] **portieres:** curtains hanging across a doorway

DAGMAR. But how?

MAMA (*quickly warning*). Nels, you do not say how!

NELS (*to* DAGMAR). So you'd better think up another name for him.

DAGMAR. I won't. He's Elizabeth. And he's going to *stay* Elizabeth.

PAPA. We could call him *Uncle* Elizabeth!

DAGMAR (*laughing delightedly*). Uncle Elizabeth! Do you hear, Elizabeth? You're called *Uncle* Elizabeth now!

JENNY. Such foolishness! Well, good-by, all. Marta. Lars.

(*Good-bys are exchanged all around, the* CHILDREN *curtseying formally.*)

MAMA. Good-by, Jenny. Good-by, Sigrid. Nels, you go tell Mr. Hyde we are ready for the reading.

(NELS *goes off. The* AUNTS *leave and* MAMA *stands in the doorway, waving good-by.*)

SIGRID (*as they go*). Well, I never thought we'd live to see Trina get married.

JENNY. She's not married yet. She's got Uncle Chris to deal with first.

(*They disappear into wings.*)

MAMA (*returning to the room and calling into the pantry*). Trina, they have gone. Dagmar, you put Elizabeth out for the night now.

DAGMAR (*correcting her*). *Uncle* Elizabeth!

MAMA. *Uncle* Elizabeth. (DAGMAR *goes out into the pantry with the cat.* TRINA *comes in as* MR. HYDE *and* NELS *return.*) Mr. Hyde, this is my sister Trina.

MR. HYDE (*bowing*). Enchanted!

MAMA (*seating herself at the table*). Mr. Hyde reads to us "The Tales from Two Cities." Is beautiful story. But sad.

TRINA (*brightly*). I like sad stories. (*She gets out her handkerchief.*)

(*The whole family group themselves around the table,* MAMA *near the table in her old chair—*PAPA *behind her.* TRINA *at one side behind table,* NELS *on the other side behind table.* DAGMAR *returning and seating herself on the floor in front of* MAMA. MR. HYDE *takes the armchair at left of table.* CHRISTINE *sits on the floor in front of table.* KATRIN *is on the steps.*)

MR. HYDE. Tonight, I would like to finish it.

MAMA. Is good.

MR. HYDE. Are you ready?

CHILDREN. Yes, please, Mr. Hyde.

MR. HYDE. I will go on from where we left off. (*He starts to read.*) "In the black prison of the Conciergerie, the doomed of the day awaited their fate. They were in number as the weeks of the year. Fifty-two were to roll that afternoon on the life-tide of the City to the boundless, everlasting sea. . . ."

(*The lights dim down slowly, leaving spots on* KATRIN *and* MR. HYDE *only.*)

KATRIN. I don't think I shall ever forget that night. It was almost midnight when he came to the end, and none of us had noticed.

MR. HYDE (*reading from the last page*). "It is a far, far better thing that I do than I have ever done; it is a far, far better rest that I go to than I have ever known." (*He closes the book.*) "The End."

(*The turntable revolves in again.* KATRIN *rises from the step and crosses to her desk on the turntable.*)

KATRIN. I wrote in my diary that night before I went to bed. (*She reads aloud from it.*) "Tonight Mr. Hyde finished *The Tale of Two Cities.* The closing chapters are indeed superb. How beautiful a thing is self-sacrifice. I wish there were someone I could die for." (*She sits looking out front.*) Mr. Hyde read us all kinds of books. He thrilled us with *Treasure Island* and terrified us with "The Hound of the Baskervilles." I can still remember the horror in his voice as he read. . . .

MR. HYDE (*still on the main stage in his spot, reading*). "Dr. Mortimer looked strangely at us for an instant, and his voice sank almost to a whisper as he answered: 'Mr. Holmes, they were the footprints of a gigantic *hound!*' " (*He closes the book.*) We will continue tomorrow night. If you are interested.

KATRIN (*looking out front*). If we were interested! You couldn't have kept us from it. It meant a lot to Mama, too, because Nels stopped going nights to the street corner to hang about with the neighborhood boys. The night they got into trouble for breaking into Mr. Dillon's store, Nels was home with us.

And sometimes Mr. Hyde read us poetry. "The Lady of the Lake" . . . and the "Rime of the Ancient Mariner."

MR. HYDE (*reading*).

> "About, about, in reel and rout
> The death-fires danced at night.
> The water, like a witch's oils,
> Burnt green and blue and white."

(*His spot goes out, and the traveler curtains close on the kitchen scene.*)

KATRIN. There were many nights I couldn't sleep for the way he had set my imagination dancing. (*Reading from her diary again.*) "What a wonderful thing is literature, transporting us to realms unknown." (*To herself.*) And all the time my schoolteacher kept telling me that I ought to write about things I knew. I did write a piece for her once about Uncle Chris, and she said it wasn't nice to write like that about a member of one's own family. Papa called Mama's Uncle Chris a black Norwegian, because of his dark hair and fierce mustache, but there were others in the family who claimed that he was black in a different way. The aunts, for example.

(*Spot goes up on turntable, representing* JENNY's *kitchen.* JENNY *and* TRINA *are discovered.* JENNY *is rolling pastry.* TRINA *is crocheting.*)

JENNY. Black! I'll say he's black. Black in his heart. Cursing and swearing. . . .

TRINA. Marta says that's only because it hurts him to walk.

JENNY. Rubbish. I know all about his limp and the accident back in the old country—but has anyone ever heard him complain? Marta's always making excuses for him.

TRINA. I know . . . but he *is* good to the children. All those oranges he's always sending them. . . .

JENNY. Oranges! What good is oranges? Turn 'em yellow. They're the only things he's ever been known to give away, anyway. He's got other uses for his money.

TRINA. What you mean?

JENNY. Bottles! And that woman who is his housekeeper.

(SIGRID *comes through the curtains. She crosses to* JENNY *and* TRINA.)

SIGRID. Jenny. Trina. What do you think? What do you think Uncle Chris has done now?

TRINA. What?

JENNY. Tell us.

SIGRID. You know my little Arne's knee—that fall he had two months ago? The man at the drugstore said it was only a bruise, but today it was hurting him again, so I left him home when I went to do the marketing. I asked Mrs. Schultz next door to keep an eye on him, and who should turn up, not ten minutes after I'd gone, but Uncle Chris. And what do you think?

JENNY. Well, tell us, if you're going to. Don't keep *asking* us.

SIGRID. He took one look at Arne's knee, bundled him into that rattletrap old automobile of his, and rushed him straight off to the hospital. I've just come from there . . . and what do you think? They've operated! They've got him in plaster of Paris!

JENNY. Without consulting you?

SIGRID. It seems the doctor is a friend of his . . . that's why he did it. No, this time he's gone too far. To put a child of Arne's age through all that pain. They wouldn't even let me *see* Arne. I'm going to tell Uncle Chris exactly what I think of him . . .

JENNY. That's right.

SIGRID. I'm going to tell him right now. (*Weakening a little.*) Come with me, Jenny.

JENNY. Well, I . . . No, I can't leave my baking.

SIGRID. You must, Jenny. We must stand together. You come, too, Trina, and ask about your dowry. *Make* him give it to you.

TRINA. Oh, but . . . Marta said Mr. Thorkelson should do that. . . .

JENNY. Well, then, go and get Mr. Thorkelson. Go down to the mortuary and get him now. Sigrid is right. We girls have got to stand together!

(*Blackout. Turntable revolves out.*)

KATRIN (*at her desk*). Nobody knew where Uncle Chris lived. That was part of the mystery about him. He used to roam up and down the state buying up farms and ranches that had gone to pieces, and bullying them back into prosperity. Then he'd sell at a profit and move on again. Two or three times a year he'd descend on the city in his automobile and come roaring and stamping into our house.

(*Her light dims. The sound of a very old and noisy Ford car changing gears is heard in the distance. A grinding and screaming as it comes to a standstill. Then* UNCLE CHRIS'S VOICE, *shouting.*)

UNCLE CHRIS'S VOICE. Marta! Lars! Children—vere are you?

(*The curtains part on the kitchen again. Outside in the street is* UNCLE CHRIS'S *car—an antique model. A woman is seated beside the empty driver's seat.* UNCLE CHRIS *is knocking on the house door. He is an elderly, powerful, swarthy man with a limp. In the kitchen,* NELS *and* CHRISTINE *are cowering.*[11])

UNCLE CHRIS. Marta! Lars!

CHRISTINE (*scared*). It's Uncle Chris.

NELS (*equally so*). I know.

CHRISTINE. What'll we do?

UNCLE CHRIS. Is nobody home? Hey, there—is nobody home? (*Banging on the door.*) Hey—someone—answer the door. (*He tries the door handle, it opens and he strides, limpingly, in. He has a strong accent, and uses the Norwegian pronunciation of the children's names.*) So, vat is—you do not answer the door? You do not hear me calling? (*The* CHILDREN *cower silently.*) I say, you do not hear me calling? I do not call loud enough?

CHRISTINE. Y-yes, Uncle Chris.

UNCLE CHRIS. Which yes? Yes, you do not hear me—or yes I do not call loud enough?

NELS. We heard you, Uncle Chris.

UNCLE CHRIS. Then why you do not come?

NELS. We . . . we were just going to.

(KATRIN *has left her desk and come up the steps.*)

UNCLE CHRIS. Let me look at you. You too, Katrinë, do not stand there—come and let me look at you. (*They line up as though for inspection. He thumps* NELS *between the shoulder blades.*) Stand tall! (*They all straighten up.*) Um-hum. By the dresser,

---

[11] **cowering**: shrinking back

where the marks are. (NELS *goes to the wall by the dresser.* UNCLE CHRIS *compares his mark with the previous one—and makes a new one on the wall, writing by it.*) Two inches. Two inches in . . . (*examining the date*) six months. Is good. Christinë. (CHRISTINE *replaces* NELS.) Show me your teeth. (*She does so.*) You brush them goot? (*She nods.*) Nils, there is a box of oranges in the automobile. You fetch them in. (NELS *goes out.* UNCLE CHRIS *measures* CHRISTINE.) Where is the little von? Dagmar?

KATRIN. She's sick, Uncle Chris.

UNCLE CHRIS (*arrested*). Sick? What is the matter with her?

KATRIN. It's her ear. She's had an earache for two days. Bad earache. Mama sent for the doctor.

UNCLE CHRIS. Goot doctor? What he say?

KATRIN. He's in there now. (*She points off. Meanwhile* CHRISTINE *has remained standing by the wall, afraid to move.*)

UNCLE CHRIS. I go in. (*He starts to the door, but* MAMA *and* DR. JOHNSON *come into the room as he does so. During this* NELS *has gone to the car, and with nervous smiles at the woman seated by the driver's seat, has heaved out a huge box of oranges. He returns with the oranges during the ensuing scene.*)

MAMA (*greeting him*). Uncle Chris.

UNCLE CHRIS. How is with Dagmar?

MAMA. Is bad. Doctor, this is my uncle, Mr. Halvorsen.

DOCTOR. How do you do, sir? (*He goes for his hat and bag which are on the bench in front of the window.*)

UNCLE CHRIS. What is with the child?

DOCTOR. We must get her to a hospital. At once. We'll have to operate.

MAMA. Operate?

DOCTOR. I'm afraid so.

MAMA. Can wait? Until my husband comes home from work?

DOCTOR. I'm afraid not. Her best chance is for us to operate immediately.

MAMA (*after a second*). We go. (*She goes to the dresser for the Little Bank.*)

UNCLE CHRIS (*who has watched her decision with approval, turns to the doctor, moving to him*). What is with the child?

DOCTOR. I'm afraid it's a mastoid.

UNCLE CHRIS. Ah . . . then you operate immediately.

DOCTOR (*resenting this*). That's what I said.

UNCLE CHRIS. Immediately!

MAMA (*who has poured the contents of the Little Bank onto the table*). Doctor . . . is enough?

DOCTOR (*at table*). I was thinking of the County Hospital.

MAMA. No. No. We pay. Is enough?

KATRIN. If there isn't, we can go to the Bank.

CHRISTINE. We've got a bank account.

MAMA. Is enough without we go to the Bank, Doctor? My husband is carpenter. Make good money.

UNCLE CHRIS. If there is need of money, *I* pay.

DOCTOR (*mainly in dislike of* UNCLE CHRIS). It'll be all right. We'll take her to the clinic. You pay what you can afford.

UNCLE CHRIS. Goot. Goot. I have a patient there already. My nephew, Arne. They operate this morning on his knee.

DOCTOR. Are you a physician, sir?

UNCLE CHRIS. I am better physician than most doctors. Nils, there, my other nephew, he become doctor when he grow up.

(NELS, *who has just returned, looks up, surprised.*)

DOCTOR (*chilly*). Oh, indeed . . . very interesting. Well, now, if you will have the child at the clinic in . . . shall we say an hour's time. . . .

UNCLE CHRIS (*striding in front of table*). The child will be at the clinic in *ten minutes'* time. I haf my automobile.

DOCTOR. I can hardly make arrangements in ten minutes.

UNCLE CHRIS (*at table*). I make arrangements. I know doctors.

MAMA. Uncle Chris, Dr. Johnson arrange. He is good doctor.

DOCTOR (*ironically*). Thank you, Madam.

MAMA. You go, Doctor. We come.

DOCTOR. Very well, in an hour, then. And Dagmar will be well taken care of, I promise you. I will do the operation myself.

UNCLE CHRIS. I watch.

DOCTOR. You will do no such thing, sir.

UNCLE CHRIS. Always I watch operations. I am head of family.

DOCTOR. I allow no one to attend my operations.

UNCLE CHRIS. Are so bad?

DOCTOR (*to* MAMA). Mrs. Hanson, if I am to undertake this operation and the care of your child, it must be on the strict understanding that this gentleman does not come near either me or my patient.

MAMA. Yes, Doctor, I talk to him. . . . You go to hospital now, please.

DOCTOR. Very well. But you understand . . . nowhere near me, or I withdraw from the case. (*He goes.*)

UNCLE CHRIS. I go see Dagmar.

MAMA (*stopping him above table*). Wait. Uncle Chris, is kind of you, but Dagmar is sick. You frighten her.

UNCLE CHRIS. I frighten her?

MAMA. Yes, Uncle Chris. You frighten everyone. . . .

UNCLE CHRIS (*amazed*). I?

MAMA. Everyone but me. Even the girls. . . . Jenny, Sigrid, Trina . . . they are frightened of you.

UNCLE CHRIS. The girls! Vomen! Pff!

MAMA. And the children, too. So Nels and I get Dagmar. You drive us to hospital in your automobile, but you do not frighten Dagmar. And you leave doctor alone. Dr. Johnson is *fine* doctor. You come with me, Nels. You carry Dagmar.

(NELS *and* MAMA *go out.* UNCLE CHRIS *stands in amazement and puzzlement. The* TWO GIRLS *watch him, hardly daring to move.*)

UNCLE CHRIS (*coming to table*). Is true? I frighten you? Christinë . . . Katrinë . . . you are frightened of me? Come, I ask you. Tell me the truth. You are frightened of me?

KATRIN (*tremulously*). A . . . a little, Uncle Chris.

UNCLE CHRIS (*on bench*). No? And you, Christinë?

CHRISTINE. Y . . . yes, Uncle Chris.

UNCLE CHRIS. But Nils . . . Nils is a boy . . . he is not frightened?

CHRISTINE. Not . . . not as much as we are. . . .

UNCLE CHRIS. But he is frightened?

CHRISTINE. Yes, Uncle Chris.

UNCLE CHRIS (*with a roar*). But why? What is there to be frightened of? I am your Uncle Chris . . . why do I frighten you?

CHRISTINE. I don't know.

UNCLE CHRIS. But that is bad. Very bad. The aunts, yes, I like to frighten them. (*The* GIRLS *giggle.*) That makes you laugh. (*He crosses to them.*) You do not like the aunts? Come, tell me. You do not like the aunts? Say!

KATRIN. Not . . . very much, Uncle Chris.

UNCLE CHRIS. And which do you not like the most? Jenny . . .
Sigrid . . . Trina. . . . Tell me—huh?

KATRIN. I think I like Aunt Jenny least. She's so . . . so bossy.

CHRISTINE. I can't stand Aunt Sigrid. Always whining and complaining.

UNCLE CHRIS (*with a great roar of laughter*). Is good. Jenny, bossy.
Sigrid, whining. Is true! But your Mama, she is different. And
she cook goot. The aunts, they cannot cook at all. Only you
do not tell your Mama we have talked of them so. It is a secret, for us. Then you cannot be frightened of me any more
. . . when we have secret. I tell you my secret, too. *I* do not
like the aunts. And so that they do not bother me, I frighten
them and shout at them. You I do not shout at if you are goot
children, and clean your teeth goot, and eat your oranges. (*He
takes out a snuffbox and partakes of its contents.*)

(*As he says "You I do not shout at," the posse of* AUNTS *appears, in outdoor clothes, accompanied by* MR. THORKELSON, *a
terrified little man. They come in at the left and start up to
the house.*)

SIGRID (*stopping in the street*). Jenny. Do you see what I see? A
woman, in his automobile.

JENNY. How shameful!

SIGRID. Ought we to bow?

JENNY. Bow? To a woman like that? We cut her. That's what we
do. I'll show you. (*She strides to the front door, ignoring the
woman in the car, and enters the house. The others follow.*
JENNY, *entering.*) Uncle Chris, Sigrid has something to say to
you.

SIGRID (*with false bravery*). Uncle Chris, you took Arne to the hospital. . . .

UNCLE CHRIS (*at table*). Yes, I take Arne to the hospital. And now
we take Dagmar to the hospital, so you do not clutter up the
place.

JENNY (*on the other side of table*). What's the matter with Dagmar?

CHRISTINE. It's her ear. Dr. Johnson's going to operate.

SIGRID (*catching her favorite word*). Operate? This is some more of
Uncle Chris's doing. Did you hear what he did to Arne?

UNCLE CHRIS (*turning on her*). Sigrid, you are a whining old fool, and you get out of here. . . .

SIGRID (*deflating*). We'd better go, Jenny. . . .

JENNY (*stoutly*). No . . . there has been enough of these high-handed goings-on. . . .

UNCLE CHRIS. And you, Jenny . . . you are a bossy old fool, and you get out of here, too, and we take Dagmar to hospital. (NELS *enters, carrying* DAGMAR *in his arms, wrapped in a blanket.*) You got her goot, Nils?

NELS. Sure, Uncle Chris.

UNCLE CHRIS. We go.

JENNY (*getting between him and the door*). No! You are going to hear me out. (*Weakening.*) That is, you are going to hear *Sigrid* out. . . .

UNCLE CHRIS. If you do not get out of the way of the door before I count three, I trow you out. And Sigrid, too, as big as she is. Von. . . . (SIGRID *moves.*) Two. . . . (JENNY *moves. He looks back at the children with a wink and a smile.*) Is goot! You put her in back of the car, Nils.

(NELS *goes out carrying* DAGMAR, *and lifts her into the car.* UNCLE CHRIS *follows and starts cranking.*)

TRINA (*running to the door after him, with* MR. THORKELSON). But, Uncle Chris, I want to introduce Mr. Thorkelson. . . . (*But* UNCLE CHRIS *ignores her, continuing to crank. She returns crest-fallen into the room with* MR. THORKELSON. MAMA *re-enters, wearing hat and coat and carrying a cheap little overnight case.*)

MAMA. Jenny . . . Trina, we go to hospital. (*She goes to* KATRIN *and* CHRISTINE.) You will be good children until Mama comes home?

THE GIRLS. Sure, Mama.

UNCLE CHRIS (*calling from the car*). Marta, we go!

MAMA (*calling back*). I come! (*She turns to the children again.*) There is milk in the cooler, and fruit and cookies for your lunch.

CHRISTINE. We'll be all right, Mama. Don't worry.

MAMA. I go now. (*She starts for the door.*)

SIGRID (*stopping her*). Marta!

MAMA. What is it?

SIGRID. You *can't* go in his automobile.

MAMA. Why not?

UNCLE CHRIS (*calling again*). Marta, we go!

MAMA. I come!

SIGRID. Because . . . because *she's* in it. The . . . the woman!

MAMA. So it will kill me, or Dagmar, if we sit in the automobile with her? I have seen her. She looks nice woman. (*Calling off, as she goes.*) I come!

UNCLE CHRIS. We go! (MAMA *climbs into the rear of the car, which backs noisily off.*)

JENNY (*to the* GIRLS). Don't stand there gaping like that, girls. (*She shoos them into the pantry.*) Go away! Go away! (*The* GIRLS *go.* JENNY *turns and sees the disappearing car through the open door.*) Oh! They've gone! We go after them! Sigrid, you lead the way! (*She gives* SIGRID *a push and the four go out, with* JENNY *dragging* MR. THORKELSON, *and* TRINA *following. Blackout. The travelers close.*)

(*Spot on turntable, representing a kind of closet room. Roller skates hang on the wall.* KATRIN *is seated on the floor and* CHRISTINE *on a small kitchen stepladder with glasses of milk, and cookies on plates.*)

KATRIN. How long have they been gone now?

CHRISTINE. About three hours. And I wish you wouldn't keep asking that.

KATRIN. How long do operations take? I heard Aunt Sigrid telling about Mrs. Bergman who was five hours on the table.

CHRISTINE. Aunt Sigrid's friends always have everything worse than anyone else. And it gets worse each time she tells it, too.

(KATRIN *smiles—drinks some milk and eats a cookie.*)

KATRIN (*with a certain melancholy enjoyment*). The house feels lonesome, doesn't it—without Mama? It's like in a book. "The sisters sat huddled in the empty house, waiting for the verdict that was to spell life or death to the little family."

CHRISTINE. Oh, don't talk such nonsense.

KATRIN. It's not nonsense.

CHRISTINE. It is, too. In the first place, we're not a little family. We're a big one. And who said anything about life or death, anyway? Always trying to make everything so dramatic!

KATRIN. Well, it *is* dramatic.

CHRISTINE. It's not. It's just . . . well, worrying. But you don't have to make a tragedy out of it.

(*Pause.*)

KATRIN. You're not eating anything.

CHRISTINE. I know that.

KATRIN. You're not drinking your milk, either. Aren't you hungry?

CHRISTINE. No. And you wouldn't be, either, if you'd any feeling for Mama and Dagmar, instead of just heartlessly sitting there eating and enjoying making a story out of it.

KATRIN. Oh, Chris, I'm not heartless. I do have feeling for them. I can't help it if it goes into words like that. Everything always does with me. But it doesn't mean I don't feel it. And I think we *ought* to eat. I think Mama would want us to.

(*Pause.* CHRISTINE *hesitates a moment, then takes a bite of a cookie. They both eat in silence. The light dims on them, and the turntable revolves out. The travelers part on the hospital corridor. A wall runs diagonally up from the front of the main stage towards the back. In front of this is a bench, on which* MAMA *and* NELS *are sitting, holding hands, looking off. Below the bench is the elevator, and above the bench, set back a little, is a closet for brooms and mops, etc. The reception desk, at which* A Nurse *is sitting, is towards the front. The wall goes up into darkness, and behind the* Nurse's *desk is darkness. As the curtains open, there is a hubbub down by the* Nurse's *desk, where the* AUNTS *are haranguing* [12] UNCLE CHRIS. MR. THORKELSON *stands slightly behind them.*)

SIGRID. But, Uncle Chris, I tell you I must see him!

UNCLE CHRIS (*storming*). You don't understand English? No visitors for twenty-four hours.

SIGRID. But *you've* seen him.

UNCLE CHRIS. I am not visitor. I am exception.

SIGRID. Well, then, his mother should be an exception, too. I'll see the doctor.

UNCLE CHRIS. *I* have seen doctor. I have told him you are not goot for Arne.

[12] **haranguing:** speaking noisily, ranting and scolding

SIGRID. Not good for my own son. . . .

UNCLE CHRIS. Not goot at all. You cry over him. I go now. (*He starts to do so, but* JENNY *pushes* TRINA *forward.*)

TRINA (*with desperate courage*). Uncle Chris . . . Uncle Chris . . . I *must* speak to you.

UNCLE CHRIS. I have business.

TRINA. But, Uncle Chris . . . I want to get married.

UNCLE CHRIS. Well, then, *get* married. (*He starts off again.*)

TRINA. No, wait, I . . . I want to marry Mr. Thorkelson. Here. (*She produces him from behind her.*) Peter, this is Uncle Chris. Uncle Chris, this is Mr. Thorkelson.

UNCLE CHRIS (*staring at him*). So?

MR. THORKELSON. How are you, sir?

UNCLE CHRIS. Busy. (*He turns again.*)

TRINA. Please, Uncle Chris . . .

UNCLE CHRIS. What is? You want to marry him? All right, marry him. I have other things to think about.

TRINA (*eagerly*). Then . . . then you give your permission?

UNCLE CHRIS. Yes, I give my permission. If you want to be a fool, I cannot stop you.

TRINA (*gratefully*). Oh, thank you, Uncle Chris.

UNCLE CHRIS. So. Is all?

TRINA (*anxious to escape*). Yes, I think is all.

JENNY (*firmly*). No! !

UNCLE CHRIS. No? (MR. THORKELSON *is pushed forward again.*)

MR. THORKELSON. Well, there . . . there was a little something else. You see, Trina mentioned . . . well, in the old country it was always usual . . . and after all, we do all come from the old country. . . .

UNCLE CHRIS. What is it? What you want?

MR. THORKELSON. Well, it's a question of Trina's . . . well, not to mince matters . . . her dowry.

UNCLE CHRIS (*shouting*). Her what?

MR. THORKELSON (*very faintly*). Her dowry . . .

UNCLE CHRIS. Ah. Her dowry. Trina wants a dowry. She is forty-two years old. . . .

TRINA (*interrupting*). No, Uncle Chris. . . .

UNCLE CHRIS (*without pausing*). And it is not enough she gets husband. She must have dowry.

NURSE (*who has been trying to interrupt, now bangs on her desk and moves toward them*). Please! Would you mind going and discussing your family matters somewhere else? This is a hospital, not a marriage bureau.

UNCLE CHRIS (*after glaring at the* NURSE, *turns to* MR. THORKELSON). You come into waiting room. I talk to you about dowry. (*He strides off into the darkness behind the* Nurse's *desk.* MR. THORKELSON, *with an appealing look back at* TRINA, *follows him. The* AUNTS *now remember* MAMA, *sitting on the bench, and cross to her.*)

JENNY. Did you hear that, Marta?

MAMA (*out of a trance*). What?

JENNY. Uncle Chris.

MAMA. No, I do not hear. I wait for doctor. Is two hours since they take Dagmar to operating room. More.

SIGRID. Two hours? That's nothing! When Mrs. Bergman had her gall bladder removed she was *six* hours on the table.

MAMA. Sigrid, I do not want to hear about Mrs. Bergman. I do not want to hear about anything. I wait for doctor. Please, you go away now. You come this evening.

TRINA. But, Marta, you can't stay here all by yourself.

MAMA. I have Nels. Please, Trina . . . I wait for doctor . . . you go now.

JENNY. We go.

TRINA. Oh, but I must wait for Peter and Uncle Chris. . . .

JENNY. We'll go next door and have some coffee. Sigrid, do you have money?

SIGRID. Yes, I . . . I have a little.

JENNY. Good. Then I treat you. We'll be next door if you want us, Marta.

(MAMA *nods without looking at them, her eyes still fixed on the elevator door. The* AUNTS *leave, going down the steps from the stage as though they were the hospital steps, and for a moment the stage is quiet. Then a scrubwoman enters, carrying a mop and pail, which she puts into the closet, and then leaves. The elevator door opens and a doctor in white coat comes out, followed by an orderly, carrying a tray of dressings. They disappear behind the desk.* MAMA *rises, agitatedly, looking after*

them. Then DR. JOHNSON *returns, carrying his hat and bag. He
sees* MAMA *and crosses to her.*)

DOCTOR. Oh, Mrs. Hanson. . . .

MAMA. Doctor. . . .

DOCTOR. Well, Dagmar's fine. She came through it beautifully. She's
back in bed now, sleeping off the anesthetic.

MAMA. Thank you, Doctor. (*She shakes hands with him.*)

DOCTOR. You're very welcome.

MAMA. Is good of you, Doctor. (*She shakes hands with him again.*)
Where is she? I go to her now.

DOCTOR. Oh, I'm sorry, but I'm afraid that's against the rules. You
shall see her tomorrow.

MAMA. Tomorrow? But, Doctor, she is so little. When she wakes
she will be frightened.

DOCTOR. The nurse will take care of her. Excellent care. You needn't
worry. You see, for the first twenty-four hours, clinic patients
aren't allowed to see visitors. The wards must be kept quiet.

MAMA. I will not make a sound.

DOCTOR. I'm very sorry. Tomorrow. And now . . . (*He glances at
his watch.*) Good afternoon. (*He puts on his hat and goes out,
down the steps and off.* MAMA *stands still a moment, looking
after him.*)

MAMA. Come, Nels. We go find Dagmar.

NELS. But, Mama, the doctor said . . .

MAMA. We find Dagmar. (*She looks vaguely around her. Then goes
to the* NURSE'*s desk.*) You tell me, please, where I can find my
daughter?

NURSE. What name?

MAMA. Dagmar.

NELS. Dagmar Hanson.

NURSE (*looking at her record book*). Hanson, Ward A. Along there.
(*She points upstage.* MAMA *starts to go up.*) Oh, just a moment. (MAMA *returns.*) When did she come in?

MAMA. This morning. They just finish operation.

NURSE. Oh, well, then, I'm afraid you can't see her today. No visitors for the first twenty-four hours.

MAMA. Am not visitor. I am her Mama.

NURSE. I'm sorry, but it's against the rules.

MAMA. Just for one minute. Please.

NURSE. I'm sorry, but it's against the rules.

(MAMA *stands staring.* NELS *touches her arm. She looks at him, nods, trying to smile, then turns and walks out with him.*)

MAMA. We must think of some way.

NELS. Mama, they'll let you see her tomorrow. They said so.

MAMA. If I don't see her today how will I know that all is well with her? What can I tell Papa when he comes home from work?

NELS. The nurses will look after her, Mama. Would you like to come next door for some coffee?

MAMA (*shaking her head*). We go home. We have coffee at home. But I must see Dagmar today. (*She plods off with* NELS.)

(*The travelers close. Spot goes up on turntable.* UNCLE CHRIS *and* MR. THORKELSON *are seated on a bench and chair, as in a waiting room. A table with a potted plant is between them. A clock on the wall points to 2:30.*)

UNCLE CHRIS (*on bench*). Well, it comes then to this. You love my niece, Trina? (MR. THORKELSON, *very scared, gulps and nods.*) You want to marry her? (MR. THORKELSON *nods again.*) You are in position to support her? (MR. THORKELSON *nods again.*) Why, then, you want dowry? (*No answer. He shouts.*) What for you want dowry?

MR. THORKELSON. Well . . . well, it would be a nice help. And it is customary.

UNCLE CHRIS. Is not customary. Who give dowries? Parents. Why? Because they are so glad they will not have to support their daughters any more, they pay money. I do not support Trina. I do not care if Trina gets married. Why then should I pay to have her married?

MR. THORKELSON. I never thought of it like that.

UNCLE CHRIS. Is insult to girl to pay dowry. If I do not give dowry, will you still marry Trina?

MR. THORKELSON. I . . . I don't know.

UNCLE CHRIS. You don't know? You don't know? You think I let Trina marry a man who will not take her without dowry?

MR. THORKELSON. No, I suppose you wouldn't.

UNCLE CHRIS. What kind of man would that be? I ask you, what kind of man would that be?

MR. THORKELSON (*fascinated—helpless*). Well, not a very nice kind of man.

UNCLE CHRIS. And are you that kind of man?

MR. THORKELSON. I . . . I don't think so.

UNCLE CHRIS (*conclusively*). Then you don't want dowry! !

MR. THORKELSON (*giving up*). No, I . . . I guess I don't.

UNCLE CHRIS (*slapping his back*). Goot. Goot. You are goot man. I like you. I give you my blessing. And I send you vedding present. I send you box of oranges!

(*While he is boisterously shaking* MR. THORKELSON'S *hand, blackout. Turntable revolves out. The curtain opens on the kitchen. It is empty.* MAMA *and* NELS *come up the hill and let themselves into the house. There is silence as they take off their hats and coats.*)

MAMA (*after a moment*). Where are the girls?

NELS. I guess they're upstairs. (*Goes to back door and calls.*) Chris! Katrin!

GIRLS' VOICES. Coming!

NELS. Shall I make you some coffee? (MAMA *shakes her head.*) You said you'd have coffee when you got home.

MAMA. Later. First I must think.

NELS. Mama, please don't worry like that. Dagmar's all right. You know she's all right.

(*The* GIRLS *come in.*)

CHRISTINE (*trying to be casual*). Well, Mama, everything all right?

MAMA (*nodding*). Is all right. You have eaten?

KATRIN. Yes, Mama.

MAMA. You drink your milk?

CHRISTINE. Yes, Mama.

MAMA. Is good.

CHRISTINE (*seeing her face*). Mama, something's the matter.

KATRIN (*overdramatically*). Mama, Dagmar's not—? She isn't—? Mama!

MAMA. No, Dagmar is fine. The doctor say she is fine. (*She rises.*) What is time?

NELS. It's three o'clock.

MAMA. Three hours till Papa come home. (*She looks around and then goes slowly into the pantry.*)

KATRIN. Nels, what is it? There *is* something the matter.

NELS. They wouldn't let Mama see Dagmar. It's a rule of the hospital.

CHRISTINE. But Dagmar's all right?

NELS. Oh, yes, she's all right.

CHRISTINE (*impatiently*). Well, then . . . !

NELS. But Mama's very upset. She started talking to me in Norwegian in the streetcar.

KATRIN (*emotionally*). What can we do?

CHRISTINE (*coldly*). You can't do anything. When *will* they let her see Dagmar?

NELS. Tomorrow.

CHRISTINE. Well, then, we'll just have to wait till tomorrow.

KATRIN. Chris, how can you be so callous? Can't you see that Mama's heart is breaking?

CHRISTINE. No. I can't. And you can't, either. People's hearts don't break.

KATRIN. They do, too.

CHRISTINE. Only in books. (MAMA *comes back, she wears an apron, and carries a scrub brush and a bucket of hot water.*) Why, Mama, what are you going to do?

MAMA (*coming down to table*). I scrub the floor. (*She gets down on her knees, facing front.*)

CHRISTINE. But you scrubbed it yesterday.

MAMA. I scrub it again. (*She starts to do so.*)

KATRIN. But, Mama . . .

MAMA (*bending low*). Comes a time when you've got to get down on your knees.

KATRIN (*to Christine*). Now do you believe me?

(CHRISTINE, *suddenly unendurably moved, turns and rushes from the room.*)

NELS. Mama, don't. Please don't. You must be tired.

KATRIN (*strangely*). Let her alone, Nels. (*They stand in silence watching* MAMA *scrub. Suddenly she stops.*) What is it, Mama? What is it?

MAMA (*sitting back on her haunches*). I tink of something! (*Slowly.*) I tink I tink of something!

(*The lights dim and the curtains close on the kitchen. From the front* UNCLE CHRIS'S VOICE *singing. The lights slowly come up on the turntable, showing* ARNE [*a child of about nine*] *in a hospital bed, with* UNCLE CHRIS *beside him.*)

UNCLE CHRIS (*singing*).

> "Ten t'ousand Svedes vent t'rough de veeds
> At de battle of Coppen-hagen.
> Ten t'ousand Svedes vent t'rough de veeds
> Chasing vun Nor-ve-gan!"

ARNE. Uncle Chris!

UNCLE CHRIS. Yes, Arne?

ARNE. Uncle Chris, does it *have* to hurt like this?

UNCLE CHRIS. If you vant it to be vell, and not to valk alvays like Uncle Chris, it does . . . for a little. Is very bad?

ARNE. It is . . . kinda . . . Oo—oo . . . !

UNCLE CHRIS. Arne, don't you know any svear vords?

ARNE. W-what?

UNCLE CHRIS. Don't you know any svear vords?

ARNE. N-no, Uncle Chris. Not real ones.

UNCLE CHRIS. Then I tell you two fine vons to use when pain is bad. Are "Damn" and "Damittohell." You say them?

ARNE. N-now?

UNCLE CHRIS. No, not now. When pain comes again. You say them then. They help plenty. I know. I haf pain, too. I say them all the time. But only if is *very* bad. Is bad now?

ARNE. No, it's . . . it's a little better.

UNCLE CHRIS. You sleep some now, maybe?

ARNE. I'll try. Will . . . will you stay here, Uncle Chris?

UNCLE CHRIS. Sure. Sure. I stay here. You are not frightened of Uncle Chris?

ARNE. No. Not any more.

UNCLE CHRIS. Goot. Goot. You like I sing some more?

ARNE. If you wouldn't mind. But maybe something a little . . . well, quieter.

UNCLE CHRIS (*tenderly*). Sure. Sure. (*He begins quietly to sing a Norwegian lullaby, in the midst,* ARNE *cries out.*)

ARNE. Oo—oo . . . Oh, *damn*. Damn. Damittohell!

UNCLE CHRIS (*delighted*). Goot! It helps—eh?

ARNE (*with pleased surprise*). Yes—yes.

UNCLE CHRIS. Then you sleep some! (*He fixes* ARNE'S *pillows for him, and resumes the lullaby, seated on his chair beside the bed. After another verse, he leans over, assuring himself that the child is asleep, and then very quietly, without interrupting his singing, takes a flask from his pocket and lifts it to his lips, as the light dims. The table revolves out.*)

(*The curtains part on the hospital corridor again. There is a different* NURSE *now at the reception desk, talking on the telephone as* MAMA *and* KATRIN *come in and go up the steps.*)

MAMA (*as they come up, in an undertone*). Is not the same nurse. Katrin, you take my hat and coat. (*She takes them off, revealing that she still wears her apron.*)

KATRIN. But, Mama, won't they . . .

MAMA (*interrupting, finger to lips*). Ssh! You let me go ahead. You wait on bench for me. (*She goes to the closet door above the bench and opens it.* KATRIN *stares after her in trepidation.*[13] MAMA *takes out a damp mop and pail, and gets down on her knees by the* Nurse's *desk, starting to clean the floor. The* Nurse *looks up.* MAMA *catches her eye, brightly.*) Very dirty floors.

NURSE. Yes, I'm glad they've finally decided to clean them. Aren't you working late?

MAMA (*quickly, lowering her head*). Floors need cleaning. (*She pushes her way, crawling on hands and knees, up behind the desk, and disappears up the corridor, still scrubbing.* KATRIN *steals to the bench, where she sits, still clutching* MAMA'S *hat and coat, looking interestedly around her. The light dims, leaving her in a single spot, as she starts to talk to herself.*)

KATRIN (*to herself*). "The Hospital" . . . A poem by Katrin Hanson. (*She starts to improvise.*[14])

> "She waited, fearful, in the hall,
> And held her bated breath."

Breath—yes, that'll rhyme with death. (*She repeats the first two lines.*)

---

[13] **trepidation:** fear, alarm
[14] **improvise:** compose on the spur of the moment

"She waited fearful in the hall
And held her bated breath.
She trembled at the least footfall,
And kept her mind on death."

(*She gets a piece of paper and pencil from her pocket and begins to scribble, as a* NURSE *comes out of the elevator, carrying some charts, which she takes to the desk, and then goes out.* KATRIN *goes on with her poem.*)

"Ah, God, 'twas agony to wait.
To wait and watch and wonder. . . ."

Wonder—under—bunder—funder—sunder. Sunder! (*Nods to herself and goes on again.*)

"To wait and watch and wonder,
About her infant sister's fate.
If Death life's bonds would sunder."

(*Then to herself again, looking front.*) That's beautiful. Yes, but it isn't true. Dagmar isn't dying. It's funny—I don't want her to die—and yet when Mama said she was all right I was almost —well, almost disappointed. It wasn't exciting any more. Maybe Christine's right, and I haven't any heart. How awful! "The girl without a heart." That'd be a nice title for a story. "The girl without a heart sat in the hospital corridor. . . ."

(*The lights come up again as* UNCLE CHRIS *appears, behind the desk. He wears his hat and is more than a little drunk. He sees* KATRIN.)

UNCLE CHRIS. Katrinë! What you do here? (*He sits on the bench beside her.*)

KATRIN (*nervously*). I'm waiting for Mama.

UNCLE CHRIS. Where is she?

KATRIN (*scared*). I . . . I don't know.

UNCLE CHRIS. What you mean . . . you don't know?

KATRIN (*whispering*). I think . . . I think she's seeing Dagmar.

UNCLE CHRIS (*shaking his head*). Is first day. They do not allow visitors first day.

KATRIN (*trying to make him aware of the* NURSE). I know. But I think that's where she is.

UNCLE CHRIS. Where *is* Dagmar?

KATRIN. I don't know.

(UNCLE CHRIS *rises and goes to the* NURSE *at the desk.*)

UNCLE CHRIS. In what room is my great-niece, Dagmar Hanson?

NURSE (*looking at her book*). Hanson . . . Hanson . . . when did she come in?

UNCLE CHRIS. This morning.

NURSE. Oh, yes. Were you wanting to see her?

UNCLE CHRIS. What room is she in?

NURSE. I asked were you wanting to see her.

UNCLE CHRIS. And *I* ask what room she is in.

NURSE. We don't allow visitors the first day.

UNCLE CHRIS. Have I said I vant to visit her? I ask what room she is in.

NURSE. Are you by any chance, Mr. . . . (*looking at her book*) Halvorsen?

UNCLE CHRIS (*proudly, and correcting her pronunciation*). Christopher Halvorsen.

NURSE. Did you say you were her uncle?

UNCLE CHRIS. Her great-uncle.

NURSE. Well, then, I'm afraid I can't tell you anything about her.

UNCLE CHRIS. Why not?

NURSE. Orders.

UNCLE CHRIS. Whose orders?

NURSE. Dr. Johnson's. There's a special note here. Patient's uncle, Mr. Halvorsen, not to be admitted or given information under any circumstances.

UNCLE CHRIS (*after a moment's angry stupefaction*). Damittohell! (*He strides away, taking out his flask, and shaking it, only to find it empty.*)

(MAMA *returns, carrying the mop and pail, walking now and smiling triumphantly.*)

MAMA (*to the* NURSE). Thank you. (*She replaces the mop and pail in the closet, and then sees* UNCLE CHRIS. *Crossing to him.*) Uncle Chris, Dagmar is fine!

UNCLE CHRIS (*amazed*). You see her?

MAMA. Sure, Uncle Chris, I see her.

UNCLE CHRIS (*reiterating,*[15] *incredulous*). You see Dagmar?

MAMA. Sure. (*She takes her hat from* KATRIN *and starts to put it on.*) Is fine hospital. But such floors! A mop is never good. Floors should be scrubbed with a brush. We go home. Uncle Chris, you come with us? I make coffee.

UNCLE CHRIS (*joining them in a little group on the steps*). Pah! Vot good is coffee? I go get drink.

MAMA (*reprovingly*). Uncle Chris!

UNCLE CHRIS. Marta, you are fine woman. Fine. But I go get drink. I get drunk.

MAMA (*quickly aside to* KATRIN). His leg hurts him.

UNCLE CHRIS. And you do not make excuses for me! I get drunk because I like it.

MAMA (*conciliating* [16] *him*). Sure, Uncle Chris.

UNCLE CHRIS (*shouting*). I like it! (*Then, with a change.*) No, is not true. You know is not true. I do not like to get drunk at all. But I do not like to come home with you, either. (*Growing slightly maudlin.*) You have family. Is fine thing. You do not know how fine. Katrinë, one day when you grow up, maybe you know what a fine thing family is. I haf no family.

KATRIN (*on the lower step*). But, Uncle Chris, Mama's always said you were the *head* of the family.

UNCLE CHRIS. Sure. Sure. I am head of the family, but I haf no family. So I go get drunk. You understand, Marta?

MAMA. Sure, Uncle Chris. You go get drunk. (*Sharply.*) But don't you feel sorry for yourself! (UNCLE CHRIS *glares at her a moment, then strides down the steps, boisterously singing his song of "Ten Thousand Swedes."* MAMA *watches him go, then takes her coat from* KATRIN.) Is fine man. Has fine ideas about family. (KATRIN *helps her on with her coat.*) I can tell Papa now that Dagmar is fine. She wake while I am with her. I explain rules to her. She will not expect us now until tomorrow afternoon.

KATRIN. You won't try and see her again before that?

MAMA (*gravely*). No. That would be against the rules! Come. We go home. (*They go off.*)

CURTAIN

[15] **reiterating**: repeating
[16] **conciliating**: pacifying

ACT II

SCENE. *Opening, exactly as in Act I.* KATRIN *at her desk.*

KATRIN (*reading*). "It wasn't very often that I could get Mama to talk—about herself, or her life in the old country, or what she felt about things. You had to catch her unawares, or when she had nothing to do, which was very, very seldom. I don't think I can ever remember seeing Mama unoccupied." (*Laying down the manuscript and looking out front.*) I do remember one occasion, though. It was the day before Dagmar came home from the hospital. And as we left, Mama suggested treating me to an ice-cream soda. (*She rises, gets her hat from beside her—a schoolgirl hat—puts it on and crosses while she speaks the next lines.*) She had never done such a thing before, and I remember how proud it made me feel—just to sit and talk to her quietly like a grown-up person. It was a kind of special *treat*-moment in my life that I'll always remember—quite apart from the soda, which was *wonderful.* (MAMA *has come from between the curtains, and starts down the steps.*)

MAMA. Katrin, you like we go next door, and I treat you to an ice-cream soda?

KATRIN (*young now, and overcome*). Mama—do you mean it?

MAMA. Sure. We celebrate. We celebrate that Dagmar is well, and coming home again. (*They cross to the turntable, which represents a drugstore, with a table and two chairs at which they seat themselves.* MAMA *is at the left of table.*) What you like to have, Katrin?

KATRIN (*with desperate earnestness*). I think a chocolate . . . no, a strawberry . . . no, a chocolate soda.

MAMA (*smiling*). You are sure?

KATRIN (*gravely*). I think so. But, Mama, can we *afford* it?

MAMA. I think this once we can afford it.

(*The* SODA CLERK *appears.*)

SODA CLERK. What's it going to be, ladies?

MAMA. A chocolate ice-cream soda, please—and a cup of coffee.

(*The* SODA CLERK *goes.*)

98

KATRIN. Mama, he called us "ladies"! (MAMA *smiles.*) Why aren't you having a soda, too?

MAMA. Better I like coffee.

KATRIN. When can I drink coffee?

MAMA. When you are grown up.

KATRIN. When I'm eighteen?

MAMA. Maybe before that.

KATRIN. When I graduate?

MAMA. Maybe. I don't know. Comes the day you are grown up, Papa and I will know.

KATRIN. Is coffee really nicer than a soda?

MAMA. When you are grown up, it is.

KATRIN. Did you used to like sodas better . . . before you were grown up?

MAMA. We didn't have sodas before I was grown up. It was in the old country.

KATRIN (*incredulous*). You mean they don't have sodas in Norway?

MAMA. Now, maybe. Now I think they have many things from America. But not when I was little girl.

(*The* SODA CLERK *brings the soda and the coffee.*)

SODA CLERK. There you are, folks. (*He sets them down and departs.*)

KATRIN (*after a good pull at the soda*). Mama, do you ever want to go back to the old country?

MAMA. I like to go back once to look, maybe. To see the mountains and the fjords.[1] I like to show them once to you all. When Dagmar is big, maybe we all go back once . . . one summer . . . like tourists. But that is how it would be. I would be tourist there now. There is no one I would know any more. And maybe we see the little house where Papa and I live when we first marry. And . . . (*her eyes grow misty and reminiscent*) something else I would look at.

KATRIN. What is that? (MAMA *does not answer.*) What would you look at, Mama?

MAMA. Katrin, you do not know you have brother? Besides Nels?

KATRIN. No! A brother? In Norway? Mama. . . .

---

[1] fjords: narrow inlets of the sea, bordered by steep cliffs

madine Misiaszek

MAMA. He is my first baby. I am eighteen when he is born.

KATRIN. Is he there now?

MAMA (*simply*). He is dead.

KATRIN (*disappointed*). Oh. I thought you meant . . . I thought you meant a real brother. A long-lost one, like in stories. When did he die?

MAMA. When he is two years old. It is his grave I would like to see again. (*She is suddenly near tears, biting her lip and stirring her coffee violently, spilling some. She gets her handkerchief from her pocketbook, dabs at her skirt, then briefly at her nose, then she returns the handkerchief and turns to* KATRIN *again. Matter-of-factly.*) Is good, your ice-cream soda?

KATRIN (*more interested now in* MAMA *than in it*). Yes. Mama . . . have you had a very *hard* life?

MAMA (*surprised*). Hard? No. No life is easy all the time. It is not meant to be. (*She pours the spilled coffee back from the saucer into her cup.*)

KATRIN. But . . . rich people . . . aren't *their* lives easy?

MAMA. I don't know, Katrin. I have never known rich people. But I see them sometimes in stores and in the streets, and they do not *look* as if they were easy.

KATRIN. Wouldn't you like to be rich?

MAMA. I would like to be rich the way I would like to be ten feet high. Would be good for some things—bad for others.

KATRIN. But didn't you come to America to *get* rich?

MAMA (*shocked*). No. We come to America because they are all here—all the others. Is good for families to be together.

KATRIN. And did you like it right away?

MAMA. Right away. When we get off the ferry boat and I see San Francisco and all the family, I say: "Is like Norway," only it is better than Norway. And then you are all born here, and I become American citizen. But not to get rich.

KATRIN. *I* want to be rich. Rich and famous. I'd buy you your warm coat. When are you going to get that coat, Mama?

MAMA. Soon now, maybe—when we pay doctor, and Mr. Hyde pay his rent. I think now I *must* ask him. I ask him tomorrow, after Dagmar comes home.

KATRIN. When I'm rich and famous, I'll buy you lovely clothes.

White satin gowns with long trains to them. And jewelry. I'll buy you a pearl necklace.

MAMA. We talk too much! (*She signs to the* SODA CLERK.) Come, finish your soda. We must go home. (*The* SODA CLERK *comes.*) How much it is, please?

SODA CLERK. Fifteen cents.

MAMA. Here are two dimes. You keep the nickel. And thank you. Was good coffee. (*They start out and up the steps towards the curtains.*) Tomorrow Dagmar will be home again. And, Katrin, you see Uncle Elizabeth is there. This afternoon again she was asking for him. You keep Uncle Elizabeth in the house all day until she comes home.

(*They disappear behind the curtains. After a second, the howls of a cat in pain are heard from behind the curtains—low at first, then rising to a heart-rending volume, and then diminishing again as the curtains part on the kitchen once more.* MAMA, PAPA, *and* DAGMAR *are entering the house.*)

DAGMAR (*standing on threshold, transfixed*). It's Uncle Elizabeth, welcoming me home! That's his song of welcome. Where is he, Mama? (*She looks around for the source of the howls.*)

MAMA. He is in the pantry . . . (*As* DAGMAR *starts to rush thither.*) But wait . . . wait a minute, Dagmar. I must tell you. Uncle Elizabeth is . . . sick.

DAGMAR. Sick? What's the matter with him?

PAPA. He has been in fight. Last night. He come home this morning very sick indeed.

(DAGMAR *starts for the pantry door, as* NELS *comes out.*)

MAMA. Nels, how is Uncle Elizabeth? Nels has been doctoring him.

NELS. He's pretty bad, Mama. I've dressed all his wounds again with boric acid, but . . . (*As* DAGMAR *tries to get past him.*) I wouldn't go and see him now, baby.

DAGMAR. I've got to. He's my cat. I haven't seen him in a whole month. More. (*She runs into the pantry and disappears.*)

MAMA. Nels, what you think?

NELS. I think we ought to have had him put away before she came home.

MAMA. But she would have been so unhappy if he was not here *at all.*

NELS. She'll be unhappier still if he dies.

(*Another howl is heard from the pantry, and then* DAGMAR *comes rushing back.*)

DAGMAR. Mama, what happened to him? What happened to him? Oh, Mama . . . when I tried to pick him up, his bandage slipped over his eye. It was bleeding. Oh, Mama, it looked awful. Oh . . . (*She starts to cry.*)

MAMA (*fondling her*). He looks like that all over. Nels, you go see to his eye again. (*Wearily,* NELS *returns to the pantry.*) Listen, Dagmar . . . *Lille Ven* . . . would it not be better for the poor thing to go quietly to sleep?

DAGMAR. You mean—go to sleep and never wake up again? (MAMA *nods gently.*) No.

PAPA. I think he die, anyway. Nels try to make him well. But I do not think he can.

DAGMAR. Mama can. Mama can do everything. (*Another howl from offstage. She clutches* MAMA *agonizedly.*) Make him live, Mama. Make him well again. *Please!*

MAMA. We see. Let us see how he gets through the night. And now, Dagmar, you must go to bed. I bring you your supper.

DAGMAR. But you will fix Uncle Elizabeth? You promise, Mama?

MAMA. I promise I try. Go now. (DAGMAR *goes out.*) I must fix her supper. (*She starts for the pantry. Howls again. She and* PAPA *stand and look at each other.* NELS *comes out.*)

NELS. Mama, it's just cruelty, keeping that cat alive.

MAMA. I know.

PAPA (*as another howl, the loudest yet, emerges*). You say we see how the cat get through the night. I ask you how do *we* get through the night? Is no use, Marta. We must put the cat to sleep. Nels, you go to the drugstore, and get something. Some chloroform, maybe. (*He gives him a coin.*)

NELS. How much shall I get?

PAPA. You ask the man. You tell him it is for a cat. He knows. (NELS *goes out and down the street. Looking at* MAMA's *face.*) Is best. Is the only thing.

MAMA. I know. But poor Dagmar. It is sad homecoming for her.

And she has been so good in hospital. Never once she cry. (*She pulls herself together.*) I get her supper. (*Another howl from off stage.*) And I take the cat outside. Right outside, where we . . . where *Dagmar* cannot hear him. (*She goes into the pantry. PAPA takes a folded newspaper from his pocket, puts on his glasses and starts to read. The back door opens gently and MR. HYDE peeps out. He wears his hat and coat and carries his suitcase and a letter. PAPA has his back to him. MR. HYDE lays the letter on the dresser and then starts to tiptoe across to the door. Then PAPA sees him.*)

PAPA. You go out, Mr. Hyde?

MR. HYDE (*pretending surprise*). Oh. . . . Oh, I did not see you, Mr. Hanson. (*He puts down the suitcase.*) I did not know you were back. As a matter of fact, I . . . I was about to leave this letter for you. (*He fetches it.*) The fact is . . . I . . . I have been called away.

PAPA. So?

MR. HYDE. A letter I received this morning necessitates my departure. My immediate departure.

PAPA. I am sorry. (*MAMA returns with a tray, on which are milk, bread, butter, and jelly.*) Mama, Mr. Hyde says he goes away.

MAMA (*coming to the table with the tray*). Is true?

MR. HYDE. Alas, dear Madam, yes. 'Tis true, 'tis pity. And pity 'tis, 'tis true. You will find here . . . (*He presents the letter.*) my check for all I owe you, and a note expressing my profoundest thanks for all your most kind hospitality. You will say good-by to the children for me? (*He bows, as MAMA takes the letter.*)

MAMA (*distressed*). Sure. Sure.

MR. HYDE (*bowing again*). Madam, my deepest gratitude. (*He kisses her hand. MAMA looks astonished. He bows to PAPA.*) Sir—my sincerest admiration! (*He opens the street door.*) It has been a privilege. *Ave atque vale!* Hail and farewell! (*He makes a gesture and goes.*)

MAMA. Was wonderful man! Is too bad. (*She opens the letter, takes out the check.*)

PAPA. How much is check for?

MAMA. Hundred ten dollar! Is four months.

PAPA. Good. Good.

MAMA. Is wonderful. Now we pay doctor everything.

PAPA. And you buy your warm coat. With fur now, maybe.

MAMA (*sadly*). But there will be no more reading. You take the check, Lars. You get the money?

PAPA (*taking it*). Sure. I get it. What does he say in his letter?

MAMA. You read it while I fix supper for Dagmar. (*She starts to butter the bread, and spread jelly, while* PAPA *reads.*)

PAPA (*reading*). "Dear Friends, I find myself compelled to take a somewhat hasty departure from this house of happiness. . . ."

MAMA. Is beautiful letter.

PAPA (*continuing*). "I am leaving you my library for the children. . . ."

MAMA. He leaves his books?

PAPA. He says so.

MAMA. But is wonderful. Go see, Lars. See if they are in his room.

(PAPA *lays down the letter and goes out.* NELS *and* CHRISTINE *appear, coming up to the house.* CHRISTINE *carries schoolbooks.*)

CHRISTINE. I'm sure it was him, Nels. Carrying his suitcase, and getting on the cable car. I'm sure he's going away.

NELS. Well, I hope he's paid Mama.

(*They open the street door.*)

CHRISTINE (*bursting in*). Mama, I saw Mr. Hyde getting on the cable car.

MAMA. I know. He leave.

CHRISTINE. Did he pay you?

MAMA. Sure, he pay me. Hundred ten dollar. . . .

NELS. Gee. . . .

MAMA (*smiling*). Is good.

CHRISTINE. Are you going to put it in the Bank?

MAMA. We need it right away. (PAPA *returns, staggering under an armload of books.*) Mr. Hyde leaves his books, too. For you.

NELS. Say! (PAPA *stacks them on the table.* NELS *and* CHRISTINE *rush to them, reading the titles.*) The Pickwick Papers, The Complete Shakespeare . . .

CHRISTINE. *Alice in Wonderland, The Oxford Book of Verse* . . .

NELS. *The Last of the Mohicans, Ivanhoe* . . .

CHRISTINE. We were right in the middle of that.

MAMA. Nels can finish it. He can read to us now in the evenings.

He has fine voice, too, like Mr. Hyde. (NELS *flushes with pleasure.*) Is wonderful. So much we can learn. (*She finishes the supper-making.*) Christine, you take the butter back to the cooler for me, and the yelly, too. (CHRISTINE *does so.*) I go up to Dagmar now. (*She lifts the tray, then pauses.*) You get it, Nels?

NELS. What? . . . Oh. . . . (*Taking a druggist's small bottle from his pocket.*) Here.

MAMA. You put it down. After I come back, we do it. You know how?

NELS. Why, no, Mama, I . . .

MAMA. You do not ask?

NELS. No, I . . . I thought Papa . . .

MAMA. You know, Lars?

PAPA. No, I don't *know* . . . but it cannot be difficult. If you *hold* the cat . . .

MAMA. And watch him die? No! I think better you get rags . . . and a big sponge, to soak up the chloroform. You put it in the box with him, and cover him over. You get them ready out there.

NELS. Sure, Mama.

MAMA. I bring some blankets.

(NELS *goes off to the pantry, as* CHRISTINE *comes back. Again* MAMA *lifts the tray and starts for the door. But there is a knock on the street door from* AUNT JENNY, *who has come to the house in a state of some excitement.*)

MAMA (*agitated*). So much goes on! See who it is, Christine.

CHRISTINE (*peeping*). It's Aunt Jenny. (*She opens the door.*)

MAMA. Jenny. . . .

JENNY (*breathless*). Marta . . . has he gone?

MAMA (*above table*). Who?

JENNY (*near table*). Your boarder . . . Mr. Hyde. . . .

MAMA. Yes, he has gone. Why?

JENNY. Did he pay you?

MAMA. Sure he pay me.

JENNY. How?

MAMA. He give me a check. Lars has it right there.

JENNY (*with meaning*). A check!

MAMA. Jenny, what is it? Christine, you give Dagmar her supper. I come soon. (CHRISTINE *takes the tray from her and goes out.*) What is it, Jenny? How do you know that Mr. Hyde has gone?

JENNY. I was at Mr. Kruper's down the street . . . you know, the restaurant and bakery . . . and he told me Mr. Hyde was there today having his lunch, and when he left he asked if he would cash a check for him. For fifty dollars. (*She pauses.*)

PAPA. Well, go on.

JENNY. Your fine Mr. Hyde didn't expect Mr. Kruper to take it to the bank until tomorrow, but he did. And what do you think? Mr. Hyde hasn't even an *account* at that bank! (NELS *returns and stands in the pantry doorway.*)

MAMA. I don't understand.

PAPA (*taking the check from his pocket*). You mean the check is no good?

JENNY. No good at all. (*Triumphantly.*) Your Mr. Hyde was a crook, just as I always thought he was, for all his reading and fine ways. Mr. Kruper said he'd been cashing them all over the neighborhood. (MAMA *stands quite still, without answering.*) How much did he owe you? Plenty, I'll bet. (*Still no answer.*) Eh? Marta, I said I bet he owed you plenty. Didn't he?

MAMA (*looks around, first at* NELS *and then down at the books on the table; she touches them*). No. No, he owed us nothing. (*She takes the check from* PAPA, *tearing it.*) Nothing.

JENNY (*persistently*). How much was that check for? (*She reaches her hand for it.*)

MAMA (*evading her*). It does not matter. He pay with better things than money. (*She goes to the stove, where she throws the check, watching it burn.*)

JENNY. I told you right in the beginning that you shouldn't trust him. But you were so sure . . . just like you always are. Mr. Hyde was a gentleman. A gentleman! I bet it must have been a hundred dollars that he rooked [2] you of. Wasn't it?

MAMA (*returning to the table*). Jenny, I cannot talk now. Maybe you don't have things to do. I have.

JENNY (*sneeringly*). What? What have *you* got to do that's so important?

---

[2] **rooked:** swindled, cheated

MAMA (*taking up the medicine bottle, fiercely*). I have to chloroform a cat!

(JENNY *steps back in momentary alarm, almost as though* MAMA *were referring to her, as she goes out into the pantry with the medicine bottle, not so very unlike Lady Macbeth with the daggers. Blackout and curtains close. After a moment, the curtains part again on the kitchen, the next morning. The books have been taken off the table, and* MAMA *is setting the breakfast dishes, with* PAPA *helping her.* DAGMAR *comes bursting into the room.*)

DAGMAR. Good morning, Mama. 'Morning, Papa. Is Uncle Elizabeth all better?

MAMA. Dagmar, there is something I must tell you.

DAGMAR. I want to see Uncle Elizabeth first. (*She runs into the pantry.* MAMA *turns helplessly to* PAPA.)

MAMA. Do something! Tell her!

PAPA. If we just let her think the cat die . . . by itself. . . .

MAMA. No. We cannot tell her lies.

(PAPA *goes to the pantry door, opening it.*)

DAGMAR (*heard in pantry, off*). What a funny, funny smell. Good morning, my darling, my darling Elizabeth. (MAMA *and* PAPA *stand stricken.* DAGMAR *comes in, carrying the cat, wrapped in an old shirt, with its head covered. She comes over to table.*) My goodness, you put enough blankets on him! Did you think he'd catch cold?

MAMA (*horror-stricken*). Dagmar, you must not. . . . (*She stops at the sight of the cat, whose tail is twitching, quite obviously alive.*) Dagmar, let me see . . . Let me see the cat! (*She goes over to her, below table front, and uncovers the cat's head.*)

DAGMAR (*overjoyed*). He's well. Oh, Mama, I *knew* you'd fix him.

MAMA (*appalled*). But, Dagmar, I didn't, I . . .

DAGMAR (*ignoring her*). I'm going to take him right up and show him to Nels. (*She runs off, calling.*) Nels! Nels! Uncle Elizabeth's well again!

MAMA (*turning to* PAPA). Is a miracle! (*She sits, dumbfounded, on the bench in front of the table.*)

PAPA (*beside her, shrugging*). You cannot have used enough chloro-

form. You just give him good sleep, and that cures him. We
rechristen the cat, Lazarus!

MAMA. But, Lars, we must tell her. Is not *good* to let her grow
up believing I can fix *everything!*

PAPA. Is best thing in the world for her to believe. (*He chuckles.*)
Besides, I know *exactly* how she feels. (*He lays his hand on
hers.*)

MAMA (*turning with embarrassment from his demonstrativeness and
slapping his hand*). We finish getting breakfast. (*She turns back
to the table.*)

(*The curtains close. Lights go up down front.* KATRIN *and* CHRIS-
TINE *enter from the wings, in school clothes, wearing hats.* CHRIS-
TINE *carries schoolbooks in a strap.* KATRIN *is reciting.*)

KATRIN. "The quality of mercy is not strained,
   It droppeth as the gentle rain from heaven
   Upon the place beneath: it is twice blest;
   It blesseth him that gives, and him that takes. . . ."

(*She dries up.*) ". . . him that takes. It blesseth him that gives
and him that takes. . . ." (*She turns to* CHRISTINE.) What comes
after that?

CHRISTINE. I don't know. And I don't care.

KATRIN. Why, Chris!

CHRISTINE. I don't. It's all I've heard for weeks. The school play,
and your graduation, and going on to High. And never a thought
of what's happening at home.

KATRIN. What do you mean?

CHRISTINE. You see—you don't even know!

KATRIN. Oh, you mean the strike?

CHRISTINE. Yes, I mean the strike. Papa hasn't worked for four
whole weeks, and a lot you care. Why, I don't believe you
even know what they're striking *for*. Do you? All you and your
friends can talk about is the presents you're going to get. You
make me ashamed of being a girl.

(*Two girls,* MADELINE *and* DOROTHY, *come through the curtains,
talking.*)

MADELINE (*to* DOROTHY). Thyra Walsh's family's going to add seven
pearls to the necklace they started for her when she was a baby.

Oh, hello, Katrin! Did you hear about Thyra's graduation present?

KATRIN (*not very happily*). Yes, I heard.

MADELINE. I'm getting an onyx ring, with a diamond in it.

KATRIN. A real diamond?

MADELINE. Yes, of course. A *small* diamond.

DOROTHY. What are *you* getting?

KATRIN. Well . . . well, they haven't actually told me, but I think . . . I think I'm going to get that pink celluloid dresser set in your father's drugstore.

DOROTHY. You mean that one in the window?

KATRIN (*to* MADELINE). It's got a brush and comb and mirror . . . and a hair-receiver. It's genuine celluloid!

DOROTHY. I wanted Father to give it to me, out of stock, but he said it was too expensive. Father's an awful tightwad. They're giving me a bangle.

MADELINE. Oh, there's the streetcar. We've got to fly. 'By, Katrin. 'By, Christine. See you tomorrow. Come on, Dorothy.

(*The* TWO GIRLS *rush off.*)

CHRISTINE. Who said you were going to get the dresser set?

KATRIN. Nobody's said so . . . for certain. But I've sort of hinted, and . . .

CHRISTINE (*going up the steps*). Well, you're not going to get it.

KATRIN. How do you know?

CHRISTINE (*turning up back; still on steps*). Because I know what you *are* getting. I heard Mama tell Aunt Jenny. Aunt Jenny said you were too young to appreciate it.

KATRIN. What is it?

CHRISTINE. Mama's giving you her brooch. Her *solje.*

KATRIN. You mean that old silver thing she wears that belonged to Grandmother? What would I want an old thing like that for?

CHRISTINE. It's an heirloom. Mama thinks a lot of it.

KATRIN. Well, then, she ought to keep it. You don't really mean that's *all* they're going to give me?

CHRISTINE. What more do you want?

KATRIN. I want the dresser set. My goodness, if Mama doesn't realize what's a suitable present . . . why, it's practically the most important time in a girl's life, when she graduates.

CHRISTINE. And you say you're not selfish!

KATRIN. It's not selfishness.

CHRISTINE. Well, I don't know what else you'd call it. With Papa not working, we need every penny we can lay our hands on. Even the Little Bank's empty. But you'll devil Mama into giving you the dresser set somehow. So why talk about it? I'm going home. (*She turns and goes through the curtains.*)

(KATRIN *stands alone with a set and stubborn mouth, and then sits on the steps.*)

KATRIN. Christine was right. I got the dresser set. They gave it to me just before supper on graduation night. Papa could not attend the exercises because there was a strike meeting to decide about going back to work. I was so excited that night I could hardly eat, and the present took the last remnants of my appetite clean away.

(*The curtains part on the kitchen.* PAPA, MAMA, *and* DAGMAR *at table, with coffee.* CHRISTINE *is clearing dishes.*)

CHRISTINE. I'll just stack the dishes now, Mama. We'll wash them when we come home. (*She carries them into the pantry.*)

PAPA (*at table, holding up a cube of sugar*). Who wants coffee-sugar? (*He dips it in his coffee.*) Dagmar? (*He hands it to her.*) Katrin? (*She rises from the steps, coming into the scene for the sugar.*)

MAMA (*at other side of table*). You get your coat, Katrin; you need it.

(KATRIN *goes out.*)

DAGMAR (*behind table*). Aunt Jenny says if we drank black coffee like you do at our age, it would turn our complexions dark. I'd like to be a black Norwegian. Like Uncle Chris. Can I, Papa?

PAPA. I like you better blonde. Like Mama.

DAGMAR. When do you get old enough for your complexion *not* to turn dark? When can we drink coffee?

PAPA. One day, when you are grown up.

(JENNY *and* TRINA *have come to the door.* JENNY *knocks.*)

MAMA. There are Jenny and Trina. (*She goes to the door.*) Is good. We can start now. (*She opens the door.* JENNY *and* TRINA *come in.*)

JENNY. Well, are you all ready? Is Katrin very excited?

PAPA (*nodding*). She ate no supper.

(MAMA *has started to put on her hat, and to put on* DAGMAR'S *hat and coat for her.* CHRISTINE *comes back from the pantry.* PAPA *gives her a dipped cube of sugar.*)

JENNY. Is that *black* coffee you dipped that sugar in? Lars, you shouldn't. It's not good for them. It'll . . .

PAPA (*finishing for her*). Turn their complexions black. I know. Well, maybe it is all right if we have *one* colored daughter.

JENNY. Lars, really!

(KATRIN *returns with her coat.*)

KATRIN. Aunt Jenny, did you see my graduation present? (*She gets it from a chair.* CHRISTINE *gives her a disgusted look, and goes out.* KATRIN *displays the dresser set above the table.*) Look! It's got a hair-receiver.

JENNY (*at left of table*). But I thought . . . Marta, I thought you were going to give her . . .

MAMA. No, you were right, Jenny. She is too young to appreciate that. She like something more gay . . . more modern.

JENNY. H'm. Well, it's very pretty, I suppose, but . . . (*She looks up as* MAMA *puts on her coat.*) You're not wearing your *solje!*

MAMA (*quickly*). No. I do not wear it tonight. Come, Trina, we shall be late.

TRINA (*behind table*). Oh, but Peter isn't here yet.

MAMA. Katrin has her costume to put on. He can follow. Or do you like to wait for Peter?

TRINA. I think . . . if you don't mind . . .

MAMA. You can stay with Lars. He does not have to go yet.

JENNY. I hope Katrin knows her part.

PAPA. Sure she knows it. *I* know it, too.

TRINA. It's too bad he can't see Katrin's debut as an actress.

MAMA. You will be back before us, Lars?

PAPA (*nodding*). I think the meeting will not last long.

MAMA. Is good. We go now. (*She goes out with* JENNY *and* DAG-MAR. CHRISTINE *and* NELS *return and follow, waiting outside for* KATRIN, *while the others go ahead.* KATRIN *puts on her hat and coat and picks up the dresser set.*)

PAPA (*to* TRINA). You like we play a game of checkers while we wait?

TRINA (*sitting at table*). Oh, I haven't played checkers in years.

PAPA. Then I beat you. (*He rises to get the checker set.* KATRIN *kisses him.*)

KATRIN. Good-by, Papa.

PAPA. Good-by, daughter. I think of you.

KATRIN. I'll see you there, Aunt Trina.

TRINA. Good luck!

PAPA. I get the checkers.

(KATRIN *goes out.* PAPA *gets the checker set from a cupboard under the dresser, brings it to the table and sets it up during the ensuing scene, which is played outside in the street.*)

CHRISTINE (*contemptuously*). Oh, bringing your cheap trash with you to show off?

KATRIN. It's not trash. It's beautiful. You're just jealous.

CHRISTINE. I told you you'd devil Mama into giving it to you.

KATRIN. I didn't. I didn't devil her at all. I just showed it to her in Mr. Schiller's window. . . .

CHRISTINE. And made her go and sell her brooch that her very own mother gave her.

KATRIN. What?

NELS. Chris . . . you weren't supposed to tell that!

CHRISTINE. I don't care. I think she ought to know.

KATRIN. Is that true? Did Mama—Nels—?

NELS. Well, yes, as a matter of fact, she did. Now, come on.

KATRIN. No, no, I don't believe it. I'm going to ask Papa.

NELS. You haven't time.

KATRIN. I don't care. (*She rushes back to the house and dashes into the kitchen.* CHRISTINE *goes off and* NELS *follows her.*) Papa—Papa—Christine says—Papa, did Mama sell her brooch to give me this?

PAPA (*above table*). Christine should not have told you that.

KATRIN. It's true, then?

PAPA. She did not sell it. She traded it to Mr. Schiller for your present.

KATRIN (*near tears*). Oh, but she shouldn't. . . . I never meant . . .

PAPA (*taking her by the shoulders*). Look, Katrin. You wanted the present. Mama wanted your happiness; she wanted it more than she wanted the brooch.

KATRIN. But I never meant her to do that. (*Crying.*) She *loved* it so. It was all she had of Grandmother's.

PAPA. She always meant it for you, Katrin. And you must not cry. You have your play to act.

KATRIN (*sobbing*). I don't want to act in it now.

PAPA. But you must. Your audience is waiting.

KATRIN (*as before*). I don't care.

PAPA. But you must care. Tonight you are not Katrin any longer. You are an actress. And an actress must act, whatever she is feeling. There is a saying—what is it—

TRINA (*brightly*). The mails must go through!

PAPA. No, no. The show must go on. So stop your crying, and go and act your play. We talk of this later. Afterwards.

KATRIN (*pulling herself together*). All right, I'll go. (*Sniffing a good deal, she picks up the dresser set and goes back to the street and off.* PAPA *and* TRINA *exchange glances, and then settle down to their checkers.*)

PAPA. Now we play.

(*The lights fade and the curtains close. Spot up on turntable. The two girls from the earlier scene are dressing in costumes for* The Merchant of Venice *before a plank dressing table.*)

DOROTHY. I'm getting worried about Katrin. If anything's happened to *her* . . .

MADELINE (*pulling up her tights*). I'll forget my lines. I know I will. I'll look out and see Miss Forrester sitting there, and forget every single line. (KATRIN *rushes in. She carries the dresser set, places it on the dressing table.*) We thought you'd had an accident, or something. . . .

KATRIN. Dorothy, is your father here tonight?

DOROTHY. He's going to be. Why?

KATRIN. I want to speak to him. (*As she pulls off her hat and coat.*) Will you tell him . . . please . . . not to go away without speaking to me? After. After the exercises.

DOROTHY. What on earth do you want to speak to Father for?

KATRIN. I've got something to say to him. Something to ask him. It's important. *Very* important.

MADELINE. Is that the dresser set? (*Picking it up.*) Can I look at it a minute?

KATRIN (*snatching it from her, violently*). No!

MADELINE. Why, what's the matter? I only wanted to look at it.

KATRIN (*emotionally*). You can't. You're not to touch it. Dorothy, you take it and put it where I can't see it. (*She thrusts it at her.*) Go on . . . Take it! Take it! Take it! !

(*Blackout. Curtains part on the kitchen.* MAMA *and* PAPA *in conclave* [3] *at the table with cups of coffee.*)

MAMA (*behind table*). I am worried about her, Lars. When it is over, I see her talking with Mr. Schiller—and then she goes to take off her costume and Nels tells me that he will bring her home. But it is long time, and is late for her to be out. And in the play, Lars, she was not good. I have heard her practice it here, and she was good, but tonight, no. It was as if . . . as if she was thinking of something else all the time.

PAPA (*at table*). I think maybe she was.

MAMA. But what? What can be worrying her?

PAPA. Marta . . . tonight, after you leave, Katrin found out about your brooch.

MAMA. My brooch? But how? Who told her?

PAPA. Christine.

MAMA (*angry*). Why?

PAPA. I do not know.

MAMA (*rising with a sternness we have not seen before, and calling*). Christine! Christine!

CHRISTINE (*emerging from the pantry, wiping a dish*). Were you calling me, Mama?

MAMA. Yes. Christine, did you tell Katrin tonight about my brooch?

CHRISTINE (*frightened, but firm*). Yes.

MAMA (*level with her*). Why did you?

[3] **conclave:** private meeting

CHRISTINE. Because I hated the smug way she was acting over that dresser set.

MAMA. Is no excuse. You make her unhappy. You make her not good in the play.

CHRISTINE. Well, she made *you* unhappy, giving up your brooch for her selfishness.

MAMA (*moving towards her, behind table*). Is not your business. I choose to give my brooch. Is not for you to judge. And you know I do not want you to tell. I am angry with you, Christine.

CHRISTINE. I'm sorry. But I'm not sorry I told. (*She goes back to the pantry with a set, obstinate face.*)

PAPA. Christine is the stubborn one.

(NELS *and* KATRIN *have approached the house outside. They stop and look at each other in the lamplight.* KATRIN *looks scared. Then* NELS *pats her, and she goes in,* NELS *following.* MAMA *looks up inquiringly and searchingly into* KATRIN's *face.* KATRIN *turns away, taking off her hat and coat, and taking something from her pocket.*)

NELS. What happened at the meeting, Papa?

PAPA. We go back to work tomorrow.

NELS. Gee, that's bully. Isn't it, Mama?

MAMA (*seated again, at table, absently*), Yes, is good.

KATRIN (*coming to* MAMA). Mama . . . here's your brooch. (*She gives it to her.*) I'm sorry I was so bad in the play. I'll go and help Christine with the dishes. (*She turns and goes into the pantry.*)

MAMA (*unwrapping the brooch from tissue paper*). Mr. Schiller give it back to her?

NELS (*behind table*). We went to his house to get it. He didn't want to. He was planning to give it to his wife for her birthday. But Katrin begged and begged him. She even offered to go and work in his store during her vacation if he'd give it back.

PAPA (*impressed*). So? So?

MAMA. And what did Mr. Schiller say?

NELS. He said that wasn't necessary. But he gave her a job all the same. She's going to work for him, afternoons, for three dollars a week.

MAMA. And the dresser set—she gave that back?

NELS. Yes. She was awful upset, Mama. It was kinda hard for her to do. She's a good kid. Well, I'll say good night. I've got to be up early.

PAPA. Good night, Nels.

NELS. Good night, Papa. (*He goes out back.*)

MAMA. Good night, Nels.

PAPA. Nels is the kind one. (*He starts to refill* MAMA's *coffee cup. She stops him, putting her hand over her cup.*) No?

MAMA (*rising and calling*). Katrin! Katrin!

KATRIN (*coming to the pantry door*). Yes, Mama?

MAMA (*sitting at table*). Come here. (KATRIN *comes to her.* MAMA *holds out the brooch.*) You put this on.

KATRIN. No . . . it's yours.

MAMA. It is your graduation present. I put it on for you. (*She pins the brooch on* KATRIN's *dress.*)

KATRIN (*near tears*). I'll wear it always. I'll keep it forever.

MAMA. Christine should not have told you.

KATRIN (*moving away*). I'm glad she did. Now.

PAPA. And I am glad, too. (*He dips a lump of sugar and holds it out to her.*) Katrin?

KATRIN (*tearful again, shakes her head*). I'm sorry, Papa. I . . . I don't feel like it. (*She crosses in front of the table and sits on the chest under the window, with her back to the room.*)

PAPA. So? So? (*He goes to the dresser.*)

MAMA. What you want, Lars? (*He does not answer, but takes a cup and saucer, comes to the table and pours a cup of coffee, indicating* KATRIN *with his head.* MAMA *nods, pleased, then checks his pouring and fills up the cup from the cream pitcher which she empties in so doing.* PAPA *puts in sugar and moves to* KATRIN.)

PAPA. Katrin. (*She turns. He holds out the cup.*)

KATRIN (*incredulous*). For me?

PAPA. For our grown-up daughter. (MAMA *nods, standing arm in arm with* PAPA. KATRIN *takes the cup, lifts it—then her emotion overcomes her. She thrusts it at* PAPA *and rushes from the room.*) Katrin is the dramatic one! Is too bad. Her first cup of coffee, and she does not drink it.

MAMA. It would not have been good for her, so late at night.

PAPA (*smiling*). And you, Marta, you are the practical one.

MAMA. You drink the coffee, Lars. We do not want to waste it. (*She pushes it across to him.*)

(*Lights dim. Curtains close. Light up on turntable, representing the parlor of* JENNY's *house. A telephone on a table, at which* TRINA *is discovered, talking.*)

TRINA (*into phone*). Yes, Peter. Yes, Peter. I know, Peter, but we don't know where he is. It's so long since we heard from him. He's sure to turn up soon. Yes, I know, Peter. I know, but . . . (*Subsiding obediently.*) Yes, Peter. Yes, Peter. (*Sentimentally.*) Oh, Peter, you know I do. Good-by, Peter. (*She hangs up, and turns, to see* JENNY, *who has come in behind her, eating a piece of toast and jam.*)

JENNY. What was all that about?

TRINA. Peter says we shouldn't wait any longer to hear from Uncle Chris. He says we should send the wedding invitations out right away. He was quite insistent about it. Peter can be very masterful sometimes . . . when he's alone with *me!*

(*The telephone rings again.* JENNY *answers it, putting down the toast, which* TRINA *takes up and nibbles at during the scene.*)

JENNY. This is Mrs. Stenborg's boardinghouse. Mrs. Stenborg speaking. Oh, yes, Marta . . . what is it? (*She listens.*)

(*Spot up on opposite turntable, disclosing* MAMA *standing at a wall telephone booth. She wears hat and coat, and has an opened telegram in her hand.*)

MAMA. Jenny, is Uncle Chris. I have a telegram. It says if we want to see him again we should come without delay.

JENNY. Where is he?

MAMA (*consulting the telegram*). It comes from a place called Ukiah. Nels says it is up north from San Francisco.

JENNY. Who is the telegram from?

MAMA. It does not say.

JENNY. That . . . woman?

MAMA. I don't know, Jenny. I think maybe.

JENNY. I won't go. (SIGRID *comes in through the curtains, dressed in hat and coat, carrying string marketing bags, full of vege-*

tables. JENNY *speaks to her, whisperingly, aside.*) It's Uncle Chris. Marta says he's dying. (*Then, back into phone.*) Why was the telegram sent to *you?* I'm the eldest.

MAMA. Jenny, is not the time to think of who is eldest. Uncle Chris is dying.

JENNY. *I* don't believe it. He's too mean to die. Ever. (NELS *comes to booth from wings and hands* MAMA *a slip of paper.*) I'm not going.

MAMA. Jenny, I cannot stop to argue. There is a train at eleven o'clock. It takes four hours. You call Sigrid.

JENNY. Sigrid is here now.

MAMA. Good. Then you tell her.

JENNY. What do you say the name of the place is?

MAMA. Ukiah. (*Spelling in Norwegian.*) U—K—I—A—H.

JENNY. I won't go.

MAMA. That *you* decide. (*She hangs up. Her spot goes out.*)

SIGRID. Uncle Chris dying!

JENNY. The wages of sin.

TRINA. Oh, he's old. Maybe it is time for him to go.

JENNY. Four hours by train, and maybe have to stay all night. All that expense to watch a wicked old man die.

SIGRID. I know, but . . . there is his will. . . .

JENNY. Huh, even supposing he's anything to leave—you know who he'd leave it *to*, don't you?

SIGRID. Yes. But all the same he's dying now, and blood is thicker than water. Especially when it's Norwegian. I'm going. I shall take Arne with me. Uncle Chris was always fond of children.

TRINA. I agree with Sigrid. I think we *should* go.

JENNY. Well, *you* can't go, anyway.

TRINA. Why not?

JENNY. Because of that woman.

TRINA. Nonsense. I've never met a woman like that. Maybe I'll never get another chance. Besides, if he's going to change his will, there's still my dowry, remember. Do you think we should take Peter?

JENNY. Peter Thorkelson? Whatever for?

TRINA. Well, after all, I mean . . . I mean, his profession . . .

JENNY. Trina, you always were a fool. Anyone would know the last person a dying man wants to see is an undertaker!

(Blackout. Turntable revolves out. Spot up on KATRIN. *She wears her schoolgirl hat.)*

KATRIN. When Mama said I was to go with her, I was excited and I was frightened. It was exciting to take sandwiches for the train, almost as though we were going on a picnic. But I was scared at the idea of seeing death, though I told myself that if I was going to be a writer, I had to experience everything. But all the same, I hoped it would be all over when we got there. *(She starts to walk up the steps.)* It was afternoon when we arrived. We asked at the station for the Halvorsen ranch, and it seemed to me that the man looked at us strangely. Uncle Chris was obviously considered an odd character. The ranch was about three miles from the town: a derelict,[4] rambling old place. There was long grass, and tall trees, and a smell of honeysuckle. We made quite a cavalcade, walking up from the gate. *(The procession comes in behind* KATRIN. MAMA, JENNY, TRINA, SIGRID *and* ARNE.*)* The woman came out on the steps to meet us.

(The procession starts moving upwards. The WOMAN *comes through the curtains, down one step. The* AUNTS *freeze in their tracks.* MAMA *goes forward to her.)*

MAMA. How is he? Is he—?
WOMAN *(with grave self-possession).* Come in, won't you? *(She holds the curtains slightly aside.* MAMA *goes in.* KATRIN *follows, looking curiously at the* WOMAN. *The* AUNTS *walk stiffly past her,* SIGRID *clutching* ARNE *and shielding him from contact with the* WOMAN. *They disappear behind the curtains. The* WOMAN *stands a moment, looking off into the distance. Then she goes in behind the curtains, too.)*

(The curtains draw apart, revealing UNCLE CHRIS's *bedroom. It is simple, and shabby. The door to the room is at the back. In the wall at left is a window, with curtains, drawn aside now. In front of it, a washstand. The afternoon sunlight comes through the window, falling onto the big double bed, in which* UNCLE CHRIS *is propped up on pillows. Beside him, on a small table, is a pitcher of water. He has a glass in his hand.* MAMA

---

[4] **derelict:** abandoned, deserted

stands to his right, JENNY *to the left. The others are ranged below the window. The* WOMAN *is not present.*)

UNCLE CHRIS (*handing* MAMA *the empty glass*). I want more. You give me more. Is still some in the bottle.

MAMA. Uncle Chris, that will not help now.

UNCLE CHRIS. It always help. (*With a glance at* JENNY.) Now especially.

JENNY (*firmly*). Uncle Chris, I don't think you realize . . .

UNCLE CHRIS. What I don't realize? That I am dying? Why else do I think you come here? Why else do I think you stand there, watching me? (*He sits upright.*) Get out. Get out. I don't want you here. Get out!

JENNY. Oh, very well. Very well. We'll be outside on the porch, if you want us. (*She starts toward the door.*)

UNCLE CHRIS. That is where I want you—on the porch! (JENNY *goes out.* TRINA *follows.* SIGRID *is about to go, too, when* UNCLE CHRIS *stops her.*) Wait. That is Arne. Come here, Arne. (ARNE, *propelled by* SIGRID, *advances toward the bed.*) How is your knee?

ARNE. It's fine, Uncle Chris.

UNCLE CHRIS. Not hurt any more? You don't use svear vords any more?

ARNE. N-no, Uncle Chris.

UNCLE CHRIS. You walk goot? Quite goot? Let me see you walk. Walk around the room. (ARNE *does so.*) Fast. Fast. Run! Run! (ARNE *does so.*) Is goot.

SIGRID (*encouraged and advancing*). Uncle Chris, Arne has always been so fond of you. . . .

UNCLE CHRIS (*shouting*). I tell you all to get out. Except Marta. (*As* KATRIN *edges with the* AUNTS *to the door.*) And Katrinë. Katrinë and I haf secret. You remember, Katrinë?

KATRIN. Yes, Uncle Chris.

MAMA. Uncle Chris, you must lie down again.

UNCLE CHRIS. Then you give me drink.

MAMA. No, Uncle Chris.

UNCLE CHRIS. We cannot waste what is left in the bottle. You do not drink it . . . who will drink it when I am gone? What harm can it do . . . now? I die, anyway. . . . You give it to me. (MAMA *goes to the washstand, pours him a drink of whisky and water, and takes it to him, sitting on the bed beside him. He drinks, then turns to her, leaning back against her arm and the pillows.*) Marta, I haf never made a will. Was never enough money. But you sell this ranch. It will not bring much. I have not had it long enough. And there is mortgage. Big mortgage. But it leave a little. Maybe two, three hundred dollars. You give to Yessie.

MAMA. Yessie?

UNCLE CHRIS. Yessie Brown. My housekeeper. She was trained nurse, but she get sick and I bring her to the country to get well again. There will be no money for *you*, Marta. Always I wanted there should be money to make Nils doctor. But there were other things . . . quick things. And now there is no time to make more. There is no money, but you make Nils doctor, all the same. You like?

MAMA. Sure, Uncle Chris. It is what Lars and I have always wanted for him. To help people who suffer. . . .

UNCLE CHRIS. Is the greatest thing in the world. It is to have a little of God in you. Always I wanted to be doctor myself. Is the only thing I have ever wanted. Nils must do it for me.

MAMA. He will, Uncle Chris.

UNCLE CHRIS. Is goot. (*He strokes her hand.*) You are the goot one. I am glad you come, *Lille Ven*. (*He moves his head restlessly.*) Where is Yessie?

MAMA. I think she wait outside.

UNCLE CHRIS. You do not mind if she is here?

MAMA. Of course not, Uncle Chris.

UNCLE CHRIS. You call her. I like you both be here. (MAMA *goes, with a quick glance at* KATRIN, *who has been standing, forgotten, listening intently.* UNCLE CHRIS *signs to* KATRIN *to come closer. She sits on the chair beside the bed.*) Katrinë, your Mama write me you drink coffee now? (*She nods. He looks at her affectionately.*) Katrinë, who will be writer. . . . You are not frightened of me now?

KATRIN. No, Uncle Chris.

UNCLE CHRIS. One day maybe you write story about Uncle Chris. If you remember.

KATRIN (*whispering*). I'll remember.

(MAMA *returns with the* WOMAN. *They come to his bed, standing on either side of it.*)

UNCLE CHRIS (*obviously exhausted and in pain*). I like you both stay with me . . . now. I think best now maybe Katrinë go away. Good-by, Katrinë (*Then he repeats it in Norwegian.*) Farvell, Katrinë.

KATRIN. Good-by, Uncle Chris.

UNCLE CHRIS. You say it in Norwegian, like I do.

KATRIN (*in Norwegian*). Farvell, Onkel Chris. (*She slips out, in tears.*)

UNCLE CHRIS. Yessie! Maybe I should introduce you to each other. Yessie, this is my niece, Marta. The only von of my nieces I can stand. Marta, this is Yessie, who have give me much happiness. . . .

(*The* TWO WOMEN *shake hands across the bed.*)

MAMA. I am very glad to meet you.

JESSIE. I am, too.

UNCLE CHRIS (*as they shake*). Is goot. And now you give me von more drink. You have drink with me . . . both of you. That way we finish the bottle. Yes?

(JESSIE *and* MAMA *look at each other.*)

MAMA. Sure, Uncle Chris.

UNCLE CHRIS. Goot. Yessie, you get best glasses. (*With a chuckle to* MAMA.) Yessie does not like to drink, but this is special occasion. (JESSIE *gets three glasses from a wall shelf.*) What is the time?

MAMA. It is about half-past four, Uncle Chris.

UNCLE CHRIS. The sun come around this side the house in afternoon. You draw the curtain a little maybe. Is strong for my eyes. (MAMA *goes over and draws the curtain over the window. The stage darkens.* JESSIE *pours three drinks, filling two of the glasses with water. She is about to put water in the third when* UNCLE CHRIS *stops her.*) No, no, I take it now without water. Always the last drink without water. Is Norwegian custom. (*To* MAMA, *with a smile.*) True? (JESSIE *sits on the bed beside him, about to feed his drink to him, but he pushes her aside.*) No.

No, I do not need you feed it to me. I can drink myself. (*He takes the glass from her.*) Give Marta her glass. (JESSIE *hands a glass to* MAMA. *The* TWO WOMEN *stand on either side of the bed, holding their glasses.*) So. . . . Skoal!

JESSIE (*clinking glasses with him*). Skoal.

MAMA (*doing likewise*). Skoal.

(*They all three drink. Slow dim to blackout. Curtains close. Spot up on turntable. A porch with a bench, and a chair, on which the three* AUNTS *are sitting.* JENNY *is dozing in the chair.*)

SIGRID (*flicking her handkerchief*). These gnats are awful. I'm being simply eaten alive.

TRINA. Gnats are always worse around sunset. (*She catches one.*)

JENNY (*rousing herself*). I should never have let you talk me into coming. To be insulted like that . . . turned out of his room . . . and then expected to sit here hour after hour without as much as a cup of coffee. . . .

SIGRID. I'd make coffee if I knew where the kitchen was.

JENNY. *Her* kitchen? It would poison me. (*Rising.*) No, I'm going home. Are you coming, Trina?

TRINA. Oh, I think we ought to wait a little longer. After all, you can't *hurry* these things. . . . I mean . . . (*She breaks off in confusion at what she has said.*)

JENNY (*to* SIGRID). And all your talk about his will. A lot of chance we got to say a word!

TRINA. Maybe Marta's been talking to him.

(MAMA *comes from between the curtains.*)

JENNY. Well?

MAMA. Uncle Chris has . . . gone.

(*There is a silence.*)

JENNY (*more gently than is her wont*). Did he . . . say anything about a will?

MAMA. There is no will.

JENNY. Well, then, that means . . . we're his nearest relatives. . . .

MAMA. There is no money, either.

SIGRID. How do you know?

MAMA. He told me. (*She brings out a small notebook that she is carrying.*)

JENNY. What's that?

MAMA. Is an account of how he spent the money.

JENNY. Bills from a liquor store.

MAMA. No, Jenny. No. I read it to you. (JENNY *sits again.*) You know how Uncle Chris was lame . . . how he walked always with limp. It was his one thought . . . lame people. He would have liked to be doctor and help them. Instead, he help them other ways. I read you the last page. . . . (*She reads from the notebook.*) "Joseph Spinelli. Four years old. Tubercular left leg. Three hundred thirty-seven dollars, eighteen cents." (*Pause.*) "Walks now. Esta Jensen. Nine years. Clubfoot. Two hundred seventeen dollars, fifty cents. Walks now." (*Then, reading very slowly.*) "Arne Solfeldt. . . ."

SIGRID (*startled*). My Arne?

MAMA (*reading on*). "Nine years. Fractured kneecap. Four hundred forty-two dollars, sixteen cents."

(KATRIN *and* ARNE *come running in.*)

ARNE (*calling as he comes running across*). Mother . . . Mother . . . Are we going to eat soon? (*He stops, awed by the solemnity of the group, and by* MAMA, *who puts out her hand gently, to silence him.*) What is it? Is Uncle Chris . . . ?

MAMA (*to the* AUNTS). It does not tell the end about Arne. I like to write "Walks now." Yes?

SIGRID (*very subdued*). Yes.

MAMA (*taking a pencil from the book*). Maybe even . . . "runs"? (SIGRID *nods, moist-eyed.* TRINA *is crying.* MAMA *writes in the book, and then closes it.*) So. Is finished. Is all. (*She touches* JENNY *on the shoulder.*) It was good.

JENNY (*after a gulping movement*). I go and make some coffee.

(*The woman,* JESSIE, *appears from between the curtains on the steps.*)

JESSIE. You can go in and see him now if you want. (JENNY *looks back, half-hesitant, at the others. Then she nods and goes in.* TRINA *follows her, mopping her eyes.* SIGRID *puts her arm suddenly around* ARNE *in a spasm of maternal affection, and they, too, go in.* MAMA, KATRIN *and* JESSIE *are left alone.* KATRIN *stands apart,* MAMA *and* JESSIE *are in front of the curtains.*) I'm moving down to the hotel for tonight . . . so that you can all stay. (*She is about to go back, when* MAMA *stops her.*)

MAMA. Wait. What will you do now . . . after he is buried? You have money? (JESSIE *shakes her head.*) Where you live?

JESSIE. I'll find a room somewhere. I'll probably go back to nursing.

MAMA. You like to come to San Francisco for a little? To our house? We have room. Plenty room.

JESSIE (*touched, moving to* MAMA). That's very kind of you, but . . .

MAMA. I like to have you. You come for a little as our guest. When you get work you can be our boarder.

JESSIE (*awkwardly grateful*). I don't know why you should bother. . . .

MAMA (*touching her*). You were good to Uncle Chris. (JESSIE *grasps her hand, deeply moved, then turns and goes quickly back through the curtains.* MAMA *turns to* KATRIN.) Katrin, you come and see him?

KATRIN (*scared*). See him? You mean . . .

MAMA. I like you see him. You need not be frightened. He looks . . . happy and at peace. I like you to know what death looks like. Then you are not frightened of it, ever.

KATRIN. Will you come with me?

MAMA. Sure. (*She stretches out her hand, puts her arm around her, and then leads her gently in through the curtains.*)

(*Spot up on turntable, representing a park bench against a hedge.* TRINA *and* MR. THORKELSON, *in outdoor clothes, are seated together.* TRINA *is cooing over a baby carriage.*)

TRINA. Who's the most beautiful Norwegian baby in San Francisco? Who's going to be three months old tomorrow? Little Christopher Thorkelson! (*To* MR. THORKELSON.) Do you know, Peter, I think he's even beginning to *look* a little like Uncle Chris! Quite apart from his black curls—and those, of course, he gets from *you.* (*To baby again.*) He's going to grow up to be a black Norwegian, isn't he, just like his daddy and his

Uncle Chris? (*Settling down beside* MR. THORKELSON.) I think there's something about his mouth . . . a sort of . . . well . . . *firmness.* Of course, it's *your* mouth, too. But then I've always thought you had quite a lot of Uncle Chris about you. (*She looks back at the baby.*) Look—he's asleep!

MR. THORKELSON. Trina, do you know what next Thursday is?

TRINA (*nodding, smiling*). Our anniversary.

MR. THORKELSON. What would you think of our giving a little party?

TRINA. A party?

MR. THORKELSON. Oh, quite a modest one. Nothing showy or ostentatious—but, after all, we have been married a year, and with your having been in mourning and the baby coming so soon and everything, we've not been able to entertain. I think it's time you . . . took your place in society.

TRINA (*scared*). What . . . sort of a party?

MR. THORKELSON. An evening party. (*Proudly.*) A soirée! I should say about ten people . . . some of the Norwegian colony . . . and Lars and Marta, of course. . . .

TRINA (*beginning to count on her fingers*). And Jenny and Sigrid. . . .

MR. THORKELSON. Oh . . . I . . . I hadn't thought of asking Jenny and Sigrid.

TRINA. Oh, we'd have to. We couldn't leave them out.

MR. THORKELSON. Trina, I hope you won't be offended if I say that I have never really felt . . . well, altogether comfortable with Jenny and Sigrid. They have always made me feel that they didn't think I was . . . well . . . *worthy* of you. Of course, I know I'm not, but . . . well . . . one doesn't like to be reminded of it . . . *all* the time.

TRINA (*taking his hand*). Oh, Peter.

MR. THORKELSON. But you're quite right. We must ask them. Now, as to the matter of refreshments . . . what would you suggest?

TRINA (*flustered*). Oh, I don't know. I . . . what would you say to . . . ice cream and cookies for the ladies . . . and coffee, of course . . . and . . . perhaps port wine for the gentlemen?

MR. THORKELSON (*anxiously*). Port wine?

TRINA. Just a little. You could bring it in already poured out, in *little* glasses. Jenny and Sigrid can help me serve the ice cream.

MR. THORKELSON (*firmly*). No. If Jenny and Sigrid come, they come as guests, like everyone else. You shall have someone in to help you in the kitchen.

TRINA. You mean a waitress? (MR. THORKELSON *nods, beaming.*) Oh, but none of us have *ever* . . . do you really think . . . I mean . . . you did say we shouldn't be ostentatious. . . .

MR. THORKELSON (*nervously, rising and starting to pace up and down*). Trina, there's something I would like to say. I've never been very good at expressing myself or my . . . well . . . *deeper* feelings—but I want you to know that I'm not only very fond of you, but very . . . well . . . very *proud* of you as well, and I want you to have the best of everything, as far as it's in my power to give it to you. (*He sits again—then, as a climax.*) I want you to have a waitress!

TRINA (*overcome*). Yes, Peter. (*They hold hands.*)

(*The lights fade and the turntable revolves out. Curtains part on kitchen, slightly changed, smartened and refurnished now.* MAMA *and* PAPA *seated as usual.* MAMA *is darning.* DAGMAR, *looking a little older, is seated on the chest, reading a solid-looking book.* NELS *enters from back door, carrying a newspaper. He wears long trousers now, and looks about seventeen.*)

NELS (*hitting* PAPA *playfully on the head with the paper*). Hello! Here's your evening paper, Papa.

(PAPA *puts down the morning paper he is reading and takes the evening one from* NELS.)

PAPA (*at table*). Is there any news?

NELS. No. (*He takes out a package of cigarettes with elaborate unconcern.* MAMA *watches with disapproval. Then, as he is about to light his cigarette, he stops, remembering something.*) Oh, I forgot. There's a letter for Katrin. I picked it up on the mat as I came in. (*Going to back door and calling.*) Katrin! Katrin! There's a letter for you.

KATRIN (*answering from off stage*). Coming!

MAMA (*at table*). Nels, you know who the letter is from?

NELS. Why, no, Mama. (*Hands it to her.*) It looks like her own handwriting.

MAMA (*gravely inspecting it*). Is bad.

PAPA. Why is bad?

MAMA. She get too many like that. I think they are stories she send to the magazines.

DAGMAR (*closing her book loudly, rising*). Well, I'll go and see if I have any puppies yet. (*Crosses below the table and then turns.*) Mama, I've just decided something.

MAMA. What have you decided?

DAGMAR. If Nels is going to be a doctor, when I grow up, I'm going to be a—(*Looking at the book title, and stumbling over the word.*)—vet-vet-veterinarian.

MAMA. And what is that?

DAGMAR. A doctor for animals.

MAMA. Is good. Is good.

DAGMAR. There are far more animals in the world than there are human beings, and far more human doctors than animal ones. It isn't fair. (*She goes to the pantry door.*) I suppose we couldn't have a horse, could we? (*This only produces a concerted laugh from the family. She turns, sadly.*) No. . . . I was afraid we couldn't. (*She goes into the pantry.*)

(KATRIN *comes in. She wears a slightly more adult dress than before. Her hair is up and she looks about eighteen.*)

KATRIN. Where's the letter?

MAMA (*handing it to her*). Here.

(KATRIN *takes it, nervously. She looks at the envelope, and her face falls. She opens it, pulls out a manuscript and a rejection slip, looks at it a moment, and then replaces both in the envelope. The others watch her covertly.[5] Then she looks up, with determination.*)

KATRIN (*above table*). Mama . . . Papa . . . I want to say something.

PAPA. What is it?

KATRIN. I'm not going to go to college.

PAPA. Why not?

KATRIN. Because it would be a waste of time and money. The only

[5] covertly: secretly

point in my going to college was to be a writer. Well, I'm not going to be one, so . . .

MAMA. Katrin, is it your letter that makes you say this? It is a story come back again?

KATRIN. Again is right. This is the tenth time. I made this one a test. It's the best I've ever written, or ever shall write. I know that. Well, it's no good.

NELS. What kind of a story is it?

KATRIN. Oh . . . it's a story about a painter, who's a genius, and he goes blind.

NELS. Sounds like *The Light That Failed*.

KATRIN. Well, what's wrong with that?

NELS (*quickly*). Nothing. Nothing!

KATRIN (*moving down*). Besides, it's not like that. My painter gets better. He has an operation and recovers his sight, and paints better than ever before.

MAMA. Is good.

KATRIN (*bitterly unhappy*). No, it isn't. It's rotten. But it's the best I can do.

MAMA. You have asked your teachers about this?

KATRIN. Teachers don't know anything about writing. They just know about literature.

MAMA. If there was someone we could ask . . . for advice . . . to tell us . . . tell us if your stories are good.

KATRIN. Yes. Well, there isn't. And they're *not*.

PAPA (*looking at the evening paper*). There is something here in the paper about a lady writer. I just noticed the headline. Wait. (*He looks back for it and reads.*) "Woman writer tells key to literary success."

KATRIN. Who?

PAPA. A lady called Florence Dana Moorhead. It gives her picture. A fat lady. You have heard of her?

KATRIN. Yes, of course. Everyone has. She's terribly successful. She's here on a lecture tour.

MAMA. What does she say is the secret?

PAPA. You read it, Katrin. (*He hands her the paper.*)

KATRIN (*grabbing the first part*). "Florence Dana Moorhead, cele-brated novelist and short story writer . . . blah-blah-blah . . . interviewed today in her suite at the Fairmont . . . blah-blah-

blah . . . pronounced sincerity the essential quality for success as a writer." (*Throwing aside the paper.*) A lot of help that is.

MAMA. Katrin, this lady . . . maybe if you sent her your stories, *she* could tell you what is wrong with them?

KATRIN (*wearily*). Oh, Mama, don't be silly.

MAMA. Why is silly?

KATRIN (*behind table*). Well, in the first place because she's a very important person . . . a celebrity . . . and she'd never read them. And in the second, because . . . you seem to think writing's like . . . well, like cooking, or something. That all you have to have is the recipe. It takes a lot more than that. You have to have a gift for it.

MAMA. You have to have a gift for cooking, too. But there are things you can learn, if you have the gift.

KATRIN. Well, that's the whole point. I haven't. I *know* . . . now. So, if you've finished with the morning paper, Papa, I'll take the want ad section, and see if I can find myself a job. (*She takes the morning paper and goes out.*)

MAMA. Is bad. Nels, what you think?

NELS. I don't know, Mama. Her stories seem all right to me, but I don't know.

MAMA. It would be good to know. Nels, this lady in the paper . . . what else does she say?

NELS (*taking up the paper*). Not much. The rest seems to be about *her* and her home. Let's see. . . . (*He reads—walking down.*) "Apart from literature, Mrs. Moorhead's main interest in life is gastronomy."

MAMA. The stars?

NELS. No—eating. "A brilliant cook herself, she says that she would as soon turn out a good soufflé as a short story, or find a new recipe as she would a first edition."

MAMA (*reaching for the paper*). I see her picture? (*She looks at it.*) Is kind face. (*Pause while she reads a moment. Then she looks up and asks.*) What is first edition?

(*Blackout. Lights up on turntable, representing the lobby of the Fairmont Hotel. A couch against a column with a palm behind it. An orchestra plays softly in the background.* MAMA *is discovered seated on the couch, waiting patiently. She wears a hat and a suit, and clutches a newspaper and a bundle of manu-scripts. A couple of guests come through the curtains and cross, disappearing into the wings.* MAMA *watches them. Then* FLORENCE DANA MOORHEAD *enters through the curtains. She is a stout, dressy, good-natured, middle-aged woman. A* BELLBOY *comes from the right, paging her.*)

BELLBOY. Miss Moorhead?

F. D. MOORHEAD. Yes?

BELLBOY. Telegram.

F. D. MOORHEAD. Oh. . . . Thank you. (*She tips him, and he goes.* MAMA *rises and moves towards her.*)

MAMA. Please . . . Please . . . Miss Moorhead . . . Miss Moor-head.

F. D. MOORHEAD (*looking up from her telegram, on the steps*). Were you calling me?

MAMA. Yes. You are . . . Miss Florence Dana Moorhead?

F. D. MOORHEAD. Yes.

MAMA. Please . . . might I speak to you for a moment?

F. D. MOORHEAD. Yes—what's it about?

MAMA. I read in the paper what you say about writing.

F. D. MOORHEAD (*with a vague social smile*). Oh, yes?

MAMA. My daughter, Katrin, wants to be writer.

F. D. MOORHEAD (*who has heard that one before*). Oh, really? (*She glances at her watch on her bosom.*)

MAMA. I bring her stories.

F. D. MOORHEAD. Look, I'm afraid I'm in rather a hurry. I'm leav-ing San Francisco this evening. . . .

MAMA. I wait two hours here for you to come in. Please, if I may talk to you for one, two minutes. That is all.

F. D. MOORHEAD (*kindly*). Of course, but I think I'd better tell you that if you want me to read your daughter's stories, it's no use. I'm very sorry, but I've had to make a rule never to read any-one's unpublished material.

MAMA (*nods—then after a pause*). It said in the paper you like to collect recipes . . . for eating.

F. D. MOORHEAD. Yes, I do. I've written several books on cooking.

MAMA. I, too, am interested in gastronomy. I am good cook. Nor-wegian. I make good Norwegian dishes. Lutefisk. And Kjötbol-ler. That is meat balls with cream sauce.

F. D. MOORHEAD. Yes, I know. I've eaten them in Christiania.[6]

MAMA. I have a special recipe for Kjötboller . . . my mother give me. She was best cook I ever knew. Never have I told this recipe, not even to my own sisters, because they are not good cooks.

F. D. MOORHEAD (*amused*). Oh?

MAMA. But . . . if you let me talk to you . . . I give it to you. I promise it is good recipe.

F. D. MOORHEAD (*vastly tickled now*). Well, that seems fair enough. Let's sit down. (*They move to the couch and sit.*) Now, your daughter wants to write, you say? How old is she?

MAMA. She is eighteen. Just.

F. D. MOORHEAD. *Does* she write, or does she just . . . *want* to write?

MAMA. Oh, she write all the time. Maybe she should not be author, but it is hard to give up something that has meant so much.

F. D. MOORHEAD. I agree, but . . .

MAMA. I bring her stories. I bring twelve.

F. D. MOORHEAD (*aghast*). Twelve!

MAMA. But if you could read maybe just one . . . To know if someone is good cook, you do not need to eat a whole dinner.

F. D. MOORHEAD. You're very persuasive. How is it your daughter did not come herself?

MAMA. She was too unhappy. And too scared . . . of you. Because you are celebrity. But I see your picture in the paper. . . .

F. D. MOORHEAD. That frightful picture!

MAMA. Is the picture of woman who like to eat good. . . .

F. D. MOORHEAD (*with a rueful*[7] *smile*). It certainly is. Now, tell me about the Kjötboller.

MAMA. When you make the meat balls you drop them in boiling stock. Not water. That is one of the secrets.

F. D. MOORHEAD. Ah!

MAMA. And the cream sauce. That is another secret. It is half *sour* cream, added at the last.

F. D. MOORHEAD. That sounds marvelous.

MAMA. You must grind the meat six times. I could write it out for you. And . . . (*Tentatively.*) while I write, you could read?

---

[6] **Christiania:** former name of Oslo, the capital of Norway
[7] **rueful:** mournful

F. D. MOORHEAD (*with a laugh*). All right. You win. Come upstairs to my apartment. (*She rises.*)

MAMA. Is kind of you. (*They start out.*) Maybe if you would read *two* stories, I could write the recipe for Lutefisk as well. You know Lutefisk . . . ?

(*They have disappeared into the wings, and the turntable revolves out.* KATRIN *is at her desk.*)

KATRIN. When Mama came back, I was sitting with my diary, which I called my Journal now, writing a Tragic Farewell to my Art. It was very seldom that Mama came to the attic, thinking that a writer needed privacy, and I was surprised to see her standing in the doorway. (*She looks up.* MAMA *is standing on the steps.*) Mama!

MAMA. You are busy, Katrin?

KATRIN (*jumping up*). No, of course not. Come in.

MAMA (*coming down*). I like to talk to you.

KATRIN. Yes, of course.

MAMA (*seating herself at the desk*). You are writing?

KATRIN (*on the steps*). No. I told you, that's all over.

MAMA. That is what I want to talk to you about.

KATRIN. It's all right, Mama. Really, it's all right. I was planning to tear up all my stories this afternoon, only I couldn't find half of them.

MAMA. They are here.

KATRIN. Did *you* take them? What for?

MAMA. Katrin, I have been to see Miss Moorhead.

KATRIN. Who's Miss . . . ? You don't mean Florence Dana Moorhead? (MAMA *nods.*) You don't mean . . . (*She comes down to her.*) Mama, you don't mean you took her my stories?

MAMA. She read five of them. I was two hours with her. We have glass of sherry. Two glass of sherry.

KATRIN. What . . . did she say about them?

MAMA (*quietly*). She say they are not good.

KATRIN (*turning away*). Well, I knew that. It was hardly worth your going to all that trouble just to be told that.

MAMA. She say more. Will you listen, Katrin?

KATRIN (*trying to be gracious*). Sure. Sure. I'll listen.

MAMA. I will try and remember. She say you write now only be-

cause of what you have read in other books, and that no one
can write good until they have felt what they write about. That for
years she write bad stories about people in the olden times,
until one day she remember something that happen in her own
town . . . something that only she could know and understand
. . . and she feels she must tell it . . . and that is how she
write her first good story. She say you must write more of things
you know. . . .

KATRIN. That's what my teacher always told me at school.

MAMA. Maybe your teacher was right. I do not know if I explain
good what Miss Moorhead means, but while she talks I think
I understand. Your story about the painter who is blind . . .
that is because . . . forgive me if I speak plain, my Katrin, but
it is important to you . . . because you are the dramatic one,
as Papa has said . . . and you think it would feel good to be
a painter and be blind and not complain. But never have you
imagined how it would really be. Is true?

KATRIN (*subdued*). Yes, I . . . guess it's true.

MAMA. But she say you are to go on writing. That you have the
gift. (KATRIN *turns back to her, suddenly aglow*.) And that when
you have written story that is real and true . . . then you send
it to someone whose name she give me. (*She fumbles for a
piece of paper*.) It is her . . . agent . . . and say she recommend you. Here. No, that is recipe she give me for goulash as
her grandmother make it . . . here . . . (*She hands over the
paper*.) It helps, Katrin, what I have told you?

KATRIN (*subdued again*). Yes, I . . . I guess it helps. Some. But
what have *I* got to write about? I haven't seen anything, or
been anywhere.

MAMA. Could you write about San Francisco, maybe? Is fine city.
Miss Moorhead write about her home town.

KATRIN. Yes, I know. But you've got to have a central character
or something. She writes about her grandfather . . . he was a
wonderful old man.

MAMA. Could you maybe write about Papa?

KATRIN. Papa?

MAMA. Papa is fine man. Is wonderful man.

KATRIN. Yes, I know, but . . .

MAMA (*rising*). I must go fix supper. Is late. Papa will be home.

(*She goes up the steps to the curtains, and then turns back.*) I like you should write about Papa. (*She goes inside.*)

KATRIN (*going back to her seat behind the desk*). Papa. Yes, but what's he ever done? What's ever happened to him? What's ever happened to *any* of us? Except always being poor and having illness, like the time when Dagmar went to hospital and Mama . . . (*The idea hits her like a flash.*) Oh. . . . Oh. . . . (*Pause—then she becomes the* KATRIN *of today.*) And that was how it was born . . . suddenly in a flash . . . the story of "Mama and the Hospital" . . . the first of all the stories. I wrote it . . . oh, quite soon after that. I didn't tell Mama or any of them. But I sent it to Miss Moorhead's agent. It was a long time before I heard anything . . . and then one evening the letter came. (*She takes an envelope from the desk in front of her.*) For a moment I couldn't believe it. Then I went rushing into the kitchen, shouting. . . . (*She rises from the desk, taking some papers with her, and rushes upstage, crying, "Mama, Mama." The curtains have parted on the kitchen—and the family tableau—*MAMA, PAPA, CHRISTINE, *and* NELS. DAGMAR *is not present.* KATRIN *comes rushing in, up the steps. The turntable revolves out as soon as she has left it.*) Mama . . . Mama . . . I've sold a story!

MAMA (*at table*). A story?

KATRIN. Yes, I got a letter from the agent . . . with a check for . . . (*Gasping.*) five hundred dollars!'

NELS (*on the chest*). No kidding? (*He rises.*)

MAMA. Katrin . . . is true?

KATRIN. Here it is. Here's the letter. Maybe I haven't read it right. (*She hands the letter.* PAPA *and* MAMA *huddle and gloat over it.*)

CHRISTINE (*behind* MAMA's *chair*). What will you *do* with five hundred dollars?

KATRIN. I don't know. I'll buy Mama her warm coat, I know that.

CHRISTINE. Coats don't cost five hundred dollars.

KATRIN. I know. We'll put the rest in the Bank.

NELS (*kidding*). Quick. Before they change their mind, and stop the check.

KATRIN. Will you, Mama? Will you take it to the Bank downtown tomorrow? (MAMA *looks vague.*) What is it?

MAMA. I do not know how.

NELS. Just give it to the man and tell him to put it in your account, like you always do.

(MAMA *looks up at* PAPA.)

PAPA. You tell them . . . now.

CHRISTINE. Tell us what?

MAMA (*desperately*). Is no bank account! (*She rises, feeling hemmed in by them—sits on bench.*) Never in my life have I been inside a bank.

CHRISTINE. But you always told us . . .

KATRIN. Mama, you've always said . . .

MAMA. I know. But was not true. I tell a lie.

KATRIN. But why, Mama? Why did you pretend?

MAMA. Is not good for little ones to be afraid . . . to not feel secure. (*Rising again.*) But now . . . with five hundred dollar . . . I think I can tell.

KATRIN (*going to her, emotionally*). Mama!

MAMA (*stopping her, quickly*). You read us the story. You have it there?

KATRIN. Yes.

MAMA. Then read.

KATRIN. Now?

MAMA. Yes. No—wait. Dagmar must hear. (*She opens pantry door and calls.*) Dagmar.

DAGMAR (*off*). Yes, Mama?

MAMA (*calling*). Come here, I want you.

DAGMAR (*off*). What is it?

MAMA. I want you. No, you leave the rabbits! (*She comes back.*) What is it called . . . the story?

KATRIN (*seating herself in the chair that* MR. HYDE *took in the opening scene.*) It's called "Mama and the Hospital."

PAPA (*delighted*). You write about Mama?

KATRIN. Yes.

MAMA. But I thought . . . I thought you say . . . I tell you . . . (*She gestures at* PAPA, *behind his back.*)

KATRIN. I know, Mama, but . . . well, that's how it came out.

(DAGMAR *comes in.*)

DAGMAR. What is it? What do you want?

MAMA. Katrin write story for magazine. They pay her five hundred dollar to print it.

DAGMAR (*completely uninterested*). Oh. (*She starts back for the pantry.*)

MAMA (*stopping her*). She read it to us. I want you should listen. (DAGMAR *sits on the floor at* MAMA's *feet.*) You are ready, Katrin?

KATRIN. Sure.

MAMA. Then read.

(*The group around the table is now a duplicate of the grouping around* MR. HYDE *in the first scene, with* KATRIN *in his place.* CHRISTINE *is in* TRINA's *chair.*)

KATRIN (*reading*). "For as long as I could remember, the house on Steiner Street had been home. All of us were born there. Nels, the oldest and the only boy . . ." (NELS *looks up, astonished to be in a story*)"my sister, Christine . . ." (CHRISTINE *does likewise*) "and the littlest sister, Dagmar. . . ."

DAGMAR. Am I in the story?

MAMA. Hush, Dagmar. We are all in the story.

KATRIN. "But first and foremost, I remember Mama." (*The lights begin to dim and the curtain slowly to fall. As it descends, we hear her voice continuing.*) "I remember that every Saturday night Mama would sit down by the kitchen table and count out the money Papa had brought home in the little envelope. . . ."

(*By now, the curtain is down.*)

For discussion

ACT I

1. What problems did Mama face early in the play? How did she teach her children about money? Did she make them aware of financial insecurity or did she make them feel secure in their family life?
2. Nels wanted to go to high school. How did he work out this problem with his family? What did this incident reveal about Papa? About Nels? Was he a selfish boy or a thoughtful one? Point out lines in Act I to support your answer.

3. Mama treated Katrin and Christine as individuals. How was this evident? What did the two girls' needs reveal about each of them? In what other ways did Mama reveal her understanding of children?

4. Aunt Trina sought Mama's advice about "something very personal." What was it? Why didn't Aunt Trina consult Sigrid or Jenny?

5. At first the aunts laughed at Trina, but Mama soon stopped that. In what way did Mama halt them? What did this incident tell you about Mama? About the two aunts?

6. Who was Mr. Hyde? What did he do for the family that "meant a great deal to Mama"? How did Katrin react to this?

7. According to Mama, Uncle Chris was the head of the family, yet the children were afraid of him. Why? In what ways did he show that he had the health of the children very much at heart?

8. Tell the story of Arne's trip to the hospital. Should Sigrid have been angry at this? Why or why not?

9. Uncle Chris told the children a "secret" that made them less afraid of him. What was the "secret"? Uncle Chris liked and admired Mama, but he quarreled with Sigrid and Jenny. Explain why you think this was so.

10. How did Mama manage to see Dagmar in the hospital in spite of the rules? What did this reveal about Mama's personality and knowledge of her children and their needs?

11. Tell how Uncle Chris changed Mr. Thorkelson's mind for him about the question of a dowry. Point out the humor in this scene.

12. Mama said of Uncle Chris, "Is fine man." Explain this in the light of his actions in Act I.

ACT II

1. What did Mama tell Katrin when they had a "special treat" at the drugstore? Why did Mama want to visit the "old country" again?

2. Mr. Hyde left suddenly, but not before giving Mama a note, his books, and a check for the rent. What did Mama learn about the check? Why did she say about Mr. Hyde: "He owed us nothing"?

3. What happened to Dagmar's Uncle Elizabeth? Why did Mama want Dagmar to know the truth? Do you agree or disagree with Papa's opinion? Why?

4. What important lesson did Katrin learn at graduation when she found out what Mama had done in order to get her the present she wanted so much? In what way did Papa show that he felt that Katrin had grown up? Why did Papa say, "Katrin is the dramatic one"?

5. Was Trina's marriage happy? How was this shown in Act II?
6. How did Mama persuade Miss Moorhead to read Katrin's stories and advise her about her writing? What was Miss Moorhead's advice to the young writer? Why wasn't Katrin sure it helped?
7. When Katrin received a check for her story, the truth came out about Mama's bank account. What was it? Do you feel that Mama had been wise to do what she did? Why or why not?
8. What did you learn about each member of the family as they discussed ways of spending the money Katrin had received?

On the play as a whole

1. The playwright uses the "flashback" technique as a framework for this play. Explain its use briefly. Look back at the opening scene to see how the flashback was done.
2. *I Remember Mama* consists of many episodes rather than any one fully-developed plot. For example, there are the incidents of Dagmar in the hospital, Mr. Hyde and his unpaid bill, and the death of Uncle Chris—to name only a few. Yet the play has unity. How, in your opinion, did Mr. Van Druten achieve this?
3. Character can be revealed through how a person acts and talks or through the reaction of other people. Using Uncle Chris as an example of this, show how his real character was revealed through the notebook found at his death.
4. List the different settings in *I Remember Mama*. Why was it necessary to have so many? Did these settings confuse you, or did the action move from one to another easily?
5. Mama is probably the most interesting character in the play. Who would you say was the next most interesting character? Give reasons to support your opinion.
6. Most good plays have character development. Choose one character and show how he or she developed during the course of the action.
7. Consider the children in the Hanson family. What characteristics did each child have that made him different from the others?
8. Although *I Remember Mama* is a quiet play, what conflict or struggle was going on? How did the playwright create suspense?
9. By rereading the dialogue spoken by Mama, find wise or significant comments that she made and list them. What do they show about her as a person?
10. In spite of difficulties, the Hanson family was happy. Why, in your opinion, was this so?

11. There is warm humor in this play. Find and discuss incidents or lines of dialogue that illustrate this. If possible, dramatize key scenes in class.

12. In your opinion is this play primarily one of plot, character, setting, or theme? Explain your answer.

For composition

1. In the play Papa says: "Christine is the stubborn one. . . . Nels is the kind one. . . . Katrin is the dramatic one." Using this approach, write a short character sketch of any one of the members of the Hanson family.

2. Employing the "flashback" technique used by Katrin, write a brief narrative of some experience from your own childhood.

3. Imagine you are the character in one of the following situations. Write an entry in your diary describing your thoughts and feelings about what is going on.

   (a) Dagmar in the hospital; (b) Nels at the beginning of the school year; (c) Katrin on her graduation night just before she goes on in the school play; (d) Papa's thoughts after Mr. Hyde has left; (e) Mama after visiting Florence Dana Moorhead; (f) Uncle Chris at the time of Arne's accident.

4. There is tasteful use of dialect in this play. Note how carefully and clearly the Norwegian way of speaking is used for effect. Write a paragraph of exposition, describing its use and effect.

5. Imagine that you are a drama critic for a large city newspaper. You have just attended the opening night of *I Remember Mama*. Write a review of the play, not exceeding three hundred words, for your newspaper. Remember that you do not wish to reveal the plot to your readers. Instead, you want to comment on the play and give your personal reaction to it.

Gore Vidal

Satire

Visit to a Small Planet

Visit to a Small Planet is a three-act television drama that combines science fiction and comedy with uproarious results. How must our civilization look to a more advanced civilization in outer space? What would happen if an inhabitant of another planet arrived on earth and wanted to "play war"?

We laugh at Kreton's strange powers and his attitude toward earth. We chuckle at Mr. Spelding's lack of understanding and the pompous authority of General Powers, who is absolutely helpless before his visitor from another planet. Yet while we laugh, we think and learn and are self-critical.

Three centuries ago, the French playwright Molière stated that the purpose of comedy is "to provoke thoughtful laughter." *Visit to a Small Planet* does just that through Gore Vidal's tongue-in-cheek dialogue, which is pointed, sophisticated, and revealing.

❧ ☙

VISIT TO A SMALL PLANET

CHARACTERS

KRETON
ROGER SPELDING
ELLEN SPELDING
MRS. SPELDING
JOHN RANDOLPH
GENERAL POWERS
AIDE
PAUL LAURENT
SECOND VISITOR
PRESIDENT OF PARAGUAY

ACT I

Stock Shot: The night sky, stars. Then slowly a luminous object arcs into view. As it is almost upon us, dissolve to the living room of the Spelding house in Maryland.

Superimpose card: "THE TIME: THE DAY AFTER TOMORROW"

The room is comfortably balanced between the expensively decorated and the homely. ROGER SPELDING *is concluding his TV broadcast. He is middle-aged, unctuous, resonant. His wife, bored and vague, knits passively while he talks at his desk. Two* TECHNICIANS *are on hand, operating the equipment. His daughter,* ELLEN, *a lively girl of twenty, fidgets as she listens.*

SPELDING (*into microphone*). . . . and so, according to General Powers . . . who should know if anyone does . . . the flying object which has given rise to so much irresponsible conjecture is nothing more than a meteor passing through the earth's orbit. It is not, as many believe, a secret weapon of this country. Nor is it a space ship as certain lunatic elements have suggested. General Powers has assured me that it is highly doubtful there is any form of life on other planets capable of building a space ship. "If any traveling is to be done in space, we will do it first." And those are his exact words. . . . Which winds up another week of news. (*Crosses to pose with wife and daughter.*) This is Roger Spelding, saying good night to Mother and Father America, from my old homestead in Silver Glen, Maryland, close to the warm pulse-beat of the nation.

TECHNICIAN. Good show tonight, Mr. Spelding.

SPELDING. Thank you.

TECHNICIAN. Yes sir, you were right on time.

144

(SPELDING *nods wearily, his mechanical smile and heartiness suddenly gone.*)

MRS. SPELDING. Very nice, dear. Very nice.

TECHNICIAN. See you next week, Mrs. Spelding.

SPELDING. Thank you, boys.

(TECHNICIANS *go.*)

SPELDING. Did you like the broadcast, Ellen?

ELLEN. Of course I did, Daddy.

SPELDING. Then what did I say?

ELLEN. Oh, that's not fair.

SPELDING. It's not very flattering when one's own daughter won't listen to what one says while millions of people . . .

ELLEN. I always listen, Daddy, you know that.

MRS. SPELDING. We love your broadcasts, dear. I don't know what we'd do without them.

SPELDING. Starve.

ELLEN. I wonder what's keeping John?

SPELDING. Certainly not work.

ELLEN. Oh, Daddy, stop it! John works very hard and you know it.

MRS. SPELDING. Yes, he's a perfectly nice boy, Roger. I like him.

SPELDING. I know. I know: he has every virtue except the most important one: he has no get-up-and-go.

ELLEN. (*precisely*). He doesn't want to get up and he doesn't want to go because he's already where he wants to be on his own farm which is exactly where I'*m* going to be when we're married.

SPELDING. More thankless than a serpent's tooth is an ungrateful child.

ELLEN. I don't think that's right. Isn't it "more deadly . . ."

SPELDING. Whatever the exact quotation is, I stand by the sentiment.

MRS. SPELDING. Please don't quarrel. It always gives me a headache.

SPELDING. I never quarrel. I merely reason, in my simple way, with Miss Know-it-all here.

ELLEN. Oh, Daddy! Next you'll tell me I should marry for money.

SPELDING. There is nothing wrong with marrying a wealthy man. The horror of it has always eluded me. However, my only wish is that you marry someone hard-working, ambitious, a man who'll make his mark in the world. Not a boy who plans to sit on a farm all his life, growing peanuts.

ELLEN. English walnuts.

SPELDING. Will you stop correcting me?

ELLEN. But, Daddy, John grows walnuts . . .

(JOHN *enters, breathlessly.*)

JOHN. Come out! Quickly. It's coming this way. It's going to land right here!

SPELDING. *What's* going to land?

JOHN. The space ship. Look!

SPELDING. Apparently you didn't hear my broadcast. The flying object in question is a meteor not a space ship.

(JOHN *has gone out with* ELLEN. SPELDING *and* MRS. SPELDING *follow.*)

MRS. SPELDING. Oh, my! Look! Something *is* falling! Roger, you don't think it's going to hit the house, do you?

SPELDING. The odds against being hit by a falling object that size are, I should say, roughly, ten million to one.

JOHN. Ten million to one or not it's going to land right here and it's *not* falling.

SPELDING. I'm sure it's a meteor.

MRS. SPELDING. Shouldn't we go down to the cellar?

SPELDING. If it's not a meteor, it's an optical illusion . . . mass hysteria.

ELLEN. Daddy, it's a real space ship. I'm sure it is.

SPELDING. Or maybe a weather balloon. Yes, that's what it is. General Powers said only yesterday . . .

JOHN. It's landing!

SPELDING. I'm going to call the police . . . the army!

(*Bolts inside.*)

ELLEN. Oh look how it shines!

JOHN. Here it comes!

MRS. SPELDING. Right in my rose garden!

ELLEN. Maybe it's a balloon.

JOHN. No, it's a space ship and right in your own backyard.

ELLEN. What makes it shine so?

JOHN. I don't know but I'm going to find out.

(*Runs off toward the light.*)

ELLEN. Oh, darling, don't! John, please! John, John come back!

(SPELDING, *wide-eyed, returns.*)

MRS. SPELDING. Roger, it's landed right in my rose garden.

SPELDING. I got General Powers. He's coming over. He said they've been watching this thing. They . . . they don't know what it is.

ELLEN. You mean it's nothing of ours?

SPELDING. They believe it . . . (*Swallows hard.*) . . . it's from outer space.

ELLEN. And John's down there! Daddy, get a gun or something.

SPELDING. Perhaps we'd better leave the house until the army gets here.

ELLEN. We can't leave John.

SPELDING. I can. (*Peers nearsightedly.*) Why, it's not much larger than a car. I'm sure it's some kind of meteor.

ELLEN. Meteors are blazing hot.

SPELDING. This is a cold one . . .

ELLEN. It's opening . . . the whole side's opening! (*Shouts.*) John! Come back! Quick. . . .

MRS. SPELDING. Why, there's a man getting out of it! (*Sighs.*) I feel much better already. I'm sure if we ask him, he'll move that thing for us. Roger, you ask him.

SPELDING (*ominously*). If it's really a man?

ELLEN. John's shaking hands with him. (*Calls.*) John darling, come on up here . . .

MRS. SPELDING. And bring your friend . . .

SPELDING. There's something wrong with the way that creature looks . . . If it is a man and not a . . . not a monster.

MRS. SPELDING. He looks perfectly nice to me.

(JOHN *and the* VISITOR *appear. The* VISITOR *is in his forties, a mild, pleasant-looking man with side-whiskers and dressed in the*

fashion of 1860. He pauses when he sees the three people, in
silence for a moment. They stare back at him, equally interested.)

VISITOR. I seem to've made a mistake. I *am* sorry. I'd better go back
and start over again.
SPELDING. My dear sir, you've only just arrived. Come in, come in.
I don't need to tell you what a pleasure this is . . . Mister . . .
Mister . . .
VISITOR. Kreton . . . This *is* the wrong costume, isn't it?
SPELDING. Wrong for what?
KRETON. For the country, and the time.
SPELDING. Well, it's a trifle old-fashioned.
MRS. SPELDING. But really awfully handsome.
KRETON. Thank you.
MRS. SPELDING (*to husband*). Ask him about moving that thing off
my rose bed.

(SPELDING *leads them all into living room.*)

SPELDING. Come on in and sit down. You must be tired after your
trip.
KRETON. Yes, I am a little. (*Looks around delightedly.*) Oh, it's better
than I'd hoped!
SPELDING. Better? What's better?
KRETON. The house . . . that's what you call it? Or is this an apartment?
SPELDING. This is a house in the State of Maryland, U.S.A.
KRETON. In the late 20th century! To think this is really the 20th
century. I must sit down a moment and collect myself. The *real*
thing!

(*He sits down.*)

ELLEN. You . . . you're not an American, are you?
KRETON. What a nice thought! No, I'm not.
JOHN. You sound more English.
KRETON. Do I? Is my accent very bad?
JOHN. No, it's quite good.
SPELDING. Where *are* you from, Mr. Kreton?
KRETON (*evasively*). Another place.

SPELDING. On this earth of course.

KRETON. No, not on this planet.

ELLEN. Are you from Mars?

KRETON. Oh dear no, not Mars. There's nobody on Mars . . . at least no one I know.

ELLEN. I'm sure you're teasing us and this is all some kind of publicity stunt.

KRETON. No, I really am from another place.

SPELDING. I don't suppose you'd consent to my interviewing you on television?

KRETON. I don't think your authorities will like that. They are terribly upset as it is.

SPELDING. How do you know?

KRETON. Well, I . . . pick up things. For instance, I know that in a few minutes a number of people from your Army will be here to question me and they . . . like you . . . are torn by doubt.

SPELDING. How extraordinary!

ELLEN. Why did you come here?

KRETON. Simply a visit to your small planet. I've been studying it for years. In fact, one might say, you people are my hobby. Especially, this period of your development.

JOHN. Are you the first person from your . . . your planet to travel in space like this?

KRETON. Oh my no! Everyone travels who wants to. It's just that no one wants to visit you. I can't think why. *I* always have. You'd be surprised what a thorough study I've made. (*Recites.*) The planet, Earth, is divided into five continents with a number of large islands. It is mostly water. There is one moon. Civilization is only just beginning. . . .

SPELDING. Just beginning! My dear sir, we have had. . . .

KRETON (*blandly*). You are only in the initial stages, the most fascinating stages as far as I'm concerned . . . I do hope I don't sound patronizing.

ELLEN. Well, we are very proud.

KRETON. I know and that's one of your most endearing, primitive traits. Oh, I can't believe I'm here at last!

(GENERAL POWERS, *a vigorous product of the National Guard, and his* AIDE *enter.*)

POWERS. All right folks. The place is surrounded by troops. Where is the monster?

KRETON. I, my dear General, am the monster.

POWERS. What are you dressed up for, a fancy-dress party?

KRETON. I'd hoped to be in the costume of the period. As you see I am about a hundred years too late.

POWERS. Roger, who is this joker?

SPELDING. This is Mr. Kreton . . . General Powers. Mr. Kreton arrived in that thing outside. He is from another planet.

POWERS. I don't believe it.

ELLEN. It's true. We saw him get out of the flying saucer.

POWERS (*to* AIDE). Captain, go down and look at that ship. But be careful. Don't touch anything. And don't let anybody else near it. (AIDE *goes*.) So you're from another planet.

KRETON. Yes. My, that's a very smart uniform but I prefer the ones made of metal, the ones you used to wear, you know: with the feathers on top.

POWERS. That was five hundred years ago . . . Are you *sure* you're not from the Earth?

KRETON. Yes.

POWERS. Well, I'm not. You've got some pretty tall explaining to do.

KRETON. Anything to oblige.

POWERS. All right, which planet?

KRETON. None that you have ever heard of.

POWERS. Where is it?

KRETON. You wouldn't know.

POWERS. This solar system?

KRETON. No.

POWERS. Another system?

KRETON. Yes.

POWERS. Look, Buster, I don't want to play games: I just want to know where you're from. The law requires it.

KRETON. It's possible that I could explain it to a mathematician but I'm afraid I couldn't explain it to you, not for another five hundred years and by then of course *you'd* be dead because you people do die, don't you?

POWERS. What?

KRETON. Poor fragile butterflies, such brief little moments in the sun. . . . You see *we* don't die.

POWERS. You'll die all right if it turns out you're a spy or a hostile alien.

KRETON. I'm sure you wouldn't be so cruel.

(AIDE *returns; he looks disturbed.*)

POWERS. What did you find?

AIDE. I'm not sure, General.

POWERS (*heavily*). Then do your best to describe what the object is like.

AIDE. Well, it's elliptical, with a fourteen foot diameter. And it's made of an unknown metal which shines and inside there isn't anything.

POWERS. Isn't anything?

AIDE. There's nothing inside the ship: No instruments, no food, nothing.

POWERS (*to* KRETON). What did you do with your instrument board?

KRETON. With my what? Oh, I don't have one.

POWERS. How does the thing travel?

KRETON. I don't know.

POWERS. You don't know. Now look, Mister, you're in pretty serious trouble. I suggest you do a bit of coöperating. You claim you traveled here from outer space in a machine with no instruments . . .

KRETON. Well, these cars are rather common in my world and I suppose, once upon a time, I must've known the theory on which they operate but I've long since forgotten. After all, General, we're not mechanics, you and I.

POWERS. Roger, do you mind if we use your study?

SPELDING. Not at all. Not at all, General.

POWERS. Mr. Kreton and I are going to have a chat. (*To* AIDE.) Put in a call to the Chief of Staff.

AIDE. Yes, General.

(SPELDING *rises, leads* KRETON *and* POWERS *into next room, a handsomely furnished study, many books and a globe of the world.*)

SPELDING. This way, gentlemen. (KRETON *sits down comfortably beside the globe which he twirls thoughtfully. At the door,* SPELDING *speaks in a low voice to* POWERS.) I hope I'll be the one to get the story first, Tom.

POWERS. There isn't any story. Complete censorship. I'm sorry but this house is under martial law. I've a hunch we're in trouble. (*He shuts the door.* SPELDING *turns and rejoins his family.*)

ELLEN. I think he's wonderful, whoever he is.

MRS. SPELDING. I wonder how much damage he did to my rose garden . . .

JOHN. It's sure hard to believe he's really from outer space. No instruments, no nothing . . . boy, they must be advanced scientifically.

MRS. SPELDING. Is he spending the night, dear?

SPELDING. What?

MRS. SPELDING. Is he spending the night?

SPELDING. Oh yes, yes. I suppose he will be.

MRS. SPELDING. Then I'd better go make up the bedroom. He seems perfectly nice to me. I like his whiskers. They're so very . . . comforting. Like Grandfather Spelding's.

(*She goes.*)

SPELDING (*bitterly*). I *know* this story will leak out before I can interview him. I just know it.

ELLEN. What does it mean, we're under martial law?

SPELDING. It means we have to do what General Powers tells us to do. (*He goes to the window as a soldier passes by.*) See?

JOHN. I wish I'd taken a closer look at that ship when I had the chance.

ELLEN. Perhaps he'll give us a ride in it.

JOHN. Traveling in space! Just like those stories. You know: intergalactic drive stuff.

SPELDING. *If* he's not an impostor.

ELLEN. I have a feeling he isn't.

JOHN. Well, I better call the family and tell them I'm all right. (*He crosses to telephone by the door which leads into hall.*)

AIDE. I'm sorry, sir, but you can't use the phone.

SPELDING. He certainly can. This is my house . . .

AIDE (*mechanically*). This house is a military reservation until the crisis is over: Order General Powers. I'm sorry.

JOHN. How am I to call home to say where I am?

AIDE. Only General Powers can help you. You're also forbidden to leave this house without permission.

SPELDING. You can't do this!

AIDE. I'm afraid, sir, we've done it.

ELLEN. Isn't it exciting!

(*Cut to study.*)

POWERS. Are you deliberately trying to confuse me?

KRETON. Not deliberately, no.

POWERS. We have gone over and over this for two hours now and all that you've told me is that you're from another planet in another solar system . . .

KRETON. In another dimension. I think that's the word you use.

POWERS. In another dimension and you have come here as a tourist.

KRETON. Up to a point, yes. What did you expect?

POWERS. It is my job to guard the security of this country.

KRETON. I'm sure that must be very interesting work.

POWERS. For all I know, you are a spy, sent here by an alien race to study us, preparatory to invasion.

KRETON. Oh, none of my people would *dream* of invading you.

POWERS. How do I know that's true?

KRETON. You don't, so I suggest you believe me. I should also warn you: I can tell what's inside.

POWERS. What's inside?

KRETON. What's inside your mind.

POWERS. You're a mind reader?

KRETON. I don't really read it. I hear it.

POWERS. What am I thinking?

KRETON. That I am either a lunatic from the earth or a spy from another world.

POWERS. Correct. But then you could've guessed that. (*Frowns.*) What am I thinking now?

KRETON. You're making a picture. Three silver stars. You're pinning them on your shoulder, instead of the two stars you now wear.

POWERS (*startled*). That's right. I was thinking of my promotion.

KRETON. If there's anything I can do to hurry it along, just let me know.

POWERS. You can. Tell me why you're here.

KRETON. Well, we don't travel much, my people. We used to but since we see everything through special monitors and recreators, there is no particular need to travel. However, I am a hobbyist. I love to gad about.

POWERS (*taking notes*). Are you the first to visit us?

KRETON. Oh, no! We started visiting you long before there were people on the planet. However, we are seldom noticed on our trips. I'm sorry to say I slipped up, coming in the way I did . . . but then this visit was all rather impromptu. (*Laughs.*) I am a creature of impulse, I fear.

(AIDE *looks in.*)

AIDE. Chief of Staff on the telephone, General.

POWERS (*picks up phone*). Hello, yes, sir. Powers speaking. I'm talking to him now. No, sir. No, sir. No, we can't determine what method of power was used. He won't talk. Yes, sir. I'll hold him here. I've put the house under martial law . . . belongs to a friend of mine, Roger Spelding, the TV commentator. Roger Spelding, the TV . . . What? Oh, no, I am sure he won't say anything. Who . . . oh, yes, sir. Yes, I realize the importance of it. Yes, I will. Good-by. (*Hangs up.*) The President of the United States wants to know all about you.

KRETON. How nice of him! And I want to know all about him. But I do wish you'd let me rest a bit first. Your language is still not familiar to me. I had to learn them all, quite exhausting.

POWERS. You speak *all* our languages?

KRETON. Yes, all of them. But then it's easier than you might think since I can see what's inside.

POWERS. Speaking of what's inside, we're going to take your ship apart.

KRETON. Oh, I wish you wouldn't.

POWERS. Security demands it.

KRETON. In that case *my* security demands you leave it alone.

POWERS. You plan to stop us?

KRETON. I already have . . . Listen.

(*Far-off shouting.* AIDE *rushes into the study.*)

AIDE. Something's happened to the ship, General. The door's shut and there's some kind of wall all around it, an invisible wall. We can't get near it.

KRETON (*to camera*). I hope there was no one inside.

POWERS (*to* KRETON). How did you do that?

KRETON. I couldn't begin to explain. Now if you don't mind, I think we should go in and see our hosts.

(*He rises, goes into living room.* POWERS *and* AIDE *look at each other.*)

POWERS. Don't let him out of your sight.

(*Cut to living room as* POWERS *picks up phone.* KRETON *is with* JOHN *and* ELLEN.)

KRETON. I don't mind curiosity but I really can't permit them to wreck my poor ship.

ELLEN. What do you plan to do, now you're here?

KRETON. Oh, keep busy. I have a project or two . . . (*Sighs.*) I can't believe you're real!

JOHN. Then we're all in the same boat.

KRETON. Boat? Oh, yes! Well, I should have come ages ago but I . . . I couldn't get away until yesterday.

JOHN. Yesterday? It only took you a *day* to get here?

KRETON. One of *my* days, not yours. But then you don't know about time yet.

JOHN. Oh, you mean relativity.

KRETON. No, it's much more involved than that. You won't know about time until . . . now let me see if I remember . . . no, I don't, but it's about two thousand years.

JOHN. What do we do between now and then?

KRETON. You simply go on the way you are, living your exciting primitive lives . . . you have no idea how much fun you're having now.

ELLEN. I hope you'll stay with us while you're here.

KRETON. That's very nice of you. Perhaps I will. Though I'm sure you'll get tired of having a visitor under foot all the time.

ELLEN. Certainly not. And Daddy will be deliriously happy. He can interview you by the hour.

JOHN. What's it like in outer space?

KRETON. Dull.

ELLEN. I should think it would be divine!

(POWERS *enters.*)

KRETON. No, General, it won't work.

POWERS. What won't work?

KRETON. Trying to blow up my little force field. You'll just plough up Mrs. Spelding's garden.

(POWERS *snarls and goes into study.*)

ELLEN. Can you tell what we're *all* thinking?

KRETON. Yes. As a matter of fact, it makes me a bit giddy. Your minds are not at all like ours. You see we control our thoughts while you . . . well, it's extraordinary the things you think about!

ELLEN. Oh, how awful! You can tell *everything* we think?

KRETON. Everything! It's one of the reasons I'm here, to intoxicate myself with your primitive minds . . . with the wonderful rawness of your emotions! You have no idea how it excites me! You simply seethe with unlikely emotions.

ELLEN. I've never felt so sordid.

JOHN. From now on I'm going to think about agriculture.

SPELDING (*entering*). You would.

ELLEN. Daddy!

KRETON. No, no. You must go right on thinking about Ellen. Such wonderfully *purple* thoughts!

SPELDING. Now see here, Powers, you're carrying this martial law thing too far . . .

POWERS. Unfortunately, until I have received word from Washington as to the final disposition of this problem, you must obey my orders: no telephone calls, no communication with the outside.

SPELDING. This is unsupportable.

KRETON. Poor Mr. Spelding! If you like, I shall go. That would solve everything, wouldn't it?

POWERS. You're not going anywhere, Mr. Kreton, until I've had my instructions.

KRETON. I sincerely doubt if you could stop me. However, I put it up to Mr. Spelding. Shall I go?

SPELDING. Yes! (POWERS *gestures a warning.*) Do stay, I mean, we want you to get a good impression of us . . .

KRETON. And of course you still want to be the first journalist to interview me. Fair enough. All right, I'll stay on for a while.

POWERS. Thank you.

KRETON. Don't mention it.

SPELDING. General, may I ask our guest a few questions?

POWERS. Go right ahead, Roger. I hope you'll do better than I did.

SPELDING. Since you read our minds, you probably already know what our fears are.

KRETON. I do, yes.

SPELDING. We are afraid that you represent a hostile race.

KRETON. And I have assured General Powers that my people are not remotely hostile. Except for me, no one is interested in this planet's present stage.

SPELDING. Does this mean you might be interested in a *later* stage?

KRETON. I'm not permitted to discuss your future. Of course my friends think me perverse to be interested in a primitive society but there's no accounting for tastes, is there? You are my hobby. I love you. And that's all there is to it.

POWERS. So you're just here to look around . . . sort of going native.

KRETON. What a nice expression! That's it exactly. I am going native.

POWERS (*grimly*). Well, it is my view that you have been sent here by another civilization for the express purpose of reconnoitering prior to invasion.

KRETON. That *would* be your view! The wonderfully primitive assumption that all strangers are hostile. You're almost too good to be true, General.

POWERS. You deny your people intend to make trouble for us?

KRETON. I deny it.

POWERS. Then are they interested in establishing communication with us? trade? that kind of thing?

KRETON. We have always had communication with you. As for trade, well, we do not trade . . . that is something peculiar only to your social level. (*Quickly.*) Which I'm not criticizing! As you know, I approve of everything you do.

POWERS. I give up.

SPELDING. You have no interest then in . . . well, trying to dominate the earth.

KRETON. Oh, yes!

POWERS. I thought you just said your people weren't interested in us.

KRETON. *They*'re not, but *I* am.

POWERS. You!

KRETON. Me . . . I mean I. You see I've come here to take charge.

POWERS. Of the United States?

KRETON. No, of the whole world. I'm sure you'll be much happier and it will be great fun for me. You'll get used to it in no time.

POWERS. This is ridiculous. How can one man take over the world?

KRETON (*gaily*). Wait and see!

POWERS (*to* AIDE). Grab him!

(POWERS *and* AIDE *rush* KRETON *but within a foot of him, they stop, stunned.*)

KRETON. You can't touch me. That's part of the game. (*He yawns.*) Now, if you don't mind, I shall go up to my room for a little lie-down.

SPELDING. I'll show you the way.

KRETON. That's all right. I know the way. (*Touches his brow.*) Such savage thoughts! My head is vibrating like a drum. I feel quite giddy, all of you thinking away. (*He starts to the door; he pauses beside* MRS. SPELDING.) No, it's not a dream, dear lady. I shall be here in the morning when you wake up. And now, good night, dear, wicked children. . . .

(*He goes as we fade out.*)

ACT II

Fade in on KRETON's *bedroom next morning. He lies fully clothed on bed with cat on his lap.*

KRETON. Poor cat! Of course I sympathize with you. Dogs *are* distasteful. What? Oh, I can well believe they do: yes, yes, how disgusting. They don't ever groom their fur! But you do *constantly*, such a fine coat. No, no, I'm not just saying that. I really mean it: exquisite texture. Of course, I wouldn't say it was *nicer* than skin but even so. . . . What? Oh, no! They *chase* you! Dogs chase you for no reason at all except pure malice? You poor creature. Ah, but you *do* fight back! That's right! give it to them: slash, bite, scratch! Don't let them get away with a trick. . . . No! Do dogs really do that? Well, I'm sure *you* don't. What . . . oh, well, yes I completely agree about mice. They *are* delicious! (Ugh!) Pounce, snap and there is a heavenly dinner. No, I don't know any mice yet . . . they're not very amusing? But after all think how you must terrify them because you are so bold, so cunning, so beautifully predatory! (*Knock at door.*) Come in.

ELLEN (*enters*). Good morning. I brought you your breakfast.

KRETON. How thoughtful! (*Examines bacon.*) Delicious, but I'm afraid my stomach is not like yours, if you'll pardon me. I don't eat. (*Removes pill from his pocket and swallows it.*) This is all I need for the day. (*Indicates cat.*) Unlike this creature, who would eat her own weight every hour, given a chance.

ELLEN. How do you know?

KRETON. We've had a talk.

ELLEN. You can *speak* to the cat?

KRETON. Not speak exactly but we communicate. I look inside and the cat coöperates. Bright red thoughts, very exciting, though rather on one level.

ELLEN. Does kitty like us?

KRETON. No, I wouldn't say she did. But then she has very few

159

thoughts not connected with food. Have you, my quadruped criminal? (*He strokes the cat, which jumps to the floor.*)

ELLEN. You know you've really upset everyone.

KRETON. I supposed that I would.

ELLEN. Can you really take over the world, just like that?

KRETON. Oh, yes.

ELLEN. What do you plan to do when you *have* taken over?

KRETON. Ah, that is my secret.

ELLEN. Well, I think you'll be a very nice President, *if* they let you of course.

KRETON. What a sweet girl you are! Marry him right away.

ELLEN. Marry John?

KRETON. Yes. I see it in your head *and* in his. He wants you very much.

ELLEN. Well, we plan to get married this summer, if father doesn't fuss too much.

KRETON. Do it before then. I shall arrange it all if you like.

ELLEN. How?

KRETON. I can convince your father.

ELLEN. That sounds awfully ominous. I think you'd better leave poor Daddy alone.

KRETON. Whatever you say. (*Sighs.*) Oh, I love it so! When I woke up this morning I had to pinch myself to prove I was really here.

ELLEN. We were all doing a bit of pinching too. Ever since dawn we've had nothing but visitors and phone calls and troops outside in the garden. No one has the faintest idea what to do about you.

KRETON. Well, I don't think they'll be confused much longer.

ELLEN. How do you plan to conquer the world?

KRETON. I confess I'm not sure. I suppose I must make some demonstration of strength, some colorful trick that will frighten everyone . . . though I much prefer taking charge quietly. That's why I've sent for the President.

ELLEN. The President? *Our* President?

KRETON. Yes, he'll be along any minute now.

ELLEN. But the President just doesn't go around visiting people.

KRETON. He'll visit me. (*Chuckles.*) It may come as a surprise to him, but he'll be in this house in a very few minutes. I think we'd better go downstairs now. (*To cat.*) No, I will not give you a mouse. You must get your own. Be self-reliant. Beast!

(*Dissolve to the study.* POWERS *is reading book entitled: "The Atom and You." Muffled explosions off-stage.*)

AIDE (*entering*). Sir, nothing seems to be working. Do we have the General's permission to try a fission bomb on the force field?

POWERS. No . . . no. We'd better give it up.

AIDE. The men are beginning to talk.

POWERS (*thundering*). Well, keep them quiet! (*Contritely.*) I'm sorry, Captain. I'm on edge. Fortunately, the whole business will soon be in the hands of the World Council.

AIDE. What will the World Council do?

POWERS. It will be interesting to observe them.

AIDE. You don't think this Kreton can really take over the world, do you?

POWERS. Of course not. Nobody can.

(*Dissolve to living room.* MRS. SPELDING *and* SPELDING *are talking.*)

MRS. SPELDING. You still haven't asked Mr. Kreton about moving that thing, have you?

SPELDING. There are too many *important* things to ask him.

MRS. SPELDING. I hate to be a nag but you know the trouble I have had getting anything to grow in that part of the garden . . .

JOHN (*enters*). Good morning.

MRS. SPELDING. Good morning, John.

JOHN. Any sign of your guest?

MRS. SPELDING. Ellen took his breakfast up to him a few minutes ago.

JOHN. They don't seem to be having much luck, do they? I sure hope you don't mind my staying here like this.

(SPELDING *glowers.*)

MRS. SPELDING. Why, we love having you! I just hope your family aren't too anxious.

JOHN. One of the G.I.'s finally called them, said I was staying here for the week-end.

SPELDING. The rest of our *lives*, if something isn't done soon.

JOHN. Just how long do you think that'll be, Dad?

SPELDING. Who knows?

(KRETON *and* ELLEN *enter.*)

KRETON. Ah, how wonderful to see you again! Let me catch my breath. . . . Oh, your minds! It's not easy for me, you know. So many crude thoughts blazing away! Yes, Mrs. Spelding, I will move the ship off your roses.

MRS. SPELDING. That's awfully sweet of you.

KRETON. Mr. Spelding, if any interviews are to be granted you will be the first. I promise you.

SPELDING. That's very considerate, I'm sure.

KRETON. So you can stop thinking *those* particular thoughts. And now where is the President?

SPELDING. The President?

KRETON. Yes, I sent for him. He should be here. (*He goes to the terrace window.*) Ah, that must be he. (*A swarthy man in uniform with a sash across his chest is standing, bewildered, on the terrace.* KRETON *opens the glass door.*) Come in, sir, come in, Your Excellency. Good of you to come on such short notice. (MAN *enters.*)

MAN (*in Spanish accent*). Where am I?

KRETON. You *are* the President, aren't you?

MAN. Of course I am the President. What am I doing here? I was dedicating a bridge and I find myself . . .

KRETON (*aware of his mistake*). Oh, dear! *Where* was the bridge?

MAN. Where do you think, you idiot, in Paraguay!

KRETON (*to others*). I seem to've made a mistake. Wrong President. (*Gestures and the man disappears.*) Seemed rather upset, didn't he?

JOHN. You can make people come and go just like that?

KRETON. Just like that.

(POWERS *looks into room from the study.*)

POWERS. Good morning, Mr. Kreton. Could I see you for a moment?

KRETON. By all means.

(*He crosses to the study.*)

SPELDING. I believe I am going mad.

(*Cut to study. The* AIDE *stands at attention while* POWERS *addresses* KRETON.)

POWERS. . . . and so we feel, the government of the United States feels, that this problem is too big for any one country, therefore we are turning the whole affair over to Paul Laurent, the Secretary-General of the World Council.

KRETON. Very sensible. I should've thought of that myself.

POWERS. Mr. Laurent is on his way here now. And I may add, Mr. Kreton, you've made me look singularly ridiculous.

KRETON. I'm awfully sorry. (*Pause.*) No, you can't kill me.

POWERS. You were reading my mind again.

KRETON. I can't really help it, you know. And such *black* thoughts today, but intense, very intense.

POWERS. I regard you as a menace.

KRETON. I know you do and I think it's awfully unkind. I do mean well.

POWERS. Then go back where you came from and leave us alone.

KRETON. I'm afraid I can't do that just yet . . .

(*Phone rings; the* AIDE *answers it.*)

AIDE. He's outside? Sure, let him through. (*To* POWERS.) The Secretary-General of the World Council is here, sir.

POWERS (*to* KRETON). I hope you'll listen to *him*.

KRETON. Oh, I shall, of course. I love listening.

(*The door opens and* PAUL LAURENT, *middle-aged and serene, enters.* POWERS *and his* AIDE *stand to attention.* KRETON *goes forward to shake hands.*)

LAURENT. Mr. Kreton?

KRETON. At your service, Mr. Laurent.

LAURENT. I welcome you to this planet in the name of the World Council.

KRETON. Thank you sir, thank you.

LAURENT. Could you leave us alone for a moment, General?

POWERS. Yes, sir.

(POWERS *and* AIDE *go.* LAURENT *smiles at* KRETON.)

LAURENT. Shall we sit down?

KRETON. Yes, yes I love sitting down. I'm afraid my manners are not quite suitable, yet.

(*They sit down.*)

LAURENT. Now, Mr. Kreton, in violation of all the rules of diplomacy, may I come to the point?

KRETON. You may.

LAURENT. Why are you here?

KRETON. Curiosity. Pleasure.

LAURENT. You are a tourist then in this time and place?

KRETON (*nods*). Yes. Very well put.

LAURENT. We have been informed that you have extraordinary powers.

KRETON. By your standards, yes, they must seem extraordinary.

LAURENT. We have also been informed that it is your intention to . . . to take charge of this world.

KRETON. That is correct. . . . What a remarkable mind you have! I have difficulty looking inside it.

LAURENT (*laughs*). Practice. I've attended so many conferences. . . . May I say that your conquest of our world puts your status of tourist in a rather curious light?

KRETON. Oh, I said nothing about *conquest.*

LAURENT. Then how else do you intend to govern? The people won't allow you to direct their lives without a struggle.

KRETON. But I'm sure they will if I ask them to.

LAURENT. You believe you can do all this without, well, without violence?

KRETON. Of course I can. One or two demonstrations and I'm sure they'll do as I ask. (*Smiles.*) Watch this. (*Pause: then shouting.* POWERS *bursts into room.*)

POWERS. Now what've you done?

KRETON. Look out the window, your Excellency. (LAURENT *goes to window. A rifle floats by, followed by an alarmed soldier.*) Nice, isn't it? I confess I worked out a number of rather melodramatic tricks last night. Incidentally, all the rifles of all the soldiers in all the world are now floating in the air. (*Gestures.*) Now they have them back.

POWERS (*to* LAURENT). You see, sir, I didn't exaggerate in my report.

LAURENT (*awed*). No, no, you certainly didn't.

KRETON. You were skeptical, weren't you?

LAURENT. Naturally. But now I . . . now I think it's possible.

POWERS. That this . . . this gentleman is going to run everything?

LAURENT. Yes, yes I do. And it might be wonderful.

KRETON. You *are* more clever than the others. You begin to see that I mean only good.

LAURENT. Yes, only good. General, do you realize what this means? We can have one government . . .

KRETON. With innumerable bureaus, and intrigue. . . .

LAURENT (*excited*). And the world could be incredibly prosperous, especially if he'd help us with his superior knowledge.

KRETON (*delighted*). I will, I will. I'll teach you to look into one another's minds. You'll find it devastating but enlightening: all that self-interest, those *lurid* emotions . . .

LAURENT. No more countries. No more wars . . .

KRETON (*startled*). What? Oh, but I like a lot of countries. Besides, at this stage of your development you're supposed to have lots of countries and lots of wars . . . innumerable wars . . .

LAURENT. But you can help us change all that.

KRETON. *Change* all that! My dear sir, I am your friend.

LAURENT. What do you mean?

KRETON. Why, your deepest pleasure is violence. How can you deny that? It is the whole point to you, the whole point to my hobby . . . and you are my hobby, all mine.

LAURENT. But our lives are devoted to *controlling* violence, and not creating it.

KRETON. Now, don't take me for an utter fool. After all, I can see into your minds. My dear fellow, don't you *know* what you are?

LAURENT. What are we?

KRETON. You are savages. I have returned to the dark ages of an insignificant planet simply because I want the glorious excitement of being among you and revelling in your savagery! There is murder in all your hearts and I love it! It intoxicates me!

LAURENT (*slowly*). You hardly flatter us.

KRETON. I didn't mean to be rude but you did ask me why I am here and I've told you.

LAURENT. You have no wish then to . . . to help us poor savages.

KRETON. I couldn't even if I wanted to. You won't be civilized for at least two thousand years and you won't reach the level of my people for about a million years.

LAURENT (*sadly*). Then you have come here only to . . . to observe?

KRETON. No, more than that. I mean to regulate your past times. But don't worry: I won't upset things too much. I've decided I don't want to be known to the people. You will go right on with your countries, your squabbles, the way you always have, while I will *secretly* regulate things through you.

LAURENT. The World Council does not govern. We only advise.

KRETON. Well, I shall advise you and you will advise the governments and we shall have a lovely time.

LAURENT. I don't know what to say. You obviously have the power to do as you please.

KRETON. I'm glad you realize that. Poor General Powers is now wondering if a hydrogen bomb might destroy me. It won't, General.

POWERS. Too bad.

KRETON. Now, your Excellency, I shall stay in this house until you have laid the groundwork for my first project.

LAURENT. And what is that to be?

KRETON. A war! I want one of your really splendid wars, with all the trimmings, all the noise and the fire . . .

LAURENT. A war! You're joking. Why at this moment we are working as hard as we know how *not* to have a war.

KRETON. But secretly you want one. After all, it's the one thing your little race does well. You'd hardly want me to deprive you of your simple pleasures, now would you?

LAURENT. I think you must be mad.

KRETON. Not mad, simply a philanthropist. Of course I myself shall get a great deal of pleasure out of a war (the vibrations must be incredible!) but I'm doing it mostly for you. So, if you don't mind, I want you to arrange a few incidents, so we can get one started spontaneously.

LAURENT. I refuse.

KRETON. In that event, I shall select someone else to head the World Council. Someone who *will* start a war. I suppose there exist a few people here who might like the idea.

LAURENT. How can you do such a horrible thing to us? Can't you see that we don't want to be savages?

KRETON. But you have no choice. Anyway, you're just pulling my leg! I'm sure you want a war as much as the rest of them do and that's what you're going to get: the biggest war you've ever had!

LAURENT (*stunned*). Heaven help us!

KRETON (*exuberant*). Heaven won't! Oh, what fun it will be! I can hardly wait! (*He strikes the globe of the world a happy blow as we fade out.*)

ACT III

Fade in on the study, two weeks later. KRETON *is sitting at desk on which a map is spread out. He has a pair of dividers, some models of jet aircraft. Occasionally he pretends to dive bomb, imitating the sound of a bomb going off.* POWERS *enters.*

POWERS. You wanted me, sir?

KRETON. Yes, I wanted those figures on radioactive fall-out.

POWERS. They're being made up now, sir. Anything else?

KRETON. Oh, my dear fellow, why do you dislike me so?

POWERS. I am your military aide, sir: I don't have to answer that question. It is outside the sphere of my duties.

KRETON. Aren't you at least happy about your promotion?

POWERS. Under the circumstances, no, sir.

KRETON. I find your attitude baffling.

POWERS. Is that all, sir?

KRETON. You have never once said what you thought of my war plans. Not once have I got a single word of encouragement from you, a single compliment . . . only black thoughts.

POWERS. Since you read my mind, sir, you know what I think.

KRETON. True, but I can't help but feel that deep down inside of you there is just a twinge of professional jealousy. You don't like the idea of an outsider playing your game better than you do. Now confess!

POWERS. I am acting as your aide only under duress.

KRETON (*sadly*). Bitter, bitter . . . and to think I chose you especially as my aide. Think of all the other generals who would give anything to have your job.

POWERS. Fortunately, they know nothing about my job.

KRETON. Yes, I do think it wise not to advertise my presence, don't you?

POWERS. I can't see that it makes much difference, since you seem bent on destroying our world.

KRETON. I'm not going to destroy it. A few dozen cities, that's all, and not very nice cities either. Think of the fun you'll have building new ones when it's over.

POWERS. How many millions of people do you plan to kill?

KRETON. Well, quite a few, but they love this sort of thing. You can't convince me they don't. Oh, I know what Laurent says. But he's a misfit, out of step with his time. Fortunately, my new World Council is more reasonable.

POWERS. Paralyzed is the word, sir.

KRETON. You don't think they like me either?

POWERS. You *know* they hate you, sir.

KRETON. But love and hate are so confused in your savage minds and the vibrations of the one are so very like those of the other that I can't always distinguish. You see, we neither love nor hate in my world. We simply have hobbies. (*He strokes the globe of the world tenderly.*) But now to work. Tonight's the big night: first, the sneak attack, then: boom! (*He claps his hands gleefully.*)

(*Dissolve to the living room, to* JOHN *and* ELLEN.)

ELLEN. I've never felt so helpless in my life.

JOHN. Here we all stand around doing nothing while he plans to blow up the world.

ELLEN. Suppose we went to the newspapers.

JOHN. He controls the press. When Laurent resigned they didn't even print his speech. (*A gloomy pause.*)

ELLEN. What are you thinking about, John?

JOHN. Walnuts. (*They embrace.*)

ELLEN. Can't we do anything?

JOHN. No, I guess there's nothing.

ELLEN (*vehemently*). Oh! I could kill him!

(KRETON *and* POWERS *enter.*)

KRETON. Very good, Ellen, *very* good! I've never felt you so violent.

ELLEN. You heard what I said to John?

KRETON. Not in words, but you were absolutely bathed in malevolence.

POWERS. I'll get the papers you wanted, sir.

(POWERS *exits.*)

KRETON. I don't think he likes me very much but your father does. Only this morning he offered to handle my public relations and I said I'd let him. Wasn't that nice of him?

JOHN. I think I'll go get some fresh air. (*He goes out through the terrace door.*)

KRETON. Oh, dear! (*Sighs.*) Only your father is really entering the spirit of the game. He's a much better sport than you, my dear.

ELLEN (*exploding*). Sport! That's it! You think we're sport. You think we're animals to be played with: well, we're not. We're people and we don't want to be destroyed.

KRETON (*patiently*). But *I* am not destroying you. You will be destroying one another of your own free will, as you have always done. I am simply a . . . a kibitzer.

ELLEN. No, you are a vampire!

KRETON. A vampire? You mean I drink blood? Ugh!

ELLEN. No, you drink emotions, our emotions. You'll sacrifice us all for the sake of your . . . your vibrations!

KRETON. Touché. Yet what harm am I really doing? It's true I'll enjoy the war more than anybody; but it will be *your* destructiveness after all, not mine.

ELLEN. You could stop it.

KRETON. So could you.

ELLEN. I?

KRETON. Your race. They could stop altogether but they won't. And I can hardly intervene in their natural development. The most I can do is help out in small, practical ways.

ELLEN. We are not what you think. We're not so . . . so primitive.

KRETON. My dear girl, just take this one household: your mother dislikes your father but she is too tired to do anything about it so she knits and she gardens and she tries not to think about him. Your father, on the other hand, is bored with all of you. Don't look shocked: he doesn't like you any more than you like him . . .

ELLEN. Don't say that!

KRETON. I am only telling you the truth. Your father wants you to marry someone important; therefore he objects to John while you, my girl . . .

ELLEN (*with a fierce cry,* ELLEN *grabs vase to throw*). You devil! (*Vase breaks in her hand.*)

KRETON. You see? That proves my point perfectly. (*Gently.*) Poor savage, I cannot help what you are. (*Briskly.*) Anyway, you will soon be distracted from your personal problems. Tonight is the night. If you're a good girl, I'll let you watch the bombing.

(*Dissolve to study. Eleven forty-five.* POWERS *and the* AIDE *gloomily await the war.*)

AIDE. General, isn't there anything we can do?

POWERS. It's out of our hands.

(KRETON, *dressed as a Hussar, with shako, enters.*)

KRETON. Everything on schedule?

POWERS. Yes, sir. Planes left for their targets at twenty-two hundred.

KRETON. Good . . . good. I myself, shall take off shortly after midnight to observe the attack first-hand.

POWERS. Yes, sir.

(KRETON *goes into the living room where the family is gloomily assembled.*)

KRETON (*enters from study*). And now the magic hour approaches! I hope you're all as thrilled as I am.

SPELDING. You still won't tell us who's attacking whom?

KRETON. You'll know in exactly . . . fourteen minutes.

ELLEN (*bitterly*). Are we going to be killed too?

KRETON. Certainly not! You're quite safe, at least in the early stages of the war.

ELLEN. Thank you.

MRS. SPELDING. I suppose this will mean rationing again.

SPELDING. Will . . . will we see anything from here?

KRETON. No, but there should be a good picture on the monitor in the study. Powers is tuning in right now.

JOHN (*at window*). Hey look, up there! Coming this way! (ELLEN *joins him.*)

ELLEN. What is it?

JOHN. Why . . . it's *another* one! And it's going to land.

KRETON (*surprised*). I'm sure you're mistaken. No one would dream of coming here. (*He has gone to the window, too.*)

ELLEN. It's landing!

SPELDING. Is it a friend of yours, Mr. Kreton?

KRETON (*slowly*). No, no, not a friend . . .

(KRETON *retreats to the study; he inadvertently drops a lace handkerchief beside the sofa.*)

JOHN. Here he comes.

ELLEN (*suddenly bitter*). Now we have two of them.

MRS. SPELDING. My poor roses.

(*The new* VISITOR *enters in a gleam of light from his ship. He is wearing a most futuristic costume. Without a word, he walks past the awed family into the study.* KRETON *is cowering behind the globe.* POWERS *and the* AIDE *stare, bewildered, as the* VISITOR *ges-*

tures sternly and KRETON *reluctantly removes shako and sword. They communicate by odd sounds.*)

VISITOR (*to* POWERS). Please leave us alone.

(*Cut to living room as* POWERS *and the* AIDE *enter from the study.*)

POWERS (*to* ELLEN). Who on earth was that?
ELLEN. It's another one, another visitor.
POWERS. Now we're done for.
ELLEN. I'm going in there.
MRS. SPELDING. Ellen, don't you dare!
ELLEN. I'm going to talk to them. (*Starts to door.*)
JOHN. I'm coming, too.
ELLEN (*grimly*). No, alone. I know what I want to say.

(*Cut to interior of the study, to* KRETON *and the other* VISITOR *as* ELLEN *enters.*)

ELLEN. I want you both to listen to me . . .
VISITOR. You don't need to speak. I know what you will say.
ELLEN. That you have no right here? That you mustn't . . .
VISITOR. I agree. Kreton has no right here. He is well aware that it is forbidden to interfere with the past.
ELLEN. The past?
VISITOR (*nods*). You are the past, the dark ages: we are from the future. In fact, we are *your* descendants on another planet. We visit you from time to time but we never interfere because it would change *us* if we did. Fortunately, I have arrived in time.
ELLEN. There won't be a war?
VISITOR. There will be no war. And there will be no memory of any of this. When we leave here you will forget Kreton and me. Time will turn back to the moment before his arrival.
ELLEN. Why did you want to hurt us?
KRETON (*heartbroken*). Oh, but I didn't! I only wanted to have . . . well, to have a little fun, to indulge my hobby . . . against the rules of course.
VISITOR (*to* ELLEN). Kreton is a rarity among us. Mentally and

morally he is retarded. He is a child and he regards your period as his toy.

KRETON. A child, now really!

VISITOR. He escaped from his nursery and came back in time to you . . .

KRETON. And *every*thing went wrong, everything! I wanted to visit 1860 . . . that's my *real* period but then something happened to the car and I ended up here, not that I don't find you nearly as interesting but . . .

VISITOR. We must go, Kreton.

KRETON (*to* ELLEN). You did like me just a bit, didn't you?

ELLEN. Yes, yes I did, until you let your hobby get out of hand. (*To* VISITOR.) What is the future like?

VISITOR. Very serene, very different . . .

KRETON. Don't believe him: it is dull, dull, dull beyond belief! One simply floats through eternity: no wars, no excitement . . .

VISITOR. It is forbidden to discuss these matters.

KRETON. I can't see what difference it makes since she's going to forget all about us anyway.

ELLEN. Oh, how I'd love to see the future . . .

VISITOR. It is against . . .

KRETON. Against the rules: how tiresome you are. (*To* ELLEN.) But, alas, you can never pay us a call because you aren't born yet! I mean where we are you are not. Oh, Ellen, dear, think kindly of me, until you forget.

ELLEN. I will.

VISITOR. Come. Time has begun to turn back. Time is bending.

(*He starts to door.* KRETON *turns conspiratorially to* ELLEN.)

KRETON. Don't be sad, my girl. I shall be back one bright day, but a bright day in 1860. I dote on the Civil War, so exciting . . .

VISITOR. Kreton!

KRETON. Only next time I think it'll be more fun if the *South* wins!

(*He hurries after the* VISITOR.)

(*Cut to clock as the hands spin backwards. Dissolve to the living room, exactly the same as the first scene:* SPELDING, MRS. SPELDING, ELLEN.)

SPELDING. There is nothing wrong with marrying a wealthy man. The horror of it has always eluded me. However, my only wish is that you marry someone hard-working, ambitious, a man who'll make his mark in the world. Not a boy who is content to sit on a farm all his life, growing peanuts . . .

ELLEN. English walnuts! And he won't just sit there.

SPELDING. Will you stop contradicting me?

ELLEN. But, Daddy, John grows walnuts . . .

(JOHN *enters*.)

JOHN. Hello, everybody.

MRS. SPELDING. Good evening, John.

ELLEN. What kept you, darling? You missed Daddy's broadcast.

JOHN. I saw it before I left home. Wonderful broadcast, sir.

SPELDING. Thank you, John.

(JOHN *crosses to window*.)

JOHN. That meteor you were talking about, well, for a while it looked almost like a space ship or something. You can just barely see it now.

(ELLEN *joins him at window. They watch, arms about one another*.)

SPELDING. Space ship! Nonsense! Remarkable what some people will believe, *want* to believe. Besides, as I said in the broadcast: if there's any traveling to be done in space we'll do it first.

(*He notices* KRETON's *handkerchief on sofa and picks it up. They all look at it, puzzled, as we cut to stock shot of the starry night against which two space ships vanish in the distance, one serene in its course, the other erratic, as we fade out*.)

For discussion

ACT I

1. In the opening moments of Act I, before Kreton's arrival, what did you learn about each member of the Spelding family?
2. Do you think Gore Vidal is poking good-natured fun at news commentators in the final words of Roger Spelding's TV broadcast? If so, what is the criticism? How does this opening speech in the play serve as exposition?
3. Point out the humor in Roger Spelding's reaction to the news that a space ship was approaching.
4. What made Kreton's physical appearance such a surprise? What did you expect? From the way he spoke, what did he reveal about the kind of planet he came from?
5. What strange powers did Kreton have that astounded the Speldings and General Powers? Why was his behavior toward the others amusing?
6. What were Kreton's views on outer space? On earth as a civilization? What criticism of people do you think may be implied here?
7. What was Kreton's purpose in coming to earth from outer space? Do you detect any social criticism in this purpose? If so, what is it?
8. Explain the humor in the characterization of General Powers. Point out lines which reveal that the playwright also had a serious purpose in creating this character.
9. In your opinion, what is particularly funny in Mrs. Spelding's reactions to Kreton?

ACT II

1. What is the mood of the opening scene of Act II? Point out details that contribute to this mood.
2. What made Kreton's mistake about the President funny?
3. What kind of person did Kreton appear to be at the beginning of the act when he promised to move his ship off the roses? How did he appear by the end of the act after his talk with Paul Laurent?
4. What was Laurent's first reaction to Kreton? Why did his opinion change? In what way did Kreton disagree with Laurent?
5. What criticism of people is to be found in Kreton's opinion of what the inhabitants of earth wanted? What criticism of Kreton might there be on this point?

6. How did Kreton visibly demonstrate his military power? What was the first project he planned to carry out? What conflict emerges clearly by the end of Act II?

7. Describe Kreton's attitude toward war. How does this contribute to the suspense in the play?

8. Show how humor and seriousness are blended in this act. Do you think this blending is successful, or do you think the humor and seriousness interfere with each other? Explain your answer.

ACT III

1. Two weeks have passed since the close of Act II. During this time, what has Kreton been doing? Point out the humor in the new relationship between Kreton and General Powers. What more serious side did General Powers reveal in his conversation with Kreton at the beginning of this act?

2. What had happened to Paul Laurent in this time? Why did Kreton call Laurent a "misfit"?

3. Why was Ellen horrified at Kreton? What purpose do you think Ellen serves in this act?

4. Kreton described to Ellen how members of the Spelding family regarded each other. Was he correct or not? Use evidence from Act I to support your opinion.

5. In what way did the mood of the play change with the arrival of the Visitor?

6. Describe the Visitor's attitude toward Kreton. What did you learn about Kreton from the Visitor? What human quality did Kreton reveal in his attitude toward life on his own planet?

7. Explain the humor in Spelding's last speech in relation to his finding Kreton's handkerchief.

8. Explain the humor in the final stage direction about the two space ships.

On the play as a whole

1. To laugh at oneself is healthy. Satire is one important way a writer does this. What type of person do you think Gore Vidal is satirizing in Mr. Spelding? General Powers? Mrs. Spelding? Give examples to support your opinion.

2. Do you think the playwright is also satirizing an aspect of modern life through Kreton? If so, show how.

3. Point out lines which reveal Kreton's attitude toward war. How did the reaction of each of the following characters to Kreton's attitude reveal something important about that character: General Powers, Roger Spelding, Paul Laurent, Mrs. Spelding, Ellen.

4. Why did Kreton find it difficult to read Paul Laurent's mind? How is this a comment on modern diplomacy?

5. What would you say the theme of this play is? In your opinion, would the playwright have made his point more effectively if he had written a serious drama rather than a comedy? Why or why not?

6. When Ellen asked, "What is the future like?" she received two different answers from Kreton and the Visitor. Compare the two answers. In what essential ways were they different? What did it show about Kreton and the Visitor?

7. What is the climax of the play? On what did you base your decision?

8. What is the subplot of the play? Is it important? If so, for what reason?

9. Minor characters are necessary because of the various functions they perform, such as providing humor, helping to forward the plot, reporting events which happen offstage, or revealing what the main characters are like. Name the minor characters in *Visit to a Small Planet* and explain what each contributed to the play.

10. The action of the play takes place "the day after tomorrow." Do you think it would have been more, or less, effective for the playwright simply to have said, "Some time in the future"? Why?

11. An important element contributing to the humor in this play is irony. For example, in Act I:

    AIDE. You don't think this Kreton can really take over the world, do you?

    POWERS. Of course not. Nobody can.

    Point out other examples of irony throughout the play.

12. Point out how *Visit to a Small Planet* mingles what is real with what is fantastic. In your opinion, how well did the playwright succeed in making the fantastic seem real? Give examples to support your opinion.

13. In some of the stage directions and in the change of scenes, it is clear that this play was written for television rather than for the stage. What evidence is there to support this statement?

14. Explain the humor implied in the title of the play.

For composition

1. Another well-known playwright and television writer, Paddy Chayef-sky, has said, "Television is the dramatic medium through which to explore our new insights into ourselves." Write a brief paper in which you discuss this statement with specific references to *Visit to a Small Planet*.

2. Write an imaginative composition in which you describe a visit to Kreton's "world." Give careful attention to details that are convincing and realistic.

3. Write a brief dialogue between a person living on another planet and yourself visiting his land. You might discuss some important issue and show how a more "civilized" mind might see it.

4. Select one character from the play whom you found particularly entertaining or important. Write a character sketch of that person, in which you bring out his (or her) outstanding traits, including how he sees himself and how he sees other people.

5. "The events in this play are definitely improbable, but not completely impossible." Do you agree or disagree with this statement? Write a paper in which you state your opinion, supporting it with specific references to the play.

6. Humor is an important element in this play. Write a short expository paper in which you give your opinion of Gore Vidal's humor. Use well-chosen lines from the play to illustrate your point.

7. In the light of your reading of *Visit to a Small Planet*, discuss Molière's statement that the purpose of comedy is "to provoke thoughtful laughter."

Louis O. Coxe and Robert Chapman

Billy Budd

Yea and Nay—
Each hath his say;
But God He keeps the middle way.

Although Herman Melville wrote those lines in another work, they apply to the terrible but fascinating sea tale of *Billy Budd*. Absolute good and absolute evil cannot live in this world together, according to Melville. Each must destroy the other, for human life is a compromise that follows the middle way. . . .

As a theatre work, *Billy Budd* is exciting. For life on board a British warship in 1798 is full of color and pageantry—the squalid life of the crew below decks, the grandeur of life among the afterguard, the austerity of discipline, the feuds between the men and officers, the interludes of wonder and calm at sea, the explosions of anger and treachery. During his seven years at sea, which ended in 1844, Melville served for fourteen months as sailor in an American warship, and he knew intimately the nature of the service. . . .

Billy Budd is extraordinarily well done. In their dramatization Mr. Coxe and Mr. Chapman have never taken cheap advantage of a melodramatic plot. They have not underwritten or overwritten. They have not stacked the cards. Some of their play is written lightly in a vein of affable comedy. The tragic portions are written with taste, firmness and intelligence. Although *Billy Budd* is the dramatization of a novel, it is a fully wrought play in its own right. There is something translucent about both script and performance. Through them comes the earnest thought of a lonely old man who had been through hell and beaten but not broken. He accepted the universal compromise but he never made it.

—Brooks Atkinson

BILLY BUDD

CHARACTERS

EDWARD FAIRFAX VERE, *Captain, Royal Navy*
PHILIP MICHAEL SEYMOUR, *First Officer*
JOHN RATCLIFFE, *First Lieutenant*
BORDMAN WYATT, *Sailing Master*
GARDINER, *a Midshipman*
REA, *a Midshipman*
SURGEON
JOHN CLAGGART, *Master-at-Arms*
SQUEAK, *Master-at-Arms' man*
THE DANSKER, *Mainmast man*
JENKINS, *Captain of the Maintop*
PAYNE, *Maintopman*

KINCAID, *Maintopman*
O'DANIEL, *Maintopman*
BUTLER, *Maintopman*
TALBOT, *Mizzentopman*
JACKSON, *Maintopman*
BILLY BUDD, *Foretopman*
HALLAM, *a Marine*
MESSBOY
STOLL, *Helmsman*
DUNCAN, *Mate of the Main Deck*
BYREN, *Relief Helmsman*
DRUMMER
OTHER SAILORS, *crew of the* Indomitable

The entire action takes place aboard H.M.S. Indomitable *at sea, August, 1798, the year following the Naval mutinies at Spithead and the Nore.*

ACT I

✥§ Scene 1

SCENE: *Although outside it is a fine morning in early August, the between-decks compartment of the crew's quarters assigned to the maintopmen is dark and shadowy except for the light spilling down the companionway from above and, through the open gun-ports, the flicker of sunlight reflected on the water. The smoking-lamp burns feebly over a wooden mess table and two benches lowered for use.*

JENKINS sits at the table mending a piece of clothing. In the shadow the DANSKER sits motionless on a low sea chest, smoking a pipe. Neither man speaks for a long minute.

Then JACKSON appears on deck at the top of the companionway and lurches down into the compartment. He is doubled up in pain.

CLAGGART (*off-stage*). You there! Jackson!

JACKSON. He's followed me!

JENKINS. Who?

JACKSON. Master-at-Arms. He'll send me aloft again sure, and I can't hang on . . .

JENKINS. What the devil's wrong with you, jack? Here, sit down.

CLAGGART (*entering down the companionway*). Why have you come down off the mainmast,[1] Jackson? Your watch over?

JACKSON. Sick, Mister Claggart, I'm bloody sick, so I'm shaking up there on the yard till I near fell off.

JENKINS. Grab an arm, mate, I'll take you along to sick-bay.

CLAGGART. Stand away from him, Jenkins. (*To JACKSON*) Just where does this sickness strike you, in the guts, or limbs? Or in the head? Does it exist at all?

JENKINS. You can see he's sick as a puking cat.

[1] mainmast: principal mast of a sailing vessel

182

CLAGGART. The role of Good Samaritan hardly fits you, Jenkins. (*To* JACKSON) Now up, man. Turn topside.[2]

JACKSON. I can't, I can't, I'm deathly sick, God help me, sir!

CLAGGART. That's hard. But this ship needs all hands. We're undermanned. The aches and pains of landsmen have their cures, but ours have none. You'll have to get aloft. Now move!

JACKSON. I ain't bluffing, sir, swear I'm not! Please, Mister Claggart . . . I got Cooper's leave, he says all right, I can come down.

CLAGGART. You have not got my leave. Cooper is captain of the maintop and ought to know better. Four men to every spar,[3] and no replacements. Now up. Back where you belong.

JACKSON (*starts up the ladder*). Sir, I can't, I can't stand it! It'll be my death, sure!

CLAGGART. No more talk, man! Up you get! Start! (JACKSON *goes painfully up the ladder and out of sight on deck.* CLAGGART *starts out after him.*)

(JENKINS *mutters.*)

CLAGGART. Did you say something, Jenkins? (JENKINS *does not answer.* CLAGGART *goes out, calling after* JACKSON.) Now Jackson, get along. Up! Up!

JENKINS. I'll stick him one day before long! I will, if I hang for it.

(*Laughter and talk in the next compartment followed by entrance of* BUTLER, TALBOT *and* KINCAID.)

BUTLER. Messboy!

TALBOT. Haul in the slops!

KINCAID. Suppose we'll get the new man? The jack they 'pressed [4] this morning off that merchantman? I see 'em come alongside just now.

TALBOT. I pity that poor fellow, so I do. I hear they get good pay on merchant ships. Eat good, too, and them treated like the Prince of Wales. (MESSBOY *enters with an iron pot of food and spits on the deck.*) Can't taste no worse.

MESSBOY. Ain't nobody making you eat it, mate. You can wash your feet in it if you like. (O'DANIEL *and* PAYNE *enter.*)

TALBOT. What's eating you, Jenkins? Ain't you going to join the banquet?

[2] Turn topside: Go up on deck.

[3] spar: mast supporting the sail of a ship

[4] 'pressed: forced into service in the navy (a custom which still existed at this time in the British Navy)

JENKINS. I seen a thing just now I won't stand for! I'm sitting here
off watch, and I seen it all. That blacksnake Claggart kicked
Jackson back aloft, and him sick as a baby in a cradle, as any fool
could see.

PAYNE. He's the Master-at-Arms, ain't he?

JENKINS. Cooper sent him down. Who's captain of the starboard
watch, him or Claggart? Cooper could have found him a relief.
Plain murder.

TALBOT. You think Claggart can get away with what he does without
Captain Starry Vere knows what's going on? Him and that red
snapper Seymour, and them other bloody officers!

JENKINS. Jackson'll fall. No man can hang to a spar sick like that.
He'll fall sure.

O'DANIEL. Tush, man, nobody falls in His Majesty's Navy. We lose
our footing. 'Tis flying we do, to be sure.

TALBOT. I tell you it's Vere that's the cause of it! Our glorious fine
Captain Vere, with a league of braid around his arm.

O'DANIEL. Vere, is it. As captains go, mate, let me tell you, he's an
angel with a harp alongside of the skipper on the *Royal George.*
Every day that one flogged a dozen men. Picked 'em by lottery.
Never took the gratings down till they was rusty with blood. Ho!
This Vere's a saint in heaven after him.

JENKINS. Ram the *Royal George* and everybody in her! Claggart's
the man we want, and the sooner the better, say I!

O'DANIEL. Ah, we'd had him puking his blood at Spithead.

BUTLER. You was there, O'Daniel? At Spithead?

O'DANIEL. Aye. I was. Wherever you do find Englishmen doing a
smart thing, you'll find an Irishman is at the bottom of it. Oho,
fine it was, every day of it, with the officers quaking in their
cabins, spitting green, and the whole English government in fear
of us! Ah, lovely it was, lovely!

TALBOT. Belay your Irish noise, you fat-mouthed mackerel-snatcher.
I'll tell you this, we need men on here is not afraid to use their
knives if it come to that. And you can be bloody sure it will come
to that, mind my word, Mickey Cork.

JENKINS. What did you ever use your knife for, Talbot, but to
scratch your lice? Ah, you're a dancing daredevil, you are for sure.

TALBOT. I'll be happy to show you, if you like.

JENKINS. Trouble will be hunting you out, mate, if you're not careful.

TALBOT. Trouble! There's not a man aboard don't know you for a coward!

JENKINS. Get out.

TALBOT. I'm not afraid of you, or your sniveling hangbys, either!

JENKINS. Move! Get out of it, or I'll run my knife to the hilts in you!

(*They attack one another with drawn knives,* JENKINS *reaching suddenly across the table to seize* TALBOT. *Silently they thrash around the compartment upsetting benches and food while the others look on unmoved.*)

O'DANIEL. Ah, I do love to see two Englishmen fighting each other. It's fonder they are of killing themselves than fighting their proper foes. (*Laughs hoarsely.*)

PAYNE. Tomorrow's rum on Jenkins. Any bets?

KINCAID. He never lost one yet.

(JENKINS *throws* TALBOT *on the deck and holds the knife at his throat for a moment before letting him up, first taking his knife. He holds out his hand.*)

JENKINS. I'm leading seaman in this compartment, mind that. (TALBOT *hits* JENKINS' *hand and goes off angrily.*)

KINCAID. You're captain, that's all right by me.

O'DANIEL. Eyes in the boat, lads. Here comes *pfft*-face.

(SQUEAK, BILLY *and* GARDINER *appear on deck and start down the companionway.*)

GARDINER. Hang it, step lively, boy! Your ship is . . . Doff your hat to officers when they speak to you! I'll teach you to touch your hat to a midshipman's coat, if it's only stuck on a broomstick to dry!

BILLY. Aye, sir. (*The men react to* GARDINER *with yawns and gestures behind his back.*)

GARDINER. Very well. Your ship is *H.M.S. Indomitable* now, and we sail her tautly, and we tolerate no nonsense. Is that clear?

BILLY. Aye, sir.

GARDINER (*to* SQUEAK). See this new man is assigned to a watch, and get him squared away. (*To* BILLY.) You're green, of course, I can see that. But I expect we'll ripen you. (*He trips going up the ladder and* SQUEAK *tries to help him.*) Carry on. (GARDINER *exits.*)

SQUEAK. My name's Squeak. I'm the Master-at-Arms' man. Have you met the Master-at-Arms yet, Mister Claggart? (BILLY *shakes his head.*) Oh you'll like him. He's a nice fellow. (o'daniel *chokes on his pipe smoke and the other men react similarly.*) Stow your gear along in there. This here's the larboard [5] section of the maintop. Captain of the watch is Jenkins. Him, there. Report to him. (*He pats* billy *on the chest and grins before starting up the ladder.*)

JENKINS. What's a green hand dumped in here for?

SQUEAK. Complaining, Jenkins?

JENKINS. I'm asking. What's wrong with that?

SQUEAK. Mister Claggart wants him here, that's why. Maybe he wants for Billy Boy to set you pigs an example. Refer any more complaints to the Master-at-Arms! (*Exits.* billy *grins at the men, who return his look.*)

BILLY. My name is Budd. Billy, if you like.

KINCAID. I'm Kincaid. This is where you swing your hammock. That's O'Daniel, this here's Payne, and Butler. This is Jenkins, captain of the watch, and that old jack's called the Dansker. Don't know why, unless maybe he's Danish. You ever had a real name, Dansker?

DANSKER. Not for many years.

BUTLER. You'd be the new impressed man?

BILLY. Aye, so I am. I just came off the *Rights of Man* this morning.

DANSKER. Forget about the Rights of Man now, lad.

JENKINS. How long you been going to sea, baby?

BILLY. About ten years, but in the merchant service.

O'DANIEL. Merchant service! Whissht! (*Laughs hoarsely.*)

BILLY. I know I'm new at Navy work, and probably there'll be some things I'll need help with.

JENKINS. No doubt, little boy.

BILLY. I'll learn fast, never fear. But she's a big old girl, this ship. I never was in a ship-of-the-line before. I'd have got lost trying to find the mess by myself. Maybe fallen in the magazine!

O'DANIEL. Ah, you get used to it. She's big, is this tub, but she's not so big you can get lost in her.

PAYNE. Sometimes I wish you could. Maybe we could lose O'Daniel. (billy *laughs and the others join.*)

BILLY. You're Irish, aren't you? I like the Irish. There was an Irishman on the *Rights of Man*, with big red whiskers . . . when I came away, he gave me a silver knife. This is it.

[5] **larboard**: left-hand side of a ship

O'DANIEL. It's a beauty. Mind you keep an eye on it.

BUTLER. What's the matter, boy?

BILLY. I was just thinking, maybe I won't ever see my friends again.

O'DANIEL. If they was Irish, don't you worry at all. The Irish is liable to turn up almost anywheres, excepting England and the fires of hell, which is much the same.

PAYNE. Danny, if it wasn't for the harps, the devil wouldn't have nothing to do. What was potato-eaters doing on a merchant ship?

BILLY. Just sailors, like me. Most of us had no other home, even the skipper. He was a kind old bloke. Looked fierce, but he always had a kind word. Used to keep a bird in a cage in his cabin. The skipper let me feed the bird sometimes. Worms right out of the ship's biscuit. That was mostly all the meat we got.

O'DANIEL. The bargemen is in Navy biscuit would eat the bird.

KINCAID. Sit down here, Bill. Maggots or not, this is what we get. You hungry?

BILLY. I'm always hungry.

KINCAID. Try your first sample of His Majesty's bounty. We don't know what it is, but we been eating it for a long time.

BUTLER. Here, eat mine. Tastes like it's been eat before, anyhow.

JENKINS. Give him more lobscouse,[6] Butler. We got to keep the roses in his cheeks, ain't we, boy?

BILLY (*laughing*). I could eat anything right now. Even this.

O'DANIEL. Help you to forget about home and mother, lad.

JENKINS. Tell us about home and mother, Baby Budd.

BILLY. There's not much to tell. I've got no home, and never had a family to remember.

JENKINS. Ain't that too bad.

BILLY. Oh, I'd feel a lot worse if I'd been 'pressed with a wife and children.

KINCAID. That's the truth.

O'DANIEL. We're all patriotic volunteers.

KINCAID. Wait till my hitch is up, you won't see no more of me.

BUTLER. Three weeks drunk in Portsmouth, then back in the ruddy fleet.

DANSKER. Men like us got no other home.

O'DANIEL. No other home, is it? Ah 'tis so thick the sweet thoughts is in here, I can scarce breathe.

---

[6] **lobscouse**: sailors' stew of meat, vegetables, and biscuits

PAYNE. Then you can strangle or get out.

JENKINS. Aye, get along. Give us some fresh air.

O'DANIEL. If you begged me to stay itself, I'd be off to where there's smarter lads. Boy, let you pay no heed to these white mice, mind what I say. And be hanged, the lot of yous! (*He starts up the ladder.*)

KINCAID. You'll catch it, Danny, if Captain holds an inspection.

O'DANIEL (*returning*). Ah whissht, I was forgetting that. And I do think that me figure shows up better here below than it does in the broad daylight.

BILLY. Inspection today?

PAYNE. Ah the Old Man crawls over the ship any time he ain't got nothing else to do. You never know when till you see him.

KINCAID. What he wants to inspect this hooker for, I can't figure. He's seen it before.

BUTLER. He ain't seen Billy.

BILLY. What's the Captain like? On the *Rights of Man*, the captain . . .

JENKINS. You going to jaw some more about that rocking horse? I suppose *you* was at Spithead, too?

BILLY. Spithead? Where is that?

JENKINS. A little party the Navy had a year ago. A mutiny, Baby, a mutiny. Know what that is?

BILLY. Why did they mutiny?

O'DANIEL. Arra, it's easy to see you're new to the Navy.

JENKINS. Jimmy-Legs is ten good reasons for it, himself.

BILLY. Who's Jimmy-Legs?

KINCAID. Master-at-Arms. We call him Jimmy-Legs.

BUTLER. Watch out for that one, Billy.

PAYNE. He's the devil himself between decks.

O'DANIEL. What d'you expect, the saints of heaven? Not in an English tub.

BILLY. Why don't you like the Master-at-Arms?

JENKINS. You'll find out soon enough, Baby.

BUTLER. Watch him, boy. Jenkins can tell you. He's had a time or two with Claggart.

JENKINS. Aye, and I'll have another one day before too long.

BUTLER. Sure, Jenkins. You look after Bill.

JENKINS. How old are you, kid? Sixteen?

BILLY. I don't know, maybe . . . twenty.

JENKINS. He don't even know how old he is!

KINCAID. Stow it, Jenkins. Come on, don't pay no attention to him. He's feeling ugly today.

JENKINS. Well now, ain't you getting holier than a bishop. Let him talk up for himself, if he don't like it.

KINCAID. Stow it, I say. You got no reason to crawl over Bill. Let him be.

BILLY. That's all right, Tom. I don't mind a joke. Black's the white of me eye, mates! (*All laugh except* JENKINS.)

JENKINS. Mama taught you pretty manners, huh? Oh! Ain't got no mama, you say? (*Laughs.*)

BILLY. Tell me what you mean, Mister Jenkins.

PAYNE. What's gnawing you, Jenkins? Can't you see the boy's trying to be friendly?

JENKINS. You forgetting who's leading seaman here? Come on, Baby, talk back, why don't you? Scared?

BILLY. N-no. Why do you think I'd be scared, M-M-Mister Jenkins?

JENKINS. He stammers! What do you know! So scared he's stammering.

BILLY. Don't say that!

JENKINS. Sounds good, ha? Sounds fine. I like the way it rolls out your mouth.

> (BILLY *strikes him.* JENKINS *staggers and falls, pulls a knife and gets up, lunging at* BILLY. PAYNE, BUTLER *and* KINCAID *get up and stand close to* BILLY, *silently protecting him.*)

JENKINS. Get away! He's got to find out who gives orders here.

KINCAID. Not this time, Jenkins. Lay off.

O'DANIEL. Belay it. You're wearing me out, the pair of yous.

BUTLER. Put away the knife. (JENKINS *sees their determination and relaxes a little, uncertain what to do.*)

BILLY. Will you shake hands? Or would you rather fight?

JENKINS. You little . . . (*He lunges forward.* BILLY *catches his arm and bends it, holding* JENKINS *cursing and powerless.*)

BILLY. That's enough, mate. Pipe down and let us be.

O'DANIEL. Good lad! Save the great strength is in you, Jenkins, for fighting the devil is after your soul.

JENKINS. All right, all right. You can let me go now.

O'DANIEL. Leave him go, lad. I won't hurt him at all.

BILLY. You're like Red Whiskers on the *Rights*, he liked to fight too. (*Freeing him.*) Will you shake hands, mate?

JENKINS (*momentarily uncertain what to do*). Shake hands, is it? . . . Well, you beat me fair. You got guts, which is more than I give you credit for. (*They shake hands.*)

KINCAID. You're some peacemaker, Bill.

PAYNE. That's the only time I ever hear Jenkins eating his own words.

O'DANIEL. Ah, that's a terrible diet, would make any man puke.

JENKINS. Don't you be getting any wrong ideas. I'm still a match for you!

KINCAID. Better belay your mess gear, Bill.

JENKINS. Where you come from, Baby?

PAYNE. Stow it! Jimmy-Legs! (BILLY *goes on talking as* CLAGGART *enters.*)

BILLY. I don't know, I guess from Portsmouth. I never lived ashore, that I can remember. Where do you come from? (*He drops a pot on deck.* CLAGGART *stands over him.*)

CLAGGART. Handsomely done, young fellow, handsomely done. And handsome is as handsome did it, too. You can wipe that up, Jenkins. (*To* BILLY.) What is your name?

BILLY. Budd, sir. William Budd, ship *Rights of Man*.

CLAGGART. Your ship is *H.M.S. Indomitable* now.

BILLY. Aye, sir.

CLAGGART. You look sturdy. What was your station aboard the merchantman?

BILLY. M-m-mizzentopman, sir.

CLAGGART. You like that station?

BILLY. Aye, sir, well enough.

CLAGGART. How long have you been at sea?

BILLY. Ten years, sir, near as I can tell.

CLAGGART. Education?

BILLY. None, sir.

CLAGGART. So. You come aboard with nothing but your face to recommend you. Well, while beauty is always welcome, that alone may not avail us much against the French. There are other requirements in the service.

BILLY. I'll learn quickly, sir.

CLAGGART. The sea's a taskmaster, young fellow. It salts the sweetness out of boyish faces. You cannot tell what motion lies asleep in that flat water. Down where the manta [7] drifts, and the shark and ray, storms wait for a wind while all the surface dazzles.

BILLY. I am a seaman, sir. I love the sea. I've hardly lived ashore.

CLAGGART. Then let the wind and sea have license to plunder at their will. As of today, a new maintopman swings between sky and water. (*He turns toward the ladder and notices the mess on deck.*) I thought I asked you to wipe that up, Jenkins.

JENKINS. That's the messboy's job.

CLAGGART. Clean up, Jenkins. (JENKINS *hesitates.*) That is an order. Turn to.

BILLY. I'll give you a hand, Jenkins. Come on.

CLAGGART. Ah, there. See how helpful Billy is. Why can't you take a leaf from this innocent young David's book, Jenkins? (*He turns away.* JENKINS *accidentally brushes against him and receives a savage cut from* CLAGGART's *rattan* [8] *across his face.*) Watch what you're doing, man!

JENKINS. I swear . . . !

CLAGGART. Yes, what is it that you swear? Well, speak. Nothing at all to say? Then hear me: I have my methods with unruly tempers.
(*On deck there is a loud crescendo scream and a crash. Running footsteps, shouts, voice calling for the* SURGEON. *The men surge toward the ladder.*)

CLAGGART. Stand fast! (SQUEAK *enters down the hatchway, whispers to* CLAGGART.) All right, I know. (SQUEAK *comes down into the compartment and runs off.*)

JENKINS. It's Jackson! I knew it! I told you so!
(*Men turn to stare at* CLAGGART *as several sailors enter down the companionway, bearing the body of* JACKSON, *inert and shattered. They carry him through the compartment and off to sick-bay.*)

SURGEON (*as he moves through the compartment*). Clear the way, you men. Take him into the sick-bay, through here. Carry him gently. Easy, now. Easy. (*Exit.*)

JENKINS (*pointing to* CLAGGART). He sent him back aloft. Killed him, he did!

O'DANIEL. Might as well have knifed him.

---

[7] **manta:** devilfish, a very large ray
[8] **rattan:** a cane or switch made from palm leaves

CLAGGART. Stand fast. Stop where you are. Your man Jackson is looked after.

O'DANIEL (*in a low voice*). Then he's a dead man surely.

CLAGGART. Who spoke?

JENKINS. We'll have a showdown now! After him, mates! Cut into him!

> (*The men move toward* CLAGGART *in a rush, drawing knives and cursing him, as* CAPTAIN VERE *appears in the companion hatchway.*)

VERE. Stand fast! Hold where you are. Master-at-Arms, what is the matter here? (*The men stop in their tracks and stare at* VERE, *who comes part way down the ladder.*)

CLAGGART. These dogs are out of temper, sir.

VERE (*to men*). You will come to attention when I address you! Let me remind you that this ship is at war. This is a wartime cruise, and this vessel sails under the Articles of War. Volunteer or 'pressed man, veteran seaman or recruit, you are no longer citizens, but sailors: a crew that I shall work into a weapon. One lawless act, one spurt of rebel temper from any man in this ship, high or low, I will pay out in coin you know of. You have but two duties: to fight and to obey, and I will bend each contumacious [9] spirit, each stiff-necked prideful soul of you, or crush the spirit in you if I must. Abide by the Articles of War and my commands, or they will cut you down. Now: choose. (*The men are silent.*) Very well. Master-at-Arms, this accident on deck, the sailor fallen from the yardarm. [10] Do you know how it occurred?

CLAGGART. I do not, sir.

VERE. You are his messmates. Does any man of you know how this occurred? (*To* BUTLER.) You?

BUTLER. No, sir.

VERE. Jenkins, do you?

JENKINS (*hesitates a moment.* CLAGGART *moves slightly, tapping his hand with the rattan*). No, sir.

VERE (*notices the cut on* JENKINS' *face*). What's this, what's this? Speak up, man. I want no random bloodshed aboard this ship.

JENKINS. I . . . fell, Captain. Fell, and . . . and cut my cheek.

VERE. I see. You fell. Master-at-Arms, you will excuse this man from duty till the Surgeon tends him.

---

[9] **contumacious**: stubborn, rebellious
[10] **yardarm**: either end of the support of a sail

CLAGGART. Aye, aye, sir.

VERE. We must not wound ourselves, draining the blood from enterprise that takes a whole man. (*He turns to go up the ladder and sees* BILLY.) Well. This is a new face. Who are you, boy?

CLAGGART. Maintopman 'pressed from the *Rights of Man* this morning, sir. William Budd.

VERE. Let him speak for himself. (BILLY *tries to speak but can only stammer incoherently*.) That's all right, boy, take your time. No need to be nervous.

BILLY. I saw a man go aloft, sir, as I came on board just a while ago. He looked sick, sir, he did. This officer was there, too, he can tell you. (*To* CLAGGART.) Don't you remember, sir?

VERE. Did you send a sick man aloft, Master-at-Arms?

CLAGGART. I did not, sir.

VERE. Very well. (*To* BILLY.) Well, Budd, I hope you take to Navy life and duty without too much regret. We go to fight the French and shall need wits and hearts about us equal to the task.

BILLY. I'll do my best, sir.

VERE. I'm sure you will. We are all here to do our several duties, and though they may seem petty from one aspect, still they must all be done. The Admiral himself looks small and idle to the man like you who can see him from the maintop, threading his pattern on the quarterdeck. The Navy's only life. (SURGEON *enters*.)

SURGEON. Captain—Jackson, the man who fell just now—he's dead, sir.

VERE (*after a pause*). Carry on, Master-at-Arms. (*He goes out up the companionway.* SURGEON *exits*.)

CLAGGART. You've made a good impression on the Captain, Billy Budd. You have a pleasant way with you. If you wish to make a good impression on me, you will need to curb your tongue. Jenkins, I thought you were ordered to sick-bay. Jump to it. And I suggest you change that shirt. See how fouled it is with a peculiar stain. Why can't you keep clean like Billy here? (*He strikes* JENKINS *viciously on the arm with his rattan, smiles at him, and exits up the ladder*.)

JENKINS. I can't stand it no more!

BILLY. I don't see what you can do, mate. He didn't mean it when he hurt you then.

JENKINS. Listen, boy, I know Jimmy-Legs. He lives on hurting people.

Stay away from him, and keep your mouth shut, if you don't want trouble.

O'DANIEL. Did you hear the lad speak up to the skipper?

PAYNE. Aye, you watch your tongue, Bill. Claggart will be after you for talking up like that.

KINCAID. He's a cool one, Billy is. None of us got the nerve.

BUTLER. It's nerve gets a man in trouble in this tub.

DANSKER. Jimmy-Legs is down on you already, Billy.

BILLY. Down on me? Why he's friendly to me.

JENKINS. Claggart don't make no friends.

O'DANIEL. You seen Jackson when they brought him below. That's how friendly he gets. (*Bosun's pipe off-stage.*)

DUNCAN (*off-stage*). Relieve the watch!

KINCAID. First watch on the *Indomitable,* Bill. Better lay up to the mainmast and report. (*Exit.*)

BUTLER. Don't slip off the yardarm.

PAYNE. Watch your step.

BILLY. Not me. You watch for me. Got to find the mainmast, and I'm in a hurry.

O'DANIEL. You'll never find your way in this old tub. I'll come along and show you. If anybody comes calling for O'Daniel while I'm out, take the message.

PAYNE. You come with me. (BILLY *and* PAYNE *go off.*)

JENKINS. I pity him, I do.

BUTLER. He's dead, ain't he? Better off than us.

JENKINS. Not Jackson. I mean the baby here. Billy.

BUTLER. We could have fared worse for a messmate.

JENKINS. Aye. He can take care of himself. Heave up the table.

✑ *Scene 2*

SCENE: *In the early evening of the same day, the off-duty sections of the crew are mustered aft*[1] *on the maindeck for* JACKSON'S *funeral. Above them* CAPTAIN VERE *stands uncovered at the forward break of the quarterdeck, reading the Committal Prayer. The westward sky is bright yellow and red, but fades into darkness as the scene progresses.*

The men are uncovered and stand at attention.

---

[1] **mustered aft:** assembled at the stern of a ship

VERE. Unto Almighty God we commend the soul of our brother departed and we commit his body to the deep, in sure and certain hope of the resurrection unto Eternal Life, through our Lord Jesus Christ, at whose coming in glorious majesty to judge the world, the sea shall give up her dead, and the corruptible bodies of those who sleep in Him shall be changed and made like unto His glorious body according to the mighty working whereby He is able to subdue all things unto Himself. Amen.

MEN. Amen.

> (*Short drum-roll followed by a muffled splash as* JACKSON's *body slips over the side. Then the bosun's pipe. Officers cover and march off.*)

CLAGGART. Ship's company: Cover! Petty officers, dismiss your divisions.

VOICE (*off-stage*). Carpenters and gunners: Dismiss!

VOICE (*off-stage*). Afterguardsmen: Dismiss!

VOICE (*off-stage*). Fore, main, and mizzentopmen: Dismiss! (*The men break formation and go off, excepting* BUTLER, JENKINS, PAYNE, KINCAID *and* BILLY, *who gather near the ratlines, at the rail.*)

BUTLER. I suppose in this clear water you could see him go down for quite a way.

BILLY. We're moving slow in this calm.

JENKINS. There'll be wind enough before dawn.

BUTLER. And that's the end of Enoch Jackson. Over the side he goes, and his mates forget him.

JENKINS. Whatever's happened to Jackson, he ain't worried none. He's got a hundred fathoms [2] over him to keep him warm and cosy.

BILLY. I'd rather be buried at sea than on the beach, when I come to die. Will you stand by the plank, Tom, so I'll shake a friendly hand before I sink? Oh! But it's dead I'll be then, come to think! (*All laugh.*)

PAYNE. Don't you worry none. By that time, you won't give a care.

KINCAID. It's only living makes sense to me, anyhow.

BILLY. Aye, I like to live. Even when it seems bad, there's a lot that's good in it.

JENKINS. Maybe for you, Bill. You wouldn't know trouble if it come up and spit in your eye.

---

[2] **fathom:** a measure of depth in the sea, six feet

BILLY. Don't you try now, mate! You might miss, and I got a clean jumper on!

PAYNE. That's the way to be, if you ask me. There's always trouble, if you know where to look for it.

BUTLER. You don't have to see nothing if you close your eyes.

KINCAID. When I close my eyes I sleep sound as a drunk marine.

BILLY. Aye, after I roll in my hammock, it's one, two, three, and I'm deep down under.

JENKINS. Well it's down under for me right now. Let's lay below.

KINCAID. Aye, we'll be on watch before long. Coming, Bill?

BILLY. I think I'll stay and watch the water for a while. I like to watch the sea at night.

JENKINS. Aye. It's deep and silent, and it can drown a man before he knows it.

BILLY. Sleep sound, mates. (*All but* JENKINS *go down the companion hatchway.*)

JENKINS. Billy: stay clear of Jimmy-Legs.

> (JENKINS *exits down the hatchway.* BILLY *is left alone staring over the side until* CLAGGART *enters. He does not see* BILLY, *but stops near the quarterdeck ladder and gazes fixedly seaward.*)

BILLY. Good evening, sir.

CLAGGART (*startled, then subtly sarcastic*). Good evening.

BILLY. Will it be all right if I stay topside a bit to watch the water?

CLAGGART. I suppose the Handsome Sailor may do many things forbidden to his messmates.

BILLY. Yes, sir. The sea's calm tonight, isn't it? Calm and peaceful.

CLAGGART. The sea's deceitful, boy: calm above, and underneath, a world of gliding monsters preying on their fellows. Murderers, all of them. Only the sharpest teeth survive.

BILLY. I'd like to know about such things, as you do, sir.

CLAGGART. You're an ingenuous [3] sailor, Billy Budd. Is there, behind that youthful face, the wisdom pretty virtue has need of? Even the gods must know their rivals, boy; and Christ had first to recognize the ills before he cured 'em.

BILLY. What, sir?

CLAGGART. Never mind. But tell me this: how have you stomach to stand here and talk to me? Are you so innocent and ignorant of

---

[3] **ingenuous**: innocent, naive

what I am? You know my reputation. Jenkins and the rest are witnesses, and certainly you've heard them talking to me. Half of them would knife me in the back some night and do it gladly; Jenkins is thinking of it. Doubtless he'll try one day. How do you dare, then? Have you not intelligence enough to be afraid of me? To hate me as all the others do?

BILLY. Why should I be afraid of you, sir? You speak to me friendly when we meet. I know some of the men . . . are fearful of you, sir, but I can't believe they're right about it.

CLAGGART. You're a fool, fellow. In time, you'll learn to fear me like the rest. Young you are, and scarcely used to the fit of your man's flesh.

BILLY. I know they're wrong, sir. You aren't like they say. Nobody could be so.

CLAGGART. So . . . ? So what, boy? Vicious, did you mean to say, or brutal? But they aren't wrong, and you would see it, but for those blue eyes that light so kindly on your fellow men.

BILLY. Oh, I've got no education, I know that. There must be a lot of things a man misses when he's ignorant. But learning's hard. Must be sort of lonely, too.

CLAGGART. What are you prating [4] of, half-man, half-child? Your messmates crowd around, admire your yellow hair and your blue eyes, do tricks and favors for you out of love, and you talk about loneliness!

BILLY. I just noticed the way you were looking off to leeward [5] as I came up, sir. Kind of sad, you were looking.

CLAGGART. Not sadness, boy. Another feeling, more like . . . pleasure. That's it. I can feel it now, looking at you. A certain . . . pleasure.

BILLY (*flattered*). Thank you, sir.

CLAGGART (*annoyed at* BILLY'S *incomprehension*). Pah.

BILLY. Just talking with you, sir, I can tell they're wrong about you. They're ignorant, like me.

CLAGGART. Compliment for compliment, eh, boy? Have you no heart for terror, fellow? You've seen this stick in use. Have you not got sense and spleen and liver to be scared, even to be cowardly?

---

[4] **prating:** talking idly or foolishly
[5] **leeward:** the direction toward which the wind blows

BILLY. No, sir, I guess not. I like talking to you, sir. But please, sir, tell me something.

CLAGGART. I wonder if I can. Well, ask it.

BILLY. Why do you want us to believe you're cruel, and not really like everybody else?

CLAGGART. I think you are the only child alive who wouldn't understand if I explained; or else you'd not believe it.

BILLY. Oh, I'd believe you, sir. There's much I could learn from you: I never knew a man like you before.

CLAGGART (*slowly*). Do you—like me, Billy Budd?

BILLY. You've always been most pleasant with me, sir.

CLAGGART. Have I?

BILLY. Yes, sir. In the mess, the day I came aboard? And almost every day you have a pleasant word.

CLAGGART. And what I have said tonight, are these pleasant words?

BILLY. Yes, sir. I was wondering . . . could I talk to you between watches, when you've nothing else to do?

CLAGGART. You're a plausible boy, Billy. Aye, the nights are long, and talking serves to pass them.

BILLY. Thank you, sir. That would mean a lot to me.

CLAGGART. Perhaps to me as well. (*He drops his rattan.* BILLY *picks it up and hands it back to him.* CLAGGART *stares at it a moment, then at* BILLY.) No. No! Charm me, too, would you! Get away!

BILLY (*surprised and puzzled*). Aye, sir. (*He exits down the hatchway. After a pause in which* CLAGGART *recovers his self-control* SQUEAK *appears.*)

CLAGGART (*without turning*). Come here. I thought I told you to put that new seaman Budd on report. Why was it not done?

SQUEAK. I tried, Mister Claggart, sir. I couldn't find nothing out of place. Gear [6] all stowed perfect.

CLAGGART. Then disarrange it. You know the practice. I want him on report.

SQUEAK. Two of his messmates is ones nearly caught me at it before.

CLAGGART. Then be more careful. Now get along and see you make out something. (SQUEAK *scurries off below decks as* VERE *comes into sight on the quarterdeck.*)

VERE. Master-at-Arms. What is that man doing above decks?

CLAGGART. Ship's corporal, sir. A routine report.

---

[6] **gear:** clothing, equipment

VERE. There is nothing in this ship of so routine a nature that I do not concern myself in it. Remember that.

CLAGGART. Aye, aye, sir. With your permission, sir. (*Exit.* VERE *walks along the deck and scans the sails as* SEYMOUR *enters.*)

SEYMOUR. Fine evening, sir.

VERE. Yes, a fine evening, Seymour. How is the glass? [7]

SEYMOUR. Falling, I believe, sir. I think we'll toss a little before morning. Well, I suppose I should be in my cabin inspecting the deck logs.[8]

VERE. Stay for a moment, Seymour. In the days and nights to come, you and I will not often have an opportunity to stand easy and talk.

SEYMOUR. Aye, sir. I expect the French will put us to our stations any hour now.

VERE. Are you impressed by omens,[9] Seymour? This seaman we've just buried: I think of him as an omen of some sort, a melancholy prologue to this voyage.

SEYMOUR. Aye, sir. Hard on the sailor, certainly, but that's the service. But we've been lucky in other ways. An accident, now, that's unavoidable.

VERE. It was more than an accident, Seymour.

SEYMOUR. This maintop sailor? How do you mean, sir?

VERE. The man was sent aloft sick, by the Master-at-Arms, contrary to my standing order. Budd, the new seaman, implied as much, and the maintop watch confirmed it. The Master-at-Arms lied to me.

SEYMOUR. What are you going to do, sir? What action can you take? He's a valuable man, one we can hardly do without as things are now.

VERE. I shall do nothing at present, only wait and observe him. No court-martial could do more than strip him of his rank for such misconduct. I will let him have his head until some act puts him squarely counter to the law, then let the law consume him.

SEYMOUR. Why trouble the natural order to no purpose? Shouldn't we let it be?

VERE. Must a man always shrug, let things alone and drift? Would to

---

[7] glass: barometer
[8] logs: daily record of a ship's progress and speed
[9] omens: signs, portents

God I could take this power of mine and break him now, smash all the laws to powder and be a man again.

SEYMOUR. We must serve the law, sir, or give up the right and privilege of service. It's how we live.

VERE. Live? Oh, you're right. Below this deck are men who at a call skip on the hurling spars against the wind, at Beat-to-quarters run as if they willed it. Yet each of us steps alone within this pattern, this formal movement centered on itself. Men live and die, taken by pattern, born to it, knowing nothing. No man can defy the code we live by and not be broken by it.

SEYMOUR. You are the Captain, sir. You maintain that code.

VERE. Keep an order we cannot understand. That's true. The world demands it: demands that at the back of every peacemaker there be the gun, the gallows and the gaol. I talk of justice, and would turn the law gentle for those who serve here; but a Claggart stands in my shadow, for I need him. So the world goes, wanting not justice, but order . . . to be let alone to hug its own iniquities. Let a man work to windward [10] of that law and he'll be hove [11] down. No hope for him, none. (*Enter* WYATT.)

WYATT. Eight o'clock report, sir. Ship inspected and all in order.

SEYMOUR. Very well, carry on. (WYATT *goes off.*) By your leave, sir. Good night. (*Exit.* VERE *remains, crosses to the hatch and looks down, then slowly upward at the set of the sails.*)

᪷ Scene 3

SCENE: *The maindeck several nights later.*

Four bells is struck off-stage. A sailor climbs wearily down the ratlines, drops to the deck and goes below. CLAGGART *stands by the larboard rail. As* BILLY *enters from below decks, he sees the Master-at-Arms.*

BILLY. Hello, sir. (CLAGGART *looks at him without answering, then turns and goes off forward. The* DANSKER *follows* BILLY *up onto the deck.*) Well, that's all there is to tell, Dansker. I always lash my hammock just so, and stow my gear same as all the others. They don't get in trouble.

[10] **windward**: direction opposed to the wind
[11] **hove**: cast

DANSKER. Mister Claggart is down upon you, Billy.

BILLY. Jimmy-Legs? Why he calls me the sweet and pleasant fellow, they tell me.

DANSKER. Does he so, Baby lad? Aye, a sweet voice has Mister Claggart.

BILLY. For me he has. I seldom pass him but there comes a pleasant word.

DANSKER. And that's because he's down upon you.

BILLY. But he's my friend. I know he talks a little strange, but he's my friend.

DANSKER. Nobody's friend is Jimmy-Legs. Yours the least of all, maybe. Lay aloft, Baby. You'll be late to relieve your watch.

BILLY. Aye, Dansker. (*He climbs up the ratlines out of sight. The* DANSKER *watches him go.* CLAGGART *appears, but the* DANSKER *ignores him and goes off aft. As* JENKINS *comes into view climbing down the ratlines,* CLAGGART *gestures off and fades into a shadowy corner of the deck near the quarterdeck ladder.* SQUEAK *enters as* JENKINS *drops to the deck, and intercepts him as he starts down the companionway.*)

SQUEAK. It's all right, mate, slack off and stay a bit.

JENKINS. What do you want? I pick my own company.

SQUEAK. So does I, mate, so does I. And if I may make so bold to say it, you'll be smarter to pick your company more careful.

JENKINS. If you got something to say to me, talk up, else I'll get below.

SQUEAK. Don't be hasty, now, mate, don't be in a sweat. It's haste gets good men into trouble. What d'you think of our new hand here, Billy Boy? Mister Claggart's taken with him, too. Fine young fellow, ha?

JENKINS. Talk plain. What d'you mean?

SQUEAK. I overheard him talking just this day. Would maybe surprise you some, what he had to say about yourself and a few other lads.

JENKINS. What?

SQUEAK. Aoh, bit of talk about his messmates. He don't fancy us! Not like his feather boys aboard the merchantman.

JENKINS. You lying cut-throat, try something else! Billy's in my mess; since he come on board he's rare been out of my sight. You're lying! I know you too well. You'll need to try some other way

to get Bill into trouble. Get away, and don't come lying to me
no more.

SQUEAK. Aoh, so it's that friendly you are! Well, now, ain't that
sweet! You're not smart, Jenkins. Remember, man: I tried to help
you out. When you're feeling the cat between your shoulders . . .

JENKINS (*seizing him*). Get back to Jimmy-Legs. And stay out of my
way! (*He throws* SQUEAK *down and exits.* SQUEAK *watches him go.*
CLAGGART *steps out of the shadows.*)

CLAGGART. I heard your little talk. You lack subtlety; but I'm the
greater fool to use you in these matters. You're inept.[1]

SQUEAK. Aoh! Why don't you do it yourself, if you don't need me!

CLAGGART. I need nobody, least of all a rum-soaked footpad from the
Old Bailey. If you wish to have free rein with your distasteful
habits, mind your cockney manners! I stand between you and the
flogging whip. Improve your style, or you stand tomorrow fore-
noon at the gratings!

SQUEAK. I only meant as you could do it better, Mister Claggart, I
wouldn't say nothing to . . .

CLAGGART (*cuts him on the arm with his rattan*). Don't touch me!
—Keep Budd in petty troubles, that you can do. Unlash his
hammock. Keep him on report.[2] In time I'll let you know what
plans I have for him. Get aft! (SQUEAK, *eager to get away, scuttles
aft as the* DANSKER *enters.*) Well, old man. Moon's in and out
tonight. There's weather somewhere. (*The* DANSKER *turns down
the night lamp over the cabin door and starts off.*) Stay and have
a pipe.

DANSKER. I have the watch.

CLAGGART. You take your duties as seriously as ever.

DANSKER. Aye. They are all of life for an old seaman like me. (*He
turns to go.*)

CLAGGART. You move away from me as though I were some kind of
stalking beast. You avoid me, too.

DANSKER. Your word, John, "too."

CLAGGART. You know what I mean. The hands detest me. You are a
hand, older than most, and older in your hatred, I have no doubt.
But why, man? You at least should see me as I am, a man who
knows how the world's made: made as I am.

---

[1] **inept:** inefficient
[2] **report:** complaint list to a person in authority

DANSKER. How can I know what goes on in your head?

CLAGGART. The enigmatic Dansker. Come, it's dark, we can drop disguises when night serves to hold the disclosing soul apart.

DANSKER. You know who you remind me of . . . maintopman: Billy Budd.

CLAGGART. More enigmas! [3] That sunny, smiling infant with no spleen nor knowledge in his head?

DANSKER. I'll leave you now.

CLAGGART. No, stay a while. This is a night for secrets and disclosures.

DANSKER. You have half the truth and Billy Budd the other. He can't see there's evil in the world, and you won't see the good.

CLAGGART. So. And I take it you come in between.

DANSKER. I keep outside. I am too old to stand between sky and water.

CLAGGART. And yet you hate me, too.

DANSKER. I hate an incomplete man.

CLAGGART. Hate me and have done. Let it alone, I say. Whatever else it is, this thing is Man, still!

DANSKER. I'll be off.

CLAGGART. Don't go. The moon's gone under. Let us talk this out. You are a wise man in your senile way.

DANSKER. Then take this for all my wisdom. You recognize the hatred of your shipmates as an honor paid to a soul they cannot understand. Your fine contempt for human love is nothing but regret.

CLAGGART. Stop there. I know the rest by heart. Nothing you say to me but clatters in my belly, watch on watch. Aye: when this arm moves out in gesture of love, it mocks me with a blow. Who lifts this arm? What officer commands this hireling flesh? Somewhere below the farthest marks and deeps, God anchors hearts, and his sea rusts mine hollow. The flukes [4] break in the bottom, and I slack and stand, go in and out forever at God's humor. Look at this sea: for all her easy swell, who knows what bones, ribs and decay are fathomed at her base and move in her motion, so that on the flattest water, the very stricture [5] of the dead can kill that beauty with a dance of death?—Here is a man. He holds, past fathom curves, drowned fleets of human agonies that gesture when the long tide pulls.

[3] **enigmas:** puzzles
[4] **flukes:** the blades at the arm of an anchor
[5] **stricture:** criticism, censure

DANSKER. Aye, John. But you must know that other men are moved so. Look up some evening at the quarterdeck for another poor thoughtful devil like you, like me, pacing all night between his doubts.

CLAGGART. What, Vere? That fine-drawn manner doesn't deceive me. There's a whited sepulchre, like all soft-spoken charmers of this world.

DANSKER. You don't believe in anything besides yourself, eh John?

CLAGGART. I've said what I have said. I know myself, and look to that. You should try it. Go to your post, old man, and your ever-lasting duties. (CLAGGART *turns away.* BILLY *scrambles into view down the ratlines and calls out excitedly.*)

BILLY. Quarterdeck ho!

RATCLIFFE (*coming forward to the forward break of the quarter-deck*). Sound off!

BILLY. Strange sail one mile off the larboard beam!

CLAGGART (*to* DANSKER). A Frenchman! Get to your station.

RATCLIFFE (*on the quarterdeck ladder*). Mister Duncan! Sound Beat-to-quarters! Clear for action!

DUNCAN (*off-stage*). Aye aye, sir!

RATCLIFFE. Gardiner! (*Enter* GARDINER.)

GARDINER. Sir?

RATCLIFFE. Report to the Captain, strange sail on the larboard beam. Then send Payne to the wheel. (*Exit* GARDINER.) Master-at-Arms, send a man to the mast to relay lookout's reports. Inspect battle stations and report to me when they are fully manned.

CLAGGART. Aye aye, sir. (*Exit.*)

VOICE (*off-stage*). She's a French frigate! Steering east by south! (*Enter* VERE *and* SEYMOUR.)

VERE. Prepare to make chase. Have your quartermaster steer small.

RATCLIFFE. Aye aye, sir.

(*Enter the* DRUMMER *and sound Beat-to-quarters. Men run on, to gun stations, rigging, crossing stage and off.*)

SEYMOUR. She's too fast for us, sir. We'll never come up with her.

VERE. We are bound to try, though we were sure to fail. And we may smell powder before this chase is over.

CLAGGART (*reentering*). Battle stations fully manned, sir!

SEYMOUR. May we try a shot at her now?

VERE. She's drawing south. Yes, commence firing, Mr. Seymour.

SEYMOUR. Larboard battery, fire one!
DUNCAN. Fire! (*Fire one gun.*)
VERE. Fire at will!
SEYMOUR. Fire at will!
    (*Guns fire dissynchronously.*[6])

[6] **dissynchronously:** at different times

ACT II

✑ Scene 1

SCENE: *The quarterdeck and part of the maindeck a few minutes before 0800.*[1] *A high wind. On the quarterdeck are* LIEUTENANT WYATT, MIDSHIPMAN REA *and the helmsman,* STOLL.

REA. I'm glad this watch is over. I'm tired.
WYATT. Make your entry in the log before your relief comes up. Bring it out here and I'll sign it.
REA. Aye, sir. What was our last position, do you remember?
WYATT. Thirteen ten west, forty-three forty north.
REA. And an easterly breeze.
WYATT. Aye, make it so. That'll make Ratcliffe happy. Last time he had an east wind, she blew his hat over the side. And put down "Running ground swell."
REA. Aye aye, sir. (*Exits.*)
WYATT. Helmsman, keep her close-hauled.
STOLL. I can't, sir. Too much cloth in the wind.
WYATT. Well hold her close as you can, and let the next watch reef sail if they like.
STOLL. Aye aye, sir. (*Enter* RATCLIFFE.)
WYATT. Morning, Johnny! You're on time!
RATCLIFFE. What's the course?
WYATT. Steady south. Wind's easterly. Glass is dropping.
RATCLIFFE. East wind? (*Enter* BYREN, *the relief helmsman.*) By the way, you forgot to sign the order book.
WYATT. All right. Thanks.
STOLL. I've been relieved, sir. Byren has the helm.

[1] 0800: 8 A.M.

WYATT. Very well. (*Exit* STOLL.) Who's mate of your watch?

RATCLIFFE. The Admiralty midshipman. That lobcock Gardiner, hang him. (*Eight bells.*)

WYATT. Where is he? It's eight. (*Enter* REA *and* GARDINER *separately, meeting.*)

RATCLIFFE. There he comes. He looks happy. That means trouble for some poor devil. (GARDINER *snatches the log out of* REA's *hands and bounds up to the quarterdeck.*)

REA. I've been relieved, sir. Horatio, Lord Gardiner has the watch.

WYATT. Ah, Midshipman Gardiner. The backbone of the British Navy. All right, Rea. You can turn in. (REA *exits.*)

RATCLIFFE. Pity we lost that Frenchman last night. A little action would season the monotony of these interminable watches.

WYATT. Did you ever hear of a ship-of-the-line running down a frigate, even with the wind? Ah, it's a magnificent morning! Thickening overcast, heavy ground swell, a fresh levanter breeze, and you, Johnny, are the Pride of the Morning!

RATCLIFFE. Mmm. Has the skipper been on deck yet?

WYATT. Not since sunrise. He came up then and paced the deck and stared off east like a sleepwalker. Then went below again without a word.

RATCLIFFE. He thinks too much.

WYATT. Well if you ever make captain, your crew won't have that to complain of, anyway. Am I relieved?

RATCLIFFE. Yes, I relieve you. (*Tosses his cap to* WYATT.) Here. Take this below, will you?

WYATT. What? You'll be out of uniform, man. Mister Gardiner wouldn't approve of your standing watch without a hat, would you, Midshipman Gardiner?

GARDINER. Sir, the Articles state that officers on watch . . .

RATCLIFFE. Well hang it, I lost twelve shillings the last time my hat went over the rail, and this is the only other one I've got. To hell with the Articles.

WYATT. Mind your language! It's downright mutinous. Well, don't expect me to stand your watches if you catch your death of cold. Good morning. (*Exit.*)

GARDINER. Midshipman Rea, sir, I don't like to say it, but his log entries are impossible.

RATCLIFFE. Then enter yourself, Mister Gardiner. So are you.

GARDINER. Yes, sir. But I do think he ought to be told . . .

RATCLIFFE. Go find the Captain and report to him the wind's abeam. Respectfully suggest we ought to take in topsails.

GARDINER. Aye aye, sir. (*He goes down stairs.*)

RATCLIFFE. And don't forget to tell him I haven't got a hat.

GARDINER. What's that, sir?

RATCLIFFE. Nothing, sir! You got my order. Dump your ballast and shove off!

GARDINER. I thought you spoke to me, sir.

RATCLIFFE. I avoid that whenever possible. Move!

GARDINER. Yes, sir.

RATCLIFFE. Ye gods, what a brat. Nothing off, helmsman. She's well enough thus.

BYREN. Nothing off, sir.

GARDINER (*nearly bumping into* VERE *as he emerges from cabin, followed by* SEYMOUR *and* HALLAM.) Atten-tion!

RATCLIFFE. Good morning, sir.

VERE. Morning, Mister Ratcliffe.

GARDINER (*starting after* VERE, *bumps into* HALLAM). Watch what you're doing!

VERE. Midshipman Gardiner.

GARDINER. Sir?

VERE. How long, pray, have you been in this ship, or any ship?

GARDINER. This is my first cruise, sir.

VERE. Your first cruise. A wartime cruise as well. And you are a midshipman. A midshipman, Mister Gardiner, let me tell you, is neither fish, flesh, nor fowl, and certainly no seaman. And unless you have a mind to be generally known as Spit-kit Gardiner, I recommend more tolerance toward the men. Now, is that clear?

GARDINER. Aye aye, sir!

VERE. Very well, you may carry on.

RATCLIFFE. We've a weather helm, sir, and bow seas.

VERE. Take in topsails, if you please, Mister Ratcliffe.

RATCLIFFE. Aye aye, sir. Mister Duncan!

DUNCAN (*enters*). Aye, sir?

RATCLIFFE. Douse your topsails and topgallants. Haul in the weather braces.

DUNCAN. Aye aye, sir. (*Exit.*) Away aloft! Hands by topgallant sheets and halyards!

GARDINER. Aloft there! Keep fast the weather sheets till the yards are down, . . . if you please!

RATCLIFFE. Get aloft yourself, Mister Gardiner, see they do it right, since you're not satisfied.

GARDINER. Sir, the Articles state that . . .

RATCLIFFE. Did you hear me?

GARDINER. Aye aye, sir. (*Exits up ratlines.*)

DUNCAN (*off-stage*). Haul taut!

VERE. You disapprove of Gardiner, Mister Ratcliffe?

RATCLIFFE. He seems to think he's the only midshipman aboard capable of doing anything properly. He's always looking at you as if your hat weren't squared.

VERE. That is an unfortunate simile under the present circumstances.

RATCLIFFE (*caught*). Oh, I—er—Keep her close to the wind, helmsman. Don't fall away!

DUNCAN (*off-stage*). Let go topgallant bowlines!

VERE. I think Gardiner has had enough correction for one day. Call him down to our level, Mister Ratcliffe.

RATCLIFFE. Aye, sir. Mister Gardiner! You may come off your perch now! (BILLY *descends rigging and starts off-stage.*) What do you think of our new man Budd, Captain?

SEYMOUR. That boy did a smart piece of work for us last night, sir. He's the nimblest man on the tops I've ever watched. Wyatt wants him for captain of the foretop.

VERE. Very well, let Budd take the post. He certainly deserves it for his actions last night during the chase. I'll speak to him myself.

SEYMOUR. He'll like hearing it from you, sir.

VERE. Hallam, go call Budd, the lad moving forward there. (*Exit* HALLAM. GARDINER *appears, looking sick.*) Well done, Gardiner. You may lay below and draw an extra tot of rum. You looks . . . chilly.

GARDINER. Thank you, sir. (*Exit.*)

SEYMOUR. By the way, sir, Budd has been on the Master-at-Arms' report once or twice for some petty misdemeanor. Nothing serious. (*Steps aside with* RATCLIFFE. BILLY *enters, followed by* HALLAM.)

BILLY. You sent for me, sir?

VERE. Yes, Budd. Your division officer recommends you for a post of more responsibility. He thinks you can perform duties of a higher station, and so do I, after last night. So I've agreed that you shall have Williams' place on the foretop.

BILLY. But—Williams is captain of the foretop, sir.

VERE. The station calls for a younger man. Lieutenant Wyatt asked for you, and the spirit you showed last night warrants it. That is a real honor for a man so new on board.

BILLY. The Navy's new to me, Captain, but I hardly know anything else but the sea and ships.

VERE. And how do you like us, now that the awesomeness has worn away a bit?

BILLY. The Navy's a bustling world, sir. Bigger than the *Rights of Man*, and I get lost sometimes. But my mates lend me a hand. Why even Jimmy-Legs—beg pardon, sir, the Master-at-Arms, I mean—he's good to me, too.

VERE. The sea and the Navy exact a discipline, but it need not be a harsh one. In some ways I envy the man who dances across the tops and seems to rule the ship and sea below. Up there is a pleach [2] of ropes for you to make a world of. Though winds have their way with tackle of your world, you live at ease against your strength and the round bole of the mast in your back. You are a king up there, while the water curds and frolics at the forefoot. I envy you that stance.

BILLY. You can trust me, Captain.

VERE. I do, boy. Very well, that's all.

BILLY. Aye aye, sir. Thank you, sir, thank you! (*He runs off.*)

VERE. Hallam, find the Master-at-Arms and bid him report to me.

HALLAM. Aye aye, sir. (*Exit.* SEYMOUR *joins* VERE.)

VERE. If I had a son, I'd hope for one like Budd.

SEYMOUR. Aye, sir. Fine boy. He's a force for order in this ship, certainly. I hope his charm's contagious.

VERE. One such is enough. Men cannot stand very much perfection. It's a disease that we stamp out at its first rash showing. (*Enter* CLAGGART. SEYMOUR *withdraws.*) Master-at-Arms, I want to make a change on the Watch, Quarter and Station Bill. I needn't have troubled you about it until later, but I am especially interested in this change.

CLAGGART. The time of day is indifferent to me, sir.

---

[2] **pleach:** interweaving

VERE. Williams, present captain of the foretop, is assigned to the afterguard. I am replacing him with Budd.

CLAGGART. William Budd, sir? You do not mean the so-called Handsome Sailor?

VERE. Aye, William Budd, the new seaman from the *Rights of Man*.

CLAGGART. I know him, sir.

VERE. Do you find anything unusual in this replacement?

CLAGGART. You must be aware, sir, that he is . . .

VERE. Well? That he is what? I know he's an able seaman.

CLAGGART. Nothing, sir. But I wondered if he were entirely trustworthy. He has been aboard such a brief time.

VERE. Long enough to prove himself to me, and to his shipmates.

CLAGGART. Very good, sir.

VERE. He is captain of the foretop. That is all.

CLAGGART. With your permission, sir. Will there not be some dissatisfaction among the foretopmen who have been aboard much longer than Budd?

VERE. Master-at-Arms: I concern myself with these matters. They are none of your function. Until such time as the senior topmen formally object to Budd for incapacity, he is captain of the foretop. Make it so on the Bill. (*Exit.*)

RATCLIFFE. What are you waiting for, man? Light to dawn? Promotion? You got the order.

CLAGGART. With your permission, sir.

(As CLAGGART *goes off*, RATCLIFFE *spits over the rail*.)

৺৳ Scene 2

SCENE: *Forward part of the deck. Night. Eight bells. A man descends the rigging and goes off.* CLAGGART *enters, stands by the hatch for a moment, then exits forward.* BILLY *comes down off watch, drops to the deck and remains in shadow, leaning over the rail, looking seaward.* JENKINS *stealthily and silently comes up from below deck.*

BILLY. Jenkins! What you doing topside . . . (JENKINS *puts his hand over* BILLY'S *mouth.*)

JENKINS (*in a whisper*). Stow the noise! (*Releases* BILLY.)

BILLY. You're after Mister Claggart, like you said you would!

JENKINS. Well? What about it? You try and stop me?

BILLY. He knows, Jenkins! I tell you, he knows! He's ready for you!

JENKINS. Then I'll oblige him! I been waiting up here every night, waiting for him to come by when it's dark. Now get away and let me do it!

BILLY. No! I won't let you hang yourself!

JENKINS. I don't give a fiddler's dam what happens to me! Move out of my way, mate!

BILLY. No! Give me the knife.

JENKINS. The knife's for Claggart. You're a nice boy, Bill, but I ain't playing with you. You get away below, quick. This game ain't for boys.

BILLY. Jenkins! You'll hang yourself!

JENKINS. Take your hands off! The moon's under, I can do it now! Leave me go!

BILLY. No!

JENKINS. Yes!

(JENKINS *strikes* BILLY; *struggle, in which* BILLY *wrests knife from* JENKINS, *and it falls on deck.* BILLY *knocks* JENKINS *down.*)

CLAGGART (*off-stage*). What's that noise? Stand where you are! (*Entering.*) You again! Well? Explain this pageant.

BILLY. He . . . I had to hit him, sir. He struck at me.

CLAGGART. Mm. And drew that knife on you, too, no doubt.

BILLY. Yes, sir.

CLAGGART. I have been waiting, forward there, for Jenkins. You intercepted him, I take it.

BILLY. I didn't know you were looking for him, sir.

CLAGGART. You shouldn't meddle, my fine young friend, in matters that don't concern you! I was expecting him. (*Enter* DANSKER.) There, help the body up. I do not thank you, boy, for cheating me of the pleasure of his punishment.

WYATT (*off-stage*). What's the disturbance there? You, forward on the spar-deck!

CLAGGART. Master-at-Arms reports all in order, sir!

WYATT (*off-stage*). Stand where you are.

CLAGGART. The sweet and pleasant fellow saved you, Jenkins. But I reserve you still for my own justice in due time. Say nothing to this officer. (*Enter* WYATT.)

WYATT. What's the matter, Master-at-Arms? It's an odd hour for star-gazing.

CLAGGART. A slight matter, sir. I found these two men together here on deck, contrary to the Captain's orders. I was sending them below when you called out.

WYATT. Oh, is that all. Carry on, then.

CLAGGART. Aye aye, sir. Now then, get below, both of you. (*Enter* VERE *followed by* HALLAM. *The* DANSKER *goes off.*) Attention!

VERE. Wyatt, what's this mean?

WYATT. Two men on deck without permission, sir.

VERE. Is there no more to this? The story's lame, man. What occurred? (*Silence.*) Very well, then. Go along, both of you.

BILLY. Aye aye, sir. Come along, mate. (*Exits with* JENKINS.)

VERE. Your knife, Master-at-Arms?

CLAGGART. William Budd's, sir, I believe.

VERE. Return it to him. (*Exits with* HALLAM *and* WYATT.)

(CLAGGART *raps rail with rattan.* SQUEAK *approaches warily.*)

CLAGGART. Listen carefully; you may make up for your late mistakes if you do this smartly. Give Budd just time enough to get to sleep. At four bells wake him. Bring him to the lee forechains. You understand?

SQUEAK. Mister Claggart, sir . . . we done enough to him. He's a good lad, Mister Claggart. Couldn't it be somebody else? Jenkins, maybe?

CLAGGART. So. He's softened your heart too, eh? Do as you're ordered, man, or I'll see your back laid raw with a flogging whip! Remember: I will be watching you. Bring him to the lee forechains. And when you're there . . .

SQUEAK. Dansker. Moving forward.

CLAGGART. Step back, you fool. Wait for me.

(*Exit* SQUEAK. *The* DANSKER *enters.*)

DANSKER. Baby saved you, eh? And you are angry.

CLAGGART. Saved me, you say? From what? I've tried to tempt Jenkins to this blow, so as to break his toplofty spirit with his neck; and I am "saved" by that guileless idiot! He'd turn the other cheek to me, in Christian kindness! Well: there's a second pleasure in striking that same face twice. I can destroy him, too, if I choose to do it!

DANSKER. Crazy, crazy!

CLAGGART. All right, old man, call it madness then. Whatever its name, it will plunder the sweetness from that face, or it will kill us both.

DANSKER. You are afraid of him.

CLAGGART. Afraid? Of Budd? What nonsense is that?

DANSKER. He usurps the crew; they turn from hating you to loving him, and leave you impotent.[1]

CLAGGART. That innocent frighten me! That witless kindness that spills from him has neither force nor aim. Stand out from between us, or you founder together, sink in five hundred fathoms with him, if I want it so!

DANSKER. Aye, then, if you take that tack, let it be both of us. You expect me to sit by and watch your deliberate arm seize him and force him under?

CLAGGART. Why not? You have always done that. I thought your practice was to stay outside. What breeds the saintly knight errant in you?

DANSKER. I am old, but I have some manhood left.

CLAGGART. What can you do? You've drifted with the tide too long, old one. You are as involved as I am now.

DANSKER. So you may say. In this ship a man lives as he can, and finds a way to make life tolerable for himself. I did so. That was a fault. But no longer.

CLAGGART. Stand clear. You haven't courage to cross me.

DANSKER. Eh, I'm not afraid of you; I see your scheme.

(CLAGGART *strikes him; the* DANSKER *falls.*)

CLAGGART. You can see only what I let you see!

DANSKER. Say what you like. I see your scheme; so will Captain if need be.

CLAGGART (*pulling him to his feet*). Take a warning for yourself, old man. And keep away! You are on watch, eh? Well, go back to sleep again, or I'll report you. (DANSKER *exits.* CLAGGART *watches him go, then violently breaks his rattan and throws the pieces over the side.*)

---

[1] impotent: powerless

SCENE: *Forward part of the main deck. Four bells.* CLAGGART *stands with one hand on the rail, waiting. After a short pause, hearing a sound, he fades into shadow.* SQUEAK *enters, bending over and running.*

SQUEAK. Hsssssssssst! (BILLY, *sleepy and rubbing his eyes, enters.*)

BILLY. You brought me all the way up here, out of my hammock. Now what do you want?

SQUEAK. I heard you're captain of the foretop, Bill. That right?

BILLY. Aye. What's that to do with you?

SQUEAK. Ah, now you can be more use to your shipmates then ever you was before.

BILLY. What?

SQUEAK. You was impressed, now, weren't you? Well, so was I. We're not the only impressed ones, Billy. There's a gang of us. Could you help . . . at a pinch?

BILLY. What do you mean?

SQUEAK. See here . . . (*Holds up two coins.*) Here's two gold guineas [1] for you, Bill. Put in with us. Most of the men aboard are only waiting for a word, and they'll follow you. There's more for you where these come from. What d'you say? If you join us, Bill, there's not a man aboard won't come along! Are you with us? The ship'll be ours when we're ready to take it!

BILLY. I don't know what you're driving at, but you had better go where you belong! (SQUEAK, *surprised, does not move.* BILLY *springs up.*) If you don't start, I'll toss you back over the rail! (SQUEAK *decamps.* BILLY *watches him and starts off himself.* DANSKER, *off-stage, calls out.*)

DANSKER. Hallo, what's the matter? (*Enters.*) Ah, Beauty, is it you again? Something must have been the matter, for you stammered. (CLAGGART *appears and comes forward.*)

CLAGGART. You seem to favor the maindeck, Billy Budd. What brings you topside at this hour, man, against my orders and the Captain's?

BILLY. I . . . found an afterguardsman in our part of the ship here, and I bid him be off where he belongs.

DANSKER. And is that all you did about it, boy?

BILLY. Aye, Dansker, nothing more.

---

[1] **guinea:** English gold coin worth approximately $3

CLAGGART. A strange sort of hour to police the deck. Name the after-guardsman.

BILLY. I . . . can't say, Mister Claggart. I couldn't see him clear enough.

DANSKER. Don't be a fool, speak up, accuse him.

CLAGGART. Well?

BILLY. I can't say, sir.

CLAGGART. You refuse? Then get below, and stay where you belong.

BILLY. Aye aye, sir. Good night, sir. Good night, Dansker. (*Exits.*)

CLAGGART. I'm glad you saw this mutinous behavior.

DANSKER. Your crazy brain squeezes out false conclusions. He has done nothing except find you out, though he's too innocent to know it.

CLAGGART. I am not hoodwinked by his weak excuse. What else would he be doing at this hour, but fanning rebel tempers like his own?

DANSKER. I stood in the shadows forward when Squeak slipped by me, running from this place. You set him on, on purpose to trap Billy.

CLAGGART. And I will do that, old man. But you will say nothing about it; see you don't. (*Enter* VERE, *followed by* HALLAM.)

VERE. Well, Master-at-Arms. You stand long watches.

CLAGGART. Sir. May I take the liberty of reserving my explanation for your private ear. I believe your interest in this matter would incline you to prefer some privacy.

VERE (*to* DANSKER *and* HALLAM). Leave us. Hallam, stand within hail. (DANSKER *and* HALLAM *go off.*) Well? What is it you wish to say, Master-at-Arms?

CLAGGART. During my rounds this night, I have seen enough to convince me that one man aboard, at least, is dangerous; especially in a ship which musters some who took a guilty part in the late serious uprisings . . .

VERE. You may spare a reference to that.

CLAGGART. Your pardon, sir. Quite lately I have begun to notice signs of some sort of movement secretly afoot, and prompted by the man in question. I thought myself not warranted, so long as this suspicion was only indistinct, in reporting it. But recently . . .

VERE. Come to the point, man.

CLAGGART. Sir, I deeply feel the cruel responsibility of making a report involving such serious consequences to the sailor mainly concerned. But God forbid, sir, that this ship should suffer the experience of the Nore.

VERE. Never mind that! You say there is one dangerous man. Name him.

CLAGGART. William Budd, the . . . captain of the foretop.

VERE. William Budd?

CLAGGART. The same, sir. But for all his youth and appealing manners, a secret, vicious lad.

VERE. How, vicious?

CLAGGART. He insinuates himself into the good will of his mates so that they will at least say a word for him, perhaps even take action with him, should it come to that. With your pardon, sir; you note but his fair face; under that there lies a man-trap.

VERE (*after a pause*). Master-at-Arms, I intend to test your accusation here and now. Hallam! (*Enter* HALLAM.)

HALLAM. Aye, sir.

VERE. Find Budd, the foretopman. Manage to tell him out of earshot that he is wanted here. Keep him in talk yourself. Go along.

HALLAM. Aye aye, sir. (*Exits.*)

VERE (*angry and perturbed*). Do you come to me with such a foggy tale, Master-at-Arms? As to William Budd, cite me an act, or spoken word of his, confirming what you here in general charge against him. Wait; weigh what you speak. Just now, and in this case, there is the yardarm end for false witness.

CLAGGART. I understand, sir. Tonight, when on my rounds, discovering Budd's hammock was unused, I combed the ship, and found him in conclave with several growlers; men, who, like himself, spread unrest and rebellion in the crew. They were collected here, near the lee forechains, and when I ordered them below, young Budd and others threatened me, and swore they'd drop me, and some officers they hate, overboard, some misty night. Should you, sir, desire substantial proof, it is not far.

(*Enter* HALLAM, *followed by* BILLY.)

VERE. Hallam, stand apart and see that we are not disturbed. (HALLAM *exits*.) And now, Master-at-Arms, tell this man to his face what you told me of him.

CLAGGART (*moving near to* BILLY, *and looking directly at him*). Certainly, sir. I said this man, this William Budd, acting so out of angry resentment against impressment and his officers, against this ship, this Service, and the King, breeds in the crew a spirit of rebellion against the officers, the mates, and me, urging some outrage like the late revolt. I myself have seen and heard him speak with manifest malingerers and men who growl of mistreatment, harshness, unfair pay and similar complaints. I say this man threatened his officers with murder, and was bent tonight on urging other men to act concertedly in mutiny. I have nothing further to say, sir.

BILLY (*tries to speak, but can make only incoherent sounds. He seems to be in pain from the contortions of his face and the gurgling which is all he can effect for speech*).

VERE. Speak, man, speak! Defend yourself! (*Remembering* BILLY's *impediment, goes to him and puts a hand on his shoulder reassuringly.*) There is no hurry, boy. Take your time, take your time.

(*After agonized dumb gesturing and stammering, increased by* VERE's *kindness,* BILLY's *arm hits out at* CLAGGART. CLAGGART *staggers, falls, lies still.*)

VERE. Stand back, man! It was a lie, then! (BILLY, *shaking, only stares at the body.* VERE *raises the body to a sitting position. Since* CLAGGART *remains inert,* VERE *lowers him again slowly, then rises.* BILLY *tries again to speak, without success; he is crying and badly frightened.*) No need to speak now, Billy. Hallam! (*Enter* HALLAM) Tell the Surgeon I wish to see him here at once. And bid Mister Seymour report to my cabin without delay. (*To* BILLY) Retire to the stateroom aft. Remain there till I summon you. (BILLY *exits.* VERE *waits, turning once to stare at* CLAGGART's *body. Enter the* SURGEON.) Surgeon, tell me how it is with him. (SURGEON *bends over* CLAGGART *briefly, then looks up in surprise.*) Come, we must dispatch. Go now. I shall presently call a drumhead court to try the man who dropped him there. Tell the lieutenants that a foretopman has, in an accidental fury, killed this man. Inform the Captain of Marines as well, and charge them to keep the matter to themselves. (SURGEON *exits.*) The divine judgment of Ananias! [2] Struck dead by the Angel of God . . . and I must judge the Angel. Can I save him? Have I that choice?

---

[2] **Ananias:** a Biblical character who was struck dead for lying

ACT III

❧ Scene 1

SCENE: *Captain* VERE's *cabin, a quarter of an hour later.* VERE *and* SEY-
MOUR.

SEYMOUR. Budd beat a man to death! What had he done?

VERE. Lied again: lied to Budd's face, hoping to kill him by it. Oh,
the boy was tempted to it past endurance.

SEYMOUR. False witness has its penalty, sir. Budd has set our justice
right.

VERE. Aye, too right. This natural, right act, done in an instinct's
fever of recognition, was late and fatal.

SEYMOUR. What are you going to do, Captain? Isn't this last lie of
the Master-at-Arms the very act you were waiting for, so as to let
the law destroy him, as you said? He should have suffered at the
yardarm if Billy hadn't killed him.

VERE. Yes. He should. But by fair process of authority. Budd has
prevented that, and turned the law against himself.

SEYMOUR. You can't condemn the boy for answering with his arm
for lack of words! The motive was clearly justified.

VERE. Aye, but was the act? (*Forcefully.*) Try, try to convince me I
am wrong!

SEYMOUR. This Master-at-Arms, you knew him for a liar, a vicious dog.

VERE. A dog's obeyed in office. Claggart was authority.

SEYMOUR. Then authority's an evil!

VERE. It often is. But it commands, and no man is its equal, not Billy,
nor you, nor I. It will strike us down, and rightly, if we resist it.

SEYMOUR. Rightly! What power gives evil its authority! We should
thank God the man's dead, and the world well rid of that particular devil.

VERE. Our life has ways to hedge its evil in. No one must go above
them; even innocents. Laws of one kind or other shape our course
from birth to death. These are the laws pronouncing Billy's guilt;
Admiralty codes are merely shadows of them.

SEYMOUR. That's tyranny, not law, forcing conformity to wrongs,
giving the victory to the devil himself!

VERE. I thought so once. But without this lawful tyranny, what

should we have but worse tyranny of anarchy and chaos? So aboard
this man-of-war. Oh, if I were a man alone, manhood would
declare for Billy.

SEYMOUR. Then do it. Put your strength and your authority behind
Budd, and let him go.

VERE. When I think I could have watched him grow in comely whole-
ness of manhood . . . all lost now. What could have been,
quenched in evil, swept out by that undertow.

SEYMOUR. It's more than anyone can have to answer for, Captain; to
his peers, or to his God. Let him go free and try on mortal flesh!
Will you urge a noose for him, marked like a common felon,[1] and
that devil still to have his wish, killing the boy at last?

VERE. Can I do otherwise? I'd give my life to save his, if I could.

SEYMOUR. It's in your hands, Captain. Only you can help him now.

VERE. Billy, Billy. What have we done to you? (*Knock.*) Yes, come
in. (*Enter* HALLAM.)

HALLAM. Lieutenants Ratcliffe and Wyatt, sir.

VERE. Let them come in. (*Enter* RATCLIFFE *and* WYATT.)

SEYMOUR. You both know why you've been summoned hither?

WYATT. Yes, sir.

RATCLIFFE. Aye, sir, in a general sort of way.

SEYMOUR. Then take your chairs. Ratcliffe. You here, Wyatt. You
are appointed members of a court-martial convened under extraordinary circumstances by Captain Vere. I am Senior Member, and
I declare this court open. (WYATT, RATCLIFFE, *and* SEYMOUR *sit.*
VERE *remains standing, apart.*) Sentry, bring the prisoner in.
(HALLAM *salutes and exits.*) As you know, the Master-at-Arms has
been killed by the foretopman, Budd. Whether by accident or by
design, and whether the act shall carry the penalty of death or
no, you are to decide. There is only one witness, Captain Vere.
I shall call upon him to give his deposition as soon as the sentry
brings in the prisoner. (*An uneasy silence.*)

WYATT. Budd wouldn't kill a minnow without good reason.

RATCLIFFE. What did the . . .

SEYMOUR. I had rather you did not express an opinion until after
you have heard the evidence. (*Another awkward silence.* HALLAM
finally enters with BILLY.) Sentry, stand outside. (*Exit* HALLAM.)
You may sit down.

[1] felon: a person who has committed a serious crime, such as murder

BILLY. Th-th-thank you, sir.

SEYMOUR. Captain: will you be good enough to give us your account?

VERE (*turning towards them*). I speak not as your Captain, but as witness before this court. The Master-at-Arms early this morning detailed to me an account of mutinous sentiments expressed by Budd, and in particular, spoke of overhearing a specific conversation last night on the mid-watch. He alleged that Budd offered him violence and threatened further violence against the officers.

WYATT. Budd a mutineer! That's absurd, he's the best-liked man . . .

SEYMOUR. Lieutenant Wyatt. Please do not interrupt the witness.

RATCLIFFE. Did the Master-at-Arms specify who the other malcontents were, sir?

VERE. He did not. He said merely that he was in possession of substantial proof of his accusation.

SEYMOUR. With your permission, sir . . . Budd, did you speak with anyone in the Master-at-Arms' hearing last night?

BILLY. I . . . spoke a little . . . with the Dansker, sir.

WYATT. Who is the Dansker?

BILLY. He's just called the Dansker, sir. He's always called so.

RATCLIFFE. I know him. A mainmast sailor.

SEYMOUR. Sentry. (*Enter* HALLAM.)

HALLAM. Sir.

SEYMOUR. Do you know a mainmast sailor referred to as "the Dansker"?

HALLAM. Aye, sir.

SEYMOUR. Go on deck and find him. Let him know apart that he is wanted here, and arrange it so that none of the other people notice his withdrawing. See you do it tactfully. I want no curiosity aroused among the men.

HALLAM. Aye aye, sir. (*Exits.*)

SEYMOUR. Please go on.

VERE. I sent at once for Budd. I ordered the Master-at-Arms to be present at this interview, to make his accusation to Budd's face.

RATCLIFFE. May I ask what was the prisoner's reaction on being confronted by the Master-at-Arms?

VERE. I perceived no sign of uneasiness in his demeanor. I believe he smiled.

RATCLIFFE. And for the Master-at-Arms?

VERE. When I directed him to repeat his accusation, he faced Budd and did so.

WYATT. Did Budd reply?

VERE. He tried to speak, but could not frame his words.

SEYMOUR. And then, sir?

VERE. He answered with blows, and his accuser fell. . . . It was apparent at once that the attack was fatal, but I summoned the Surgeon to verify the fact. That is all. (*He turns away.*)

SEYMOUR (*to* BILLY). You have heard Captain Vere's account. Is it, or is it not, as he says?

BILLY. Captain Vere tells the truth. It is just as Captain Vere says, but it is not as the Master-at-Arms said. I have eaten the King's bread, and I am true to the King.

VERE. I believe you, boy.

BILLY. God knows . . . I . . . thank you, sir.

SEYMOUR. Was there any malice between you and the Master-at-Arms?

BILLY. I bore no malice against the Master-at-Arms. I'm sorry he is dead. I did not mean to kill him. If I'd found my tongue, I would not have struck him. But he lied foully to my face, and I . . . had to say . . . something . . . and I could only say it . . . with a blow. God help me.

SEYMOUR. One question more—you tell us that what the Master-at-Arms said against you was a lie. Now, why should he have lied with such obvious malice, when you have declared that there was no malice between you? (BILLY *looks appealingly at* VERE.) Did you hear my question?

BILLY. I . . . I . . .

VERE. The question you put to him comes naturally enough. But can he rightly answer it? Or anyone else, unless, indeed, it be he who lies within there. (*Knock and enter immediately* HALLAM.)

HALLAM. The mainmast man, sir.

SEYMOUR. Send him in. (HALLAM *nods off and the* DANSKER *enters.* HALLAM *withdraws, closing door.*) State your name and station.

DANSKER. I have no name. I'm called the Dansker, that's all I know. Mainmast man.

SEYMOUR. You have been summoned in secrecy to appear as a witness before this court, of which I am Senior Member. I may not at this time disclose to you the nature of the offense being tried.

However, the offender is William Budd, foretopman. (*Pause.*) Do you consent to give this court your testimony, though ignorant of the case at trial, and further, to keep in strictest confidence all that passes here?

DANSKER. Aye.

SEYMOUR (*pushes forward a Bible*). Do you so swear?

DANSKER (*touching the Bible*). I do.

SEYMOUR. Then this is my question. In your opinion, is there malice between Budd and the Master-at-Arms?

DANSKER. Aye.

VERE (*wheeling around*). How!

SEYMOUR. Explain your statement.

DANSKER. How should he not have hated him?

SEYMOUR. Be plain, man. We do not deal in riddles here.

DANSKER. Master-at-Arms bore malice towards a grace he could not have. There was no reason for it.

RATCLIFFE. In other words, this malice was one-sided?

DANSKER. Aye.

RATCLIFFE. And you cannot explain how it arose?

DANSKER. Master-at-Arms hated Billy . . .

SEYMOUR. One moment. I notice that you have been using the past tense in your testimony. Why?

DANSKER. I look around and sense finality here.

WYATT. You cannot explain further the cause of Claggart's hate for Budd?

DANSKER. Master-at-Arms made his world in his own image. Pride was his demon, and he kept it strong by others' fear of him. Billy could not imagine such a nature, saw nothing but a lonely man, strange, but a man still, nothing to be feared. So Claggart, lest his world be proven false, planned Billy's death. The final reason is beyond my thinking. *injustice*

VERE. Aye, that is thoughtfully put. There is a mystery in iniquity. But it seems to me, Seymour, that the point we seek here is hardly material.

SEYMOUR. Aye, sir. Very well, you may go.

DANSKER. One thing more. Since this Master-at-Arms first came on board from God knows where, I have seen his shadow lengthen along the deck, and being under it, I was afraid. Whatever happened here, I am in part to blame—more than this lad. (*To* BILLY) I am an old man, Billy. You—try to—forgive me. (*Exits.*)

SEYMOUR. Have you any further questions to put to the accused?

RATCLIFFE. No.

WYATT. None.

SEYMOUR. William Budd, if you have anything further to say for yourself, say it now.

BILLY (*after glance at* VERE). I have said all, sir.

SEYMOUR. Sentry. (*Enter* HALLAM.) Remove the prisoner to the after compartment. (HALLAM *and* BILLY *exit. A long pause.*) Have you anything to say, Ratcliffe?

RATCLIFFE. Yes, sir. Claggart was killed because Budd couldn't speak. In that sense, that he stammers, he's a cripple. You don't hang a man for that, for speaking the only way he could.

WYATT. If you condemn him, it's the same thing as condoning the apparent lie the Master-at-Arms clearly told. I'd have struck him, too. The boy is clearly innocent, struck him in self-defense.

RATCLIFFE. Aye. I'm ready to acquit him now.

SEYMOUR. Good. Then we can reach a verdict at once.

VERE. Hitherto I have been a witness at this trial, no more. And I hesitate to interfere, except that at this clear crisis you ignore one fact we cannot close our eyes to.

SEYMOUR. With your pardon, sir, as Senior Member of this court, I must ask if you speak now as our commanding officer or as a private man.

VERE. As convening authority, Seymour. I summoned this court, and I must review its findings and approve them before passing them on to the Admiralty.

SEYMOUR. Aye, sir, that is your right.

VERE. No right. Which of us here has rights? It is my duty, and I must perform it. Budd has killed a man—his superior officer.

SEYMOUR. We have found a verdict, sir.

VERE. I know that, Seymour. Your verdict sets him free, and so would I wish to do. But are we free to choose as we would do if we were private citizens? The Admiralty has its code. Do you suppose it cares who Budd is? Who you and I are?

SEYMOUR. We don't forget that, sir. But surely Claggart's tales were simply lies. We've established that.

VERE. Aye. But the Nore and Spithead were brute facts, and must not come again. The men were starved out before, but if they should think we are afraid . . .

RATCLIFFE. Captain, how could they? They certainly know Budd is no mutineer.

WYATT. Of course not. Since he came on board, he's done more to keep the crew in hand than any of us.

SEYMOUR. That's true. The men took naturally to him.

VERE. As officers we are concerned to keep this ship effective as a weapon. And the law says what we must do in such a case as this. Come now, you know the facts, and the Mutiny Act's provisions. At sea, in time of war, an impressed man strikes his superior officer, and the blow is fatal. The mere blow alone would hang him, at least according to the Act. Well then, the men on board know that as well as you and I. And we acquit him. They have sense, they know the proper penalty to follow, and yet it does not follow.

SEYMOUR. But they know Budd, sir, and Claggart too, I daresay. Would they not applaud the decision that frees Budd? They would thank us.

WYATT. String him to a yard, and they'll turn round and rescue him, and string us up instead!

RATCLIFFE. Aye, that's a point. It's twice as dangerous to hang the boy as it would be to let him go. If there's a mutinous temper in the crew, condemning Budd would surely set it off.

VERE. That is possible. Whatever step we take, the risk is great; but it is ours. That is what makes us officers. Yet if in fear of what our office demands we shirk our duty, we only play at war, at being men. If by our lawful rigor mutiny comes, there is no blame for us. But if in fear, miscalled a kind of mercy, we pardon Budd against specific order, and then the crew revolts, how culpable [2] and weak our verdict would appear! The men on board know what our case is, how we are haunted by the Spithead risings. Have they forgotten how the panic spread through England? No. Your clemency would be accounted fear, and they would say we flinch from practising a lawful rigor lest new outbreaks be provoked. What shame to us! And what a deadly blow to discipline!

RATCLIFFE. I concede that, sir. But this case is exceptional, and pity, if we are men, is bound to move us, Captain.

[2] culpable: blameworthy

VERE. So am I moved. Yet we cannot have warm hearts betraying heads that should be cool. In such a case ashore, an upright judge does not allow the pleading tears of women to touch his nature. Here at sea, the heart, the female in a man, weeps like a woman. She must be ruled out, hard though it be. (*Pause.*) Still silent? Very well, I see that something in all your downcast faces seems to urge that not alone the heart moves hesitancy. Conscience, perhaps. The private conscience moves you.

WYATT. Aye, that's it, sir. How can we condemn this man and live at peace again within ourselves? We have our standards; ethics, if you like.

VERE. Challenge your scruples! They move as in a dusk. Come, do they import something like this: if we are bound to judge, regardless of palliating circumstances,[3] the death of Claggart as the prisoner's deed, then does that deed appear a capital crime whereof the penalty is mortal? But can we adjudge to summary and shameful death a fellow creature innocent before God, and whom we feel to be so? Does that state the case rightly?

SEYMOUR. That is my feeling, sir.

VERE. You all feel, I am sure, that the boy in effect is innocent; that what he did was from an unhappy stricture of speech that made him speak with blows. And I believe that, too; believe as you do, that he struck his man down, tempted beyond endurance. Acquit him, then, you say, as innocent?

RATCLIFFE. Exactly! Oh I know the Articles prescribe death for what Budd has done, but that . . .

WYATT. Oh, stow the Articles! They don't account for such a case as this. You yourself say Budd is innocent.

VERE. In intent, Wyatt, in intent.

WYATT. Does that count for nothing? His whole attitude, his motive, count for nothing? If his intent . . .

VERE. The intent or non-intent of Budd is nothing to the purpose. In a court more merciful than martial it would extenuate, and shall, at the last Assizes, set him free. But here we have these alternatives only: condemn or let go.

SEYMOUR. But it seems to me we've got to consider the problem as a moral one, sir, despite the fact that we're not moralists. When

[3] **palliating circumstances:** circumstances which make a crime appear less grave

Claggart told you his lie, the case immediately went beyond the scope of military justice.

VERE. I, too, feel that. But do these gold stripes across our arms attest that our allegiance is to Nature?

RATCLIFFE. To our country, sir.

VERE. Aye, Ratcliffe; to the King. And though the sea, which is inviolate Nature primeval, though it be the element whereon we move and have our being as sailors, is our official duty hence to Nature? No. So little is that true that we resign our freedom when we put this on. And when war is declared, are we, the fighters commissioned to destroy, consulted first?

WYATT. Does that deny us the right to act like men? We're not trying a murderer, a dockside cut-throat!

VERE. The gold we wear shows that we serve the King, the Law. What does it matter that our acts are fatal to our manhood, if we serve as we are forced to serve? What bitter salt leagues move between our code and God's own judgments! We are conscripts, every one, upright in this uniform of flesh. There is no truce to war born in the womb. We fight at command.

WYATT. All I know is that I can't sit by and see Budd hanged!

VERE. I say we fight by order, by command of our superiors. And if our judgments approve the war, it is only coincidence. And so it is with all our acts. So now, would it be so much we ourselves who speak as judges here, as it would be martial law operating through us? For that law, and for its rigor, we are not responsible. Our duty lies in this: that we are servants only.

RATCLIFFE. The Admiralty doesn't want service like that. What good would it do? Who'd profit by Budd's death?

WYATT. You want to make us murderers!

SEYMOUR. Wyatt! Control yourself!

VERE. What is this vessel that you serve in. Wyatt, an ark of peace? Go count her guns; then tell your conscience to lie quiet, if you can.

RATCLIFFE. But that is war. This would be downright killing!

SEYMOUR. It's all war, Ratcliffe; war to the death, for all of us.

VERE. You see that, Seymour? That this war began before our time?

SEYMOUR. And will end long after it.

VERE. Here we have the Mutiny Act for justice. No child can own a closer tie to parent than can that Act to what it stems from:

War. This is a wartime cruise and in this ship are Englishmen who fight against their wills, perhaps against their conscience, 'pressed by war into the service of the King. Though we as fellow creatures understand their lot, what does it matter to the officer, or to the enemy? The French will cut down conscripts in the same swath [4] with volunteers, and we will do as much for them. War has no business with anything but surfaces. War's child, the Mutiny Act, is featured like the father.

RATCLIFFE. Couldn't we mitigate the penalty if we convict him?

VERE. No, Ratcliffe. The penalty is prescribed.

RATCLIFFE. I'd like to think it over, Captain. I'm not sure.

VERE. I repeat, then, that while we ponder and you hesitate over anxieties I confess to sharing, the enemy comes nearer. We must act, and quickly. The French close in on us; the crew will find out shortly what has happened. Our consciences are private matters, Ratcliffe. But we are public men, controlling life and death within this world at sea. Tell me whether or not in our positions we dare let our consciences take precedence of the code that makes us officers and calls this case to trial.

RATCLIFFE (*after a pause; quietly*). No, sir.

WYATT. Can you stand Budd's murder on your conscience?

SEYMOUR. Wyatt! Hold your tongue!

WYATT (*jumping up*). I say let him go!

SEYMOUR. Sit down, sir!

VERE. Let him speak.

WYATT. I won't bear a hand to hang a man I know is innocent! My blood's not cold enough. I can't give the kind of judgment you want to force on us! I ask to be excused from sitting upon this court.

SEYMOUR. Do you know what you're saying? Sit down and hold your tongue, man!

VERE. The kind of judgment I ask of you is only this, Wyatt: that you recognize your function in this ship. I believe you know it quite as well as we, yet you rebel. Can't you see that you must first strip off the uniform you wear, and after that your flesh, before you can escape the case at issue here? Decide you must, Wyatt. Oh you may be excused and wash your hands of it, but someone must decide. We are the law; law orders us to act, and

[4] swath: stroke

shows us how. Do you imagine Seymour, or Ratcliffe here, or I, would not save this boy if we could see a way consistent with our duties? Acquit Budd if you can. God knows I wish I could. If in your mind as well as in your heart, you can say freely that his life is not forfeit to the law we serve, reason with us! Show us how to save him without putting aside our function. Or if you can't do that, teach us to put by our responsibility and not betray ourselves. Can you do this? Speak, man, speak! Show us how! Save him, Wyatt, and you save us all. (WYATT *slowly sits down*.) You recognize the logic of the choice I force upon you. But do not think me pitiless in thus demanding sentence on a luckless boy. I feel as you do for him. But even more, I think there is a grace of soul within him that shall forgive the law we bind him with, and pity us, stretched on the cross of choice. (*He turns away*.)

SEYMOUR. Well, gentlemen. Will you decide? (*Officers write their verdicts on paper before them, and hand them to* SEYMOUR, *who rises, draws his dirk and places it on the table, pointing forward*.) He is condemned, sir. Shall we appoint the dawn?

dirk – dagger

✤ Scene 2

SCENE: CAPTAIN VERE'S *cabin, 0400. Ship's bell strikes off-stage.* VERE *sitting alone at his desk. Knock at the door.*

VERE. Come in. (*Enter* SEYMOUR.) Oh, it's you, Seymour.

SEYMOUR. It's eight bells, Captain.

VERE. What's the hour of sunrise?

SEYMOUR. Four fifty-two, sir.

VERE. Eight bells. And one bell at four-thirty. Odd and even numbers caught between two hands. Budd shall not live to hear the odd made even or wrong made right.—Call all hands to quarters at four-thirty.

SEYMOUR. Aye aye, Captain. (*He turns irresolutely*.)

VERE. The wind has slackened, I think. How is the glass?

SEYMOUR. It's risen slightly. Sea has flattened out.

VERE. Fair weather after foul . . . it's all nature, nature and law. How exigent are these Mediterranean climates of the heart, and temperate zones of mind!

SEYMOUR. Have you been here all night, sir?

VERE. All night, Seymour . . . all my life moving between dark and dark. It has been a long night, but day will be quick and deadly on the mainyard. D'you think, Seymour, a man can forgive a wrong done of the heart's own election?

SEYMOUR. Most people are decent enough. You can forgive them trespasses.

VERE. No. There's wickedness alive. It's dead now in one man, but it's alive to feel and smell at night. . . . Seymour, go below. Get Budd and bring him here.

SEYMOUR. But Captain . . .

VERE. Do as you're told. Get Budd and bring him here. (SEYMOUR *exits.* VERE *sits motionless for a few moments, then rises and goes to the cabin door.*) Sentry.

HALLAM. Yes, sir?

VERE. Who has the deck this watch?

HALLAM. Mister Ratcliffe, Captain.

VERE. Very well. (*Pause.*) Sentry!

HALLAM. Sir?

VERE. When Mister Seymour has returned, admit him right away.

HALLAM. Aye aye, Captain.

VERE. The wind's still sharp. You must be cold there, Hallam. Go to the leeward side. I'll be responsible.

HALLAM. Thank you, sir. This is the coldest hour now, just before sunrise.

VERE (*closes door, returns slowly to his desk*). The lamp holds steady when the vessel heels. Does the law hang straight in crooked lives? It burns, and shapes nothing but shadows here, plumb in the twisting cabin of the mind. (*Footsteps, voices.* VERE *turns to door. Enter* SEYMOUR, BILLY, *and* HALLAM.) Take off the manacles. (HALLAM *frees* BILLY.)

SEYMOUR (*to* HALLAM). Outside, man. Bear a hand. (*Exits with* HALLAM.)

VERE. Sit down. No, it's better that I stand.

BILLY. I was thinking, locked up below there . . . the Captain knows the rights of all this. He'll save me if it's right. Then you sent for me. Is there hope for me, Captain?

VERE. Billy, what hope is there?

BILLY. Tell me why. I only want to understand.

VERE. How young you still are, Billy! Oh I can tell you this: nothing is lost of anything that happens. I have given you the judgment of the world . . . deadly constraint . . . a length of hemp and a yard-arm. I have done this to you, no one else.

BILLY. I can't get the rights of all that's happened.

VERE. There's not much right, Billy. Only necessity. You and Claggart broke man's compromise with good and evil, and both of you must pay the penalty.

BILLY. Penalty? What for? Would anyone make laws just to be broken by fellows like me?

VERE. Aye, boy. You have learned this late. Most of us find out early and trim to a middle course.

BILLY. Do you mean . . . it's better to be like that?

VERE. Better as this world goes. When a man is born, he takes a guilt upon him, I can't say how or why. And life takes its revenge on those who hurt its pride with innocence.

BILLY. Do you think Claggart knew it would come to this?

VERE. He knew he would kill you, and he died to gain that end. But if you trust me, he'll not win entirely.

BILLY. How could he hate me like that?

VERE. The world we breathe is love and hatred both, but hatred must not win the victory.

BILLY. Claggart is dead. Now I'm to hang. Doesn't that show the law is wrong, when it can't choose between him and me?

VERE. Yes, it's all wrong, all wrong.

BILLY. I don't know, Captain. I never was a hand to wonder about things, but now I think that maybe there's a kind of cruelty in people that's just as much a part of them as kindness, say, or honesty, or m-m-m . . . I can't find words, I guess, Captain.

VERE. There are no words. We are all prisoners of deadly forms that are made to break us to their measure. Nothing has power to overcome them, except forgiveness . . . Can you forgive what I have done?

BILLY. I *can* trust you, can't I? *Can* you show me it's all right, my being . . .

VERE (*turns away; a long pause*). It's nearly dawn, lad. In the Spanish villages they're lighting fires.

BILLY. I'm not afraid, sir. (*He steps toward* VERE.) It's getting light.

VERE. There's no time for either of us left. Go, take the morning. God knows you have the right to it. And when you are on the main-yard, think of me, and pray for those who must make choices. Hallam. (*Enter* HALLAM *in doorway.*) Take Budd into your charge. (BILLY *and* HALLAM *go out.*) Time has run out.

◄§ Scene 3

SCENE: *Main deck aft. Drum-to-formation. Crew forming up.* WYATT, MIDSHIPMEN GARDINER *and* REA.

WYATT. Bear a hand. Form the men up in ranks.

GARDINER. Aye, sir. All right, you! Close ranks! Move up, Stoll. That's better. Talbot, square your hat. Form up straight there! (*Drum.* MEN *come to attention.*)

WYATT. Division commanders report!

VOICE (*off-stage*). Carpenters and gunners, present or accounted for, sir!

VOICE (*off-stage*). Marine Detachment, present or accounted for, sir!

VOICE (*off-stage*). Afterguard, present or accounted for, sir!

GARDINER. Fore, main and mizzentopmen . . . one absentee!

WYATT. All hands will stand by to witness punishment! Stand easy.

VOICES (*off-stage*). Stand easy. (WYATT *walks away from men. Murmur in ranks.*)

KINCAID. Where is Billy? He wasn't in his hammock when they piped us up.

O'DANIEL. He'll be getting himself in trouble if he don't fall in.

KINCAID. Who they punishing, and what for?

JENKINS. It's got to be flogging, or they wouldn't have us all up here.

KINCAID. Vere never flogs anybody. And there ain't no gratings up.

DANSKER. They flog men at noon. The early morning's for hanging.

KINCAID. Hanging! (*The word travels back.*) Who? What for?

O'DANIEL. The skipper, he don't confide in me no more.

KINCAID. I thought they waited till they got ashore before they hanged a man.

DANSKER. Not in wartime.

JENKINS. He goes up them ratlines, out on the yard, they slips a noose around his neck, and then he jumps and hangs himself.

O'DANIEL. They'd have the devil's work getting O'Daniel to jump.

KINCAID. It's jump, or get pushed.

JENKINS. Where's Claggart? You don't suppose it's Claggart! Oh, Judas, let it be that fishblooded nark!

KINCAID. Not him. He's too smart, he is.

JENKINS. Where is he, then? He ain't here.

DANSKER. He is here.

KINCAID. Where? I don't see him.

DANSKER. He is here.

KINCAID. Ah . . . you're balmy, old man.

(*Enter* VERE, SEYMOUR, RATCLIFFE *and the* SURGEON. *Drum sounds Attention.*)

WYATT (*to* SEYMOUR). Ship's company present to witness execution, sir.

SEYMOUR. Very well. (*To* VERE.) Ship's company present to witness execution, sir.

VERE (*nods*).

SEYMOUR (*to* WYATT). Lieutenant Wyatt, have the prisoner brought forward.

WYATT. Aye aye, sir. (*Marches to wing.*) Sentries, bring forward the prisoner. (*Marches back to his post.*)

(*Enter* BILLY *with two sentries. Astonished murmur through the crew, who momentarily break ranks.*)

WYATT. No talking in ranks! (*Continued restless movement and murmurings.*) Form up!

GARDINER. You men are at attention!

WYATT (*over subdued muttering*). You hear me? Silence in ranks! (*Silence.* SENTRIES *lead* BILLY *to the foot of the ropes.* SEYMOUR *looks at* VERE, *who nods.* SEYMOUR *steps forward and reads.*)

SEYMOUR. Proceedings of the court-martial held aboard *H.M.S. Indomitable* on the eighth August, 1798. Convened under the authority of Edward Fairfax Vere, Senior Captain, Royal Navy, and composed of the First Officer, the Sailing Master, and the First Lieutenant of said vessel. In the case of William Budd, foretopman, Royal Navy. While attached and so serving in the aforesaid vessel, he did, on the 8th day of August, 1798, strike and

kill his superior officer, one John Claggart, Master-at-Arms, Royal
Navy.

(*Crew breaks out uneasily, astonished, talking excitedly.*)

JENKINS. Billy! Did you, boy? ⎫
VOICE. Good lad! ⎪
VOICE. Serves him proper! ⎬ *All together*
KINCAID. Hi, Billy! Hurrah! ⎭

WYATT. Quiet! Silence, you men! Form up!

GARDINER. Stand at attention, hang you! Silence in the ranks!

WYATT. Do you hear? (*Excited muttering, low voices.*)

SEYMOUR. You will be silent and remain at strict attention until dis-
missed. (*Silence.*) . . . Master-at-Arms, Royal Navy. Therefore,
the court sentences the aforementioned William Budd, foretopman, Royal Navy, to die by hanging on the first watch of the day
following these proceedings. By authority of his Gracious Majesty
George Rex and Alan Napier, Viscount Kelsey, First Sea Lord.
Signed, Philip Seymour, Senior Member.

(*During the last phrases of the reading, the crew, upon hearing the sentence, breaks out again, some stepping forward,
shouting; they are in an ugly temper.*)

VOICES. No he don't! ⎫
Not if I know it! ⎪
Hang the jemmies instead, I say! ⎪
Not Billy, you bloody swineheads! ⎬ *All together*
You ain't hanging Billy! ⎪
Let them dance on a rope's end! ⎭

WYATT. Stand back! Sentries, guard your prisoner, if you have to
fire!

GARDINER. Stand back, you clods! Keep back!

SEYMOUR (*steps forward*). Silence there! You will resume discipline
instantly! Be warned. (*He waits a silent moment. Men stop in dis-
ordered formation.*) Stand back into ranks.

GARDINER. Form up again, quick about it now! (*There is a surly movement into irregular lines.*)

SEYMOUR (*warily resuming procedure*). Prisoner, have you anything
to say? (BILLY *shakes his head.*) If you have nothing to say, when
the drum roll is sounded, you will proceed to carry out the sentence of this court. (*He signals to* WYATT.)

WYATT. Sound off!

> (*Drum roll.* BILLY *turns and starts up the ropes.*)

VOICES. Get him! Now!

> Bill! Stay where you are, boy, don't do it!
>
> Wait, Billy! Wait!   *All together*
>
> Rush the deck, mates! Don't let them do it!
>
> We're here, Bill, don't you worry!

BILLY (*stops, turns forward, looks at* VERE, *and shouts out loud and clear, without trace of stammer*). God bless Captain Vere!

> (*A second's pause;* VERE *is profoundly shaken;* BILLY *goes quickly up the ropes and out of sight. The crew moves back a step, is silent; officers and men in deep breathless quiet watch him out of sight and are staring overhead as the curtain falls.*)

CURTAIN

NOTES ON THE PLAY

IT IS difficult now, in retrospect, to determine how and why we arrived at a decision to make Melville's novel into a play. We had, of course, been familiar with the story for some time, and when in 1947 we actually began discussing the dramatic problems entailed in writing a play on the theme Melville gives us, we had only recently been very close to the novel. Perhaps the "Melville Revival" influenced us; it may have been the desire to find a theme and action that was inherently poetic and non-realistic. Above all, one idea or purpose seems clear: that we saw in *Billy Budd* a morality play.

History and the literature of the past serve many functions for the present. Men like to think that they look at the past and its works objectively, with an evaluating eye, yet most of us know that any age seeks from the past justifications and flatteries; looks for ideas in a literature of another time and selects from them those that seem peculiarly perti- nent [1] to the seeker, whether the ideas found be actually *there* or not. For us, as inchoate [2] playwrights, in January of 1947, Melville's story of good, evil, and the way the world takes such absolutes was material enough for two veterans of a war, a depression, and the moving cold front.

Today morality is not popular; perhaps it has never really been so. In our day it is popularly lamented and celebrated *in absentia*,[3] much modern criticism being devoted to the discovery of morality in the least likely places. Yet to find the stuff of dramatic morality pure is no easy task, since, however hard one may try, Freud [4] will turn up and all one's efforts will post off to the clinic and the analyst's couch to work out there a modern salvation. Thus a critic can say of our play that such a phenomenon as Claggart could never appear in our world with all we known of the psyche [5] and the ego. We doubt that. We are certain that neither a Billy nor a Claggart ever was or could be, and, to undercut a little ground, we add that the same is true of an Oedipus.[6] But all these personae are true as symbol, figuring as they do certain permanent atti- tudes, qualities, moral images. It is just this figuring forth that Mel- ville's novel so preeminently effects for our time, and if we do indeed lament a lack of standards for this age we can at least see in *Billy Budd* the potentiality of a new vision, a vision that allows a man to think

[1] **pertinent:** to the point
[2] **inchoate:** beginning
[3] **in absentia:** in its absence
[4] **Freud:** founder of psychoanalysis
[5] **psyche:** the mind
[6] **Oedipus:** tragic hero of Greek legend

235

generally about absolutes without feeling he is violating "truth" because he has not polled a sample of his generation to get the "facts." The trouble is, Melville has stated a fact, but it is not the kind of fact men either like or know what to do with.

Perhaps all this has less to do than we think with how our play got written or even started. Once that start was made, however, we found ourselves bound by the novel, and it was only after some experimentation that we realized how little Melville had given us that was theatrical or, perhaps, finished. There was certainly little reason why he should; the drama is surely in the novel, but it is an inner, imagined drama. Our job was to put it on a stage and give flesh to the finely articulated skeleton—no small task in view of the deceptive nature of the novel. What seems to the casual reader mere padding in *Billy Budd* (the novel) is vital information—about the great mutinies, the Napoleonic Wars, the British Navy, the moral and social climate. And Melville was assuming an audience of some culture (if at this stage he was able to assume an audience at all) which would know about the Rights of Man, the Terror, and what manner of man Captain Vere is intended to represent. All this we had to show, to bring to life and to give to the audience in such a way that the information might not arrive as information but as an ambience.[7] We do not say that we have done this, only that it must be done if there is to be a real play. This is a morality play and we do not apologize for its being such.

The version presented here is that of the final Broadway production. The play in this form has passed through several stages. The original version, given by the Experimental Theatre in 1949, was in stricter poetic form and was more austere in tone and structure; much of it seemed to us too bald and expository.[8] We have tried to thicken the texture of the play with much added dramatic incident, conflict, and realistic speech. There is, of course, some danger that we have fallen between two stools: what we have done may not entirely please either the average theatregoer or the Melville scholar. But for our part we have done! Our original faith in the novel remains and supports our faith in our own work. We will look far before we find another theme of equal interest or vitality.

LOUIS O. COXE
ROBERT CHAPMAN

[7] **ambience:** surrounding, background
[8] **expository:** explanatory

For discussion

ACT I

1. What did the incident about Jackson's illness reveal about Claggart? About the attitude of the men toward Claggart?

2. What did you find out about Billy Budd and Jenkins from the fight they had? Refer to specific lines to support your answer.

3. In your opinion, why did Claggart become so angry when Jenkins brushed against him? What did it reveal about his attitude toward people?

4. The setting for this play is the year 1798 when the English were at war with France. Two naval mutinies at Nore and Spithead had occurred the year before. What bearing might this have had on the tone of Captain Vere's speech to the men in Scene 1?

5. Why do you think neither the men nor Jenkins took the opportunity to tell Captain Vere the truth when he questioned them?

6. From the way Captain Vere talked in this scene, what kind of person did he seem to be? What quality did Billy Budd reveal when the Captain inquired about Jackson's accident?

7. Explain the irony in Billy's being impressed from *The Rights of Man* to the *Indomitable*.

8. From the conversation between Billy Budd and Claggart in Scene 2, what would you say Billy's attitude toward Claggart was? What effect did Billy have on Claggart?

9. Why did Claggart want Billy "on report"? Do you think it was for a specific reason? Was it because of what Billy represented? Explain.

10. What humor do you see in Squeak's name being what it was?

11. Do you think Captain Vere was right to let Claggart "have his head"? Why or why not?

12. State the main ideas about good and evil as discussed by Claggart and Dansker. What relation did Dansker see between Claggart and Billy?

13. What purpose did the playwrights have in ending the act with the naval action against a French frigate?

ACT II

1. What do you think is the purpose of the first few minutes of Act II? What function does Gardiner serve?

2. What was the attitude of the Captain toward Billy? Why did he promote him? What was Claggart's reaction to the promotion?

3. Billy's stopping Jenkins in his plan did not please Claggart. Why was this typical of the Master-at-Arms?

4. In the conversation between Claggart and Dansker, what was revealed about Dansker's role aboard ship in the past? In your opinion, was Dansker correct or not in having adopted this role? Why do you think he changed?

5. In this conversation, what did you find out about Claggart's deep antagonism to Billy?

6. What was Captain Vere's purpose in having Billy confront Claggart? Why didn't it work out as the Captain had planned? What was the Captain's terrible dilemma at the end of Act II?

ACT III

1. What was Seymour's attitude toward what Billy had done? In what way did he and Captain Vere disagree on the question of authority?

2. State the arguments for and against Billy as expressed by the naval court and the Captain. Why was there a conflict between "conscience" and "law"?

3. "Our consciences are private matters, but we are public men." Discuss this statement in the light of the court action.

4. In your opinion, was the verdict of the court just? Why or why not?

5. Discuss Billy's statement: "I think that maybe there's a kind of cruelty in people that's just as much a part of them as kindness. . . ."

6. In your opinion, did love or hatred win out in what occurred? Give reasons for your opinion.

7. What was the men's reaction when they discovered Billy's fate?

8. How do you explain Billy Budd's final words? What do they show about him?

11. *bring out characters, give contrast in play — develops theme on different levels*

On the play as a whole

1. Comment on your reaction to the outcome of the play. Did you find it convincing? Would you have found a different ending more satisfactory? Explain.

2. Despite the ending, *Billy Budd* has been seen as having a deeply affirmative meaning. What is that meaning? Can you give other instances from real life or literature that show where a tragic ending also had an affirmative meaning? *Love overcomes evil*

3. Why did Billy not suspect Claggart of wanting to harm him? What did this reveal about Billy's nature?

innocent
Billy's honesty reproached Claggart's dishonesty

4. Discuss the meaning of why Claggart hated Billy. Did Claggart have any other emotion about Billy? If so, what did this seem to show? *hate + jealousy, fear*

5. The word *vere* means truth. Discuss this in the light of Captain Vere's character.

6. Discuss the dilemma in which Captain Vere found himself. Present arguments for or against his decision.

7. *Billy Budd* is more than a realistic sea play about specific individuals. It is also an allegory, in which the characters represent abstract moral ideas. Explain. *Claggart - evil Billy - good*

8. Using the glossary on page 247, study the meaning of the terms *rising action, conflict, climax, falling action*. Apply each of these terms to the plot of *Billy Budd*.

9. Look up the meaning of the word *foreshadowing* in the glossary. What does the opening of Act I, Scene 2 foreshadow? Point out other specific lines of dialogue or incidents which illustrate the use of foreshadowing in the play.

10. Why did the playwrights present so much brutality in the opening scene? With what is it in contrast? How did the opening scene contrast in mood with the closing scene? What did the playwrights achieve through this?

11. Some of Captain Vere's speeches are abstract discussions of justice and duty. The seamen's speeches are a mixture of realistic banter and complaining. Choose two selections which show this marked contrast in style and read them aloud for comparison. Do these contrasts in style go well together? Why or why not?

12. Claggart does not speak in a realistic manner, particularly in his conversations with Billy Budd and Dansker. How does he speak? Why do you think this is so?

13. Read a selection from Melville's *Billy Budd*. Then find the corresponding section in the play. Compare and contrast the two literary forms. Discuss the use of dialogue, minor characters, description, and exposition in each passage. Summarize your conclusions.

For composition

1. Imagine you are Claggart. Write an entry in your diary describing your private impressions of Billy Budd and what you thought of him after he had come aboard.

2. Imagine you are Captain Vere. Write a letter to an intimate friend at home in England, telling him what happened to Billy Budd and your personal views concerning the outcome.

Rising action - Scene 2
Climax - fatal blow

3. Choose any two of the following statements from the play and develop each of the ideas expressed in a carefully written paragraph.
   (a) "There is mystery in iniquity." (Captain Vere)
   (b) "Pride was his [Claggart's] demon, and he kept it strong by others' fear of him." (Dansker)
   (c) "We are the law; law orders us to act, and shows us how." (Captain Vere)
   (d) "I think there is a grace of soul within him that shall forgive the law we bind him with, and pity us, stretched on the cross of choice." (Captain Vere speaking of Billy)
   (e) "The world we live in is love and hatred both, but hatred must not win the victory." (Captain Vere)
   (f) "I am a seaman, sir. I love the sea. I've hardly lived ashore." (Billy)
   (g) "You don't believe in anything besides yourself. I hate an incomplete man." (Dansker speaking to Claggart)
4. *Billy Budd* has been called both an allegory and a morality play. Write a short composition defining these terms and show how they apply to this play.
5. In a well-developed paragraph, express your opinion of *Billy Budd* as a drama of adventure and as a drama of deeper significance. Do you think either of these aspects is presented more convincingly than the other? Do you think the two aspects are well blended? Give examples from the play to support your opinions.

ABOUT THE PLAYWRIGHTS

Robert Chapman (1919–   ) was born in Illinois and is at present an Associate Professor of English at Harvard University. He is the Director of the Loeb Drama Center at Harvard. Mr. Chapman also directs plays, teaches classical acting, and is interested in Oriental theater. As a playwright, he is best known for *Billy Budd,* which he wrote with Louis O. Coxe.

Louis O. Coxe (1915–   ) was born in Manchester, New Hampshire. He grew up in Salem, Massachusetts, and attended Princeton University, where he received his Bachelor of Arts degree in 1940. Coxe served in the United States Navy from 1942 to 1946, an interesting fact in the light of his later dramatic adaptation of Melville's *Billy Budd.*

From 1949 to 1955, Coxe taught at the University of Minnesota. After receiving a *Sewanee Review* Fellowship in 1955, he began teaching at Bowdoin College. Louis O. Coxe has published poems and other plays, and appears as one of the significant new names in recent American writing.

Reginald Rose (1921–   ) published his first book, *Six Television Plays,* in 1956. Before this, he had a varied career as publicist for Warner Brothers, advertising account executive, and copy chief. His first television play, *The Bus to Nowhere,* appeared in 1951. He has written adaptations and original scripts which rank among the best in television. *Twelve Angry Men* won him an Emmy Award for excellence in dramatic writing. It was later made into a highly praised movie.

John Van Druten (1901–1957) was born and educated in London. In 1926 he came to the United States, and in 1944 he became an American citizen. Concerning his decision, Van Druten writes, "I know that I am happy here and that I like American people . . . But I am an American by choice, not by accident of birth." As a lawyer, Van Druten turned to the academic side of his profession as Special Lecturer in Eng-

241

lish Law and Legal History at the University College of Wales. During this time he wrote poems, short stories, and plays. After 1922, he devoted himself to writing. His dramas include *Young Woodley, There's Always Juliet*, and *The Voice of the Turtle*. One of his best works is *I Remember Mama*, an adaptation of Kathryn Forbes' *Mama's Bank Account*.

Gore Vidal (1926–   ) was born in West Point, New York. From 1943 to 1946 he served on an army ship in the Aleutians. There, at the age of nineteen, he wrote *Williwaw*, his first novel. This was followed by eight successful novels. Now he is almost equally well known for his television plays, many of which have been published. The noted critic John Crosby has described Gore Vidal as "a writer of unusual talent and authority."

SUGGESTED READING LIST

Plays of Human Interest

The Diary of Anne Frank	*Frances Goodrich & Albert Hackett*
Gideon	*Paddy Chayefsky*
Green Pastures	*Marc Connelly*
Marty	*Paddy Chayefsky*
Member of the Wedding	*Carson McCuller*
The Miracle Worker	*William Gibson*
My Heart's in the Highlands	*William Saroyan*
Our Town	*Thornton Wilder*
The Philadelphia Story	*Philip Barry*
The Sandbox	*Edward Albee*
The Show-Off	*George Kelly*
The Skin of Our Teeth	*Thornton Wilder*
The Teahouse of the August Moon	*John Patrick*

Plays with Music

Amahl and the Night Visitors	*Gian-Carlo Menotti*
Brigadoon	*Alan Jay Lerner & Frederick Loewe*
Camelot	*Alan Jay Lerner & Frederick Loewe*
Carousel	*Richard Rodgers & Oscar Hammerstein II*
Finian's Rainbow	*E. Y. Harburg & Burton Lane*
The King and I	*Richard Rodgers & Oscar Hammerstein II*
My Fair Lady	*Alan Jay Lerner & Frederick Loewe*

Plays with an American Background

Abe Lincoln in Illinois	*Robert Sherwood*
The Magnificent Yankee	*Emmet Lavery*
The Patriots	*Sidney Kingsley*
Sunrise at Campobello	*Dore Schary*
Valley Forge	*Maxwell Anderson*
Yellow Jack	*Sidney Howard*

Plays of Dramatic Conflict

Ile	
In the Zone	*3 one-act plays by Eugene O'Neill*
Where the Cross Is Made	
The Caine Mutiny Court Martial	*Herman Wouk*
The Crucible	*Arthur Miller*
The Elder Statesman	*T. S. Eliot*
Elizabeth the Queen	*Maxwell Anderson*
Ethan Frome	*Owen Davis & Donald Davis*
The Glass Menagerie	*Tennessee Williams*
The Little Foxes	*Lillian Hellman*
A Raisin in the Sun	*Lorraine Hansberry*

Plays of the American Catholic Theater

Brother Orchid	*Leo Brady*
The City of Kings	*Urban Nagle, O. P.*
The Dream Slayers	*Richard Breen*
The First Legion	*Emmet Lavery*
Savanarola	*Urban Nagle, O. P.*
Who Ride on White Horses	*Richard Breen & Harry Schnibbe*

Plays for Amusement

Arsenic and Old Lace	*Joseph Kesselring*
Junior Miss	*Jerome Chodorov*
Life with Father	*Howard Lindsay & Russel Crouse*
The Matchmaker	*Thornton Wilder*
Mrs. McThing	*Mary Chase*
You Can't Take It with You	*Moss Hart & George S. Kaufman*

GLOSSARY OF TERMS

act: one of the main divisions of the action of a play, generally separated from other acts by an intermission.

action: the psychological, emotional, and physical happenings that convey the meaning and story of the play. See *rising action* and *falling action.*

allegory: a literary work in which objects, persons, or events are equated with meanings outside the work itself.

antagonist: the force that opposes the central character or protagonist. The antagonist may be some weakness, desire, or belief within the protagonist himself. Or it may be some outside force, such as another character, circumstances, nature or environment, Fate or Providence.

anticlimax: an outcome that is disappointing because it falls short of what the preceding action led the reader or viewer to expect.

aside: a remark made by one character in the presence of others but assumed not to be heard by them.

atmosphere: the over-all feeling of a play; for example, the brooding atmosphere in a Eugene O'Neill play.

character: a person in a play. A *dynamic character* undergoes some change or development during the course of the play. A *static character* undergoes little if any change during the course of the play.

characterization: the development of a character through what he says and does and through what other characters say about him.

climax: the moment of greatest dramatic intensity; the turning point in the action, usually followed by a decrease in suspense.

comedy: a form of drama that is light and amusing and typically has a happy ending. Many comedies poke fun at—satirize—manners, customs, social or political institutions, or types of people.

conflict: the struggle between two opposing forces, ideas, or beliefs, which is the basis of the plot. In most plays the conflict is resolved when one force—usually the protagonist—succeeds or fails in overcoming the opposing force. Sometimes, the protagonist gives up the struggle as too difficult or not worthwhile. The term *inner conflict* refers to a struggle within the heart and mind of the protagonist. The term *external conflict* refers to a struggle between the protagonist and an outside force.

245

denouement: the "working out" of the plot, following the climax. In this
　　final part of the play—usually brief but sometimes a full act—the
　　playwright brings the conflict to an end and explains how and why
　　everything turned out as it did.

dialogue: the conversation between two or more characters in a play.

dramatic irony: a mode of expression in which a statement or action
　　of a character has a meaning unperceived by himself but understood
　　by the audience. For example, a character—unaware that he has a
　　poisoned drink—might say, "Ah! This will refresh me!"

dramatic purpose: the purpose which a character, incident, or particular
　　line, or lines, serves in furthering the action of the play, creating sus-
　　pense, changing or intensifying the mood, increasing the emotional
　　effect, contributing to the humor, or helping to reveal character.

epigram: a short witty saying, sometimes having a satirical or ironical
　　meaning.

episode: an event, or set of events, that helps to make up the main plot
　　or, at times, is incidental to it.

exposition: the background information that reveals "how it all began";
　　namely, what happened prior to the time covered in the play, what
　　the main characters are like (sometimes before they appear), and
　　what situation has arisen that will lead to a problem that must be
　　solved.

falling action: the action following the climax; also referred to as *resolu-
　　tion* or *denouement*.

fantasy: a play involving such unreal characters and improbable events
　　that the reader is not expected to believe it. Some fantasies are in-
　　tended merely to entertain; others have a serious purpose as well;
　　namely, to poke fun at outmoded customs or at the stupidity of certain
　　people or groups of people.

farce: a form of drama in which the humorous effect is achieved largely
　　through the creation of exaggerated or far-fetched situations or
　　characters.

flashback: a dramatic device by which the playwright interrupts the main
　　action of the play to present a situation or incident which occurred
　　at an earlier time.

foreshadowing: the technique of dropping hints or suggestions that lead
　　the reader or theater audience to anticipate subsequent events or
　　situations.

irony: a mode of expression in which the intended meaning of the words used is the direct opposite of the literal or usual meaning; also, an outcome of events contrary to what would naturally be hoped for or expected. See *dramatic irony*.

legitimate theater: drama performed on a stage. The term is used to differentiate stage drama from motion pictures, television plays, etc.

melodrama: a drama with sensational and often violent action, and usually with a happy ending.

monologue: a long speech of one character in a play.

mood: the frame of mind or state of feeling created by the setting, the lines spoken by the characters, or a particular situation or sequence of events.

moral: the lesson or "teaching" that is brought out through the action of the play or is explicitly stated or implied by one of the characters.

plot: the series of events or episodes that make up the action of the play.

poetic justice: an outcome of events that rewards the virtuous and punishes the vicious; an ending in which each character gets exactly what he deserves.

protagonist: the opposing force in the conflict most responsible for bringing the conflict to an end; usually the central or leading character.

realism: a manner of writing in which people, scenes, and events are presented as they are in real life, without romantic or idealistic coloring.

resolution: the events following the climax of the play; sometimes called *falling action*.

rising action: the series of events, preceding the climax, which intensify the conflict and, thereby, create a feeling of suspense about the outcome.

satire: the use of irony, sarcasm, or ridicule to expose, denounce, or poke fun at customs, manners, individuals, or social or political institutions.

scene: a short episode in which the time, and possibly the place, are different from that of a previous episode; also, an incident or happening in the play that develops naturally out of the preceding action and flows into the action that follows.

scenery: the backdrop, walls, furniture, etc., used onstage to represent the place in which the action of a scene occurs.

setting: the time and place in which the events in a play occur.

soliloquy: lines spoken by a character to himself rather than to another character; a kind of "thinking out loud" for the purpose of revealing information about the character or about events which the reader or theater audience needs to know.

stage directions: the words, phrases, sentences, and even paragraphs, printed in italics and enclosed in parentheses, through which the playwright indicates what is taking place on the stage and how he wants the characters to speak, feel, or act. Occasionally, he uses the stage directions to comment on a character or situation or to suggest the particular mood to be created at that point in the play.

stock character: a character who has been used in so many plays that the audience immediately recognizes him and knows how he will think and act.

style: the distinctive manner in which the playwright uses language: his choice and arrangement of words.

subplot: a secondary series of events or episodes that is subordinate to the main plot but, in most cases, contributes to it.

suspense: a feeling of excitement, curiosity, or expectation about the outcome of the play.

theme: the idea, view of life, or commentary on human behavior that is dramatized through the words and deeds of the characters.

tone: the feeling conveyed by a playwright through style and choice of words, which reveals his attitude toward his subject; for example, a satirical tone.

tragedy: a form of drama in which the protagonist undergoes a morally significant struggle and is defeated, sometimes because of a flaw in his own character, more often because he is unable to overcome the force, or forces, that oppose him.

unity: the quality in a play that gives it the effect of being a harmonious whole.